The Intelligent Design D and the Temptation of Sc

The controversy over Intelligent Design (ID) has now continued for over two decades, with no signs of ending. For its defenders, ID is revolutionary new science, and its opposition is merely ideological. For its critics, ID is both bad science and bad theology. But the polemical nature of the debate makes it difficult to understand the nature of the arguments on all sides.

A balanced and deep analysis of a controversial debate, this volume argues that beliefs about the purposiveness or non-purposiveness of nature should not be based merely on science. Rather, the philosophical and theological nature of such questions should be openly acknowledged.

Dr. Erkki Vesa Rope Kojonen is a postdoctoral researcher at the University of Helsinki, Faculty of Theology. He is also the editor of the Finnish Science and Theology magazine Areiopagi.fi, and has participated widely in discussions on science and theology both in his home country and internationally. His research interests also include the general discussion between faith and reason, philosophy of science as well as theology more generally. He was born in 1982, is married and lives in Espoo, Finland with his wife and three children.

Routledge Science and Religion Series

Series Editors:

Roger Trigg, *Emeritus Professor, University of Warwick, and Academic Director of the Centre for the Study of Religion in Public Life, Kellogg College, Oxford*

J. Wentzel van Huyssteen, *Princeton Theological Seminary, USA*

Science and religion have often been thought to be at loggerheads but much contemporary work in this flourishing interdisciplinary field suggests this is far from the case. The *Routledge Science and Religion Series* presents exciting new work to advance interdisciplinary study, research and debate across key themes in science and religion, exploring the philosophical relations between the physical and social sciences on the one hand and religious belief on the other. Contemporary issues in philosophy and theology are debated, as are prevailing cultural assumptions arising from the 'post-modernist' distaste for many forms of reasoning. The series enables leading international authors from a range of different disciplinary perspectives to apply the insights of the various sciences, theology and philosophy and look at the relations between the different disciplines and the rational connections that can be made between them. These accessible, stimulating new contributions to key topics across science and religion will appeal particularly to individual academics and researchers, graduates, postgraduates and upper-undergraduate students.

The Roots of Religion
Exploring the Cognitive Science of Religion
Edited by Roger Trigg and Justin L. Barrett

Being as Communion
A Metaphysics of Information
William A. Dembski

Christian Moral Theology in the Emerging Technoculture
From Posthuman Back to Human
Brent Waters

The Intelligent Design Debate and the Temptation of Scientism

Erkki Vesa Rope Kojonen

LONDON AND NEW YORK

First published 2016
by Routledge

2 Park Square, Milton Park, Abingdon, Oxfordshire OX14 4RN
52 Vanderbilt Avenue, New York, NY 10017

Routledge is an imprint of the Taylor & Francis Group, an informa business

First issued in paperback 2019

British Library Cataloguing in Publication Data
A catalogue record for this book is available from the British Library

Library of Congress Cataloging-in-Publication Data
Kojonen, Erkki V. R. The intelligent design debate and the temptation of scientism / by Erkki V. R. Kojonen.
pages cm.—(Ashgate science and religion series)
Includes bibliographical references and index.
ISBN 978-1-4724-7250-2 (hardcover : alk. paper) —
ISBN 978-1-4724-7251-9 (ebook)—ISBN 978-1-4724-7252-6 (epub)
1. Intelligent design (Teleology) 2. Evolution (Biology)—Religious aspects—Christianity. 3. Scientism. I. Title.
BS659.K65 2016
124—dc23
2015031559

ISBN: 978-1-4724-7250-2 (hbk)
ISBN: 978-0-367-88158-0 (pbk)

Typeset in Bembo
by Apex CoVantage, LLC

Contents

Acknowledgements

The discussion on Intelligent Design is controversial and the rhetoric is often volatile. Someone like me, who finds both something to like and something to criticize in Intelligent Design, can feel like a 'lonely duck', as theologian Thomas Jay Oord has stated.[1] With this research monograph, I am joining this society of lonely ducks. My goal with this book has been to write an eirenic, balanced and deep analysis of the debate, from which readers of varying viewpoints could benefit, regardless of whether they agree with every position defended in the book. I am also glad to be able to give a voice to all the other lonely ducks out there.

This study began its life as a dissertation, and is the result of several years of research, writing and dialogue with proponents of various views on Intelligent Design. As such the book would have been impossible to complete without the support of many people and institutions, whom I now wish to thank. Pauli Annala, Heikki Helanterä, Toivo Holopainen, Timo Koistinen, Jeffrey Koperski, Pekka Kärkkäinen, Leo Näreaho, Juha Pihkala, Anne Runehov, Miikka Ruokanen, Robert J. Russell and others read parts of the manuscript and provided invaluable feedback on it from their often very different perspectives. In addition, Aku Visala, Olli-Pekka Vainio and many other friends, colleagues, students and readers of our Finnish *Areiopagi.fi webmagazine* have spent countless hours discussing theology, philosophy and the natural sciences with me, which has provided great stimulus for the development of my thought. I have done my best to benefit from the excellent advice I have received. However, my conversation partners should not be assumed to agree with each other, or with everything that I have written.

The Faculty of Theology at the University of Helsinki has provided an intellectually stimulating environment that is open to different approaches and discussion between them. International visits to the Center for Theology and the Natural Sciences (Berkeley, California) and the Ian Ramsey Centre (Oxford) were invaluable for broadening my perspective on the international discussion in the field of religion and science studies. The funding for the research project

1 Oord 2010.

culminating in this book was received from the Finnish Doctoral Programme of Theology, the Faculty of Theology at the University of Helsinki, the Church Research Institute of the Finnish Evangelical-Lutheran church, the Emil Aaltonen Foundation and the Karl Schlect Stiftung. Their funding made it possible for me to seize the moment and devote the needed time for this study.

My family has been supportive of my doctoral pursuit from the beginning, and our home has been a place to experience the wonder of life which makes the questions of this dissertation so much more interesting. The support and friendship of my wife Senja Kojonen has meant that this lonely duck has some company close by after all.

Erkki Vesa Rope Kojonen

1 Introduction

The purpose of this book

The controversy over Intelligent Design (ID) has now continued for over two decades, with no signs of ending. For its defenders, ID is revolutionary new science, and its opposition is merely ideological. The conclusion that nature is designed is argued to be the clear result of the cumulative efforts of the various natural sciences, and proponents of ID believe this conclusion to be 'so unambiguous and so significant that it must be ranked as one of the greatest achievements in the history of science'.[1] However, for its varied critics, ID is both bad science and bad theology. But the polemical nature of the debate makes it difficult to understand the real nature of the arguments on each side.

The purpose of this book is to provide a balanced analysis of the strengths and weaknesses of different positions in the debate. The book analyses the central philosophical and theological questions of the ID discussion, aiming to show how all sides can improve their argumentation. Although the empirical arguments for and against are also touched upon, the main focus is on the theological and philosophical questions.

This may be a surprising emphasis, since many participants of the debate agree that the natural sciences should be the main factor driving our conclusions about whether nature is purposefully designed or not. As Nathaniel C. Comfort has noted: 'One point on which anti-Darwinists and anticreationists agree is that this is a pitched battle between dogmatic religious fanatics on the one hand, and rigorous, fair-minded scientists on the other. However, which side is which depends on who you read'.[2] Although both critics and defenders of ID often explain the beliefs of the other side as the result of ideological or religious bias, the importance of the philosophical and theological assumptions on one's own side is not usually emphasized. However, it is my contention that using philosophical and theological arguments in this debate is actually necessary, and all sides depend on such arguments in addition to evidence from the natural sciences.

1 Behe 2006a, 232–233.

2 Comfort 2007, 3.

Teasing out the theological and philosophical background of the debate might be interpreted as a critique of the various positions, since all sides would rather identify with the scientists than with the religious fanatics described by Comfort. Of course we are right to be wary of fanaticism and dogmatism. But all theology and philosophy are not distorting ideology, and it is my intent simply to shed light on this part of the debate. I argue that the sidelining of theology and philosophy from the debate is actually an example of the influence of scientism, defined as the belief that science is the only way to gain reliable knowledge about the world. Not many in the debate consciously advocate such a position; often proponents of ID even state their rejection of scientism explicitly. The influence of scientism on the debate is more subtle, implicit in some of the arguments and emphases of the debate.

Because of the usefulness of the natural sciences for contemporary Western societies, it is understandable to experience a temptation to think that scientific methods are also the best or only way to settle age-old philosophical and religious questions, such as whether the cosmos is purposefully created or not. Because science commands near-universal respect in our culture, it is tempting to restrict one's arguments to this highly respected medium, rather than engaging in more controversial, openly philosophical and theological dialogue. However, this leads to a problematic devaluing of those forms of rationality that fall outside the natural sciences. Of course, it is not uncontroversial that there is some problem in such a devaluing. For example, biologist Jerry Coyne argues that it is simply reasonable, since science is rational, and religion is not: 'Science and religion, then, are competitors in the business of finding out what is true about our universe. In this goal religion has failed miserably, for its tools for discerning "truth" are useless'.[3] One of the goals of the present volume is to show how philosophical and theological discussion of such matters continues to have value.

So, in addition to advancing understanding of the central positions and arguments in the debate, the purpose of this book is also to reconnect the discussion on ID into the broader philosophical and theological discussion of the same themes. In this way, the book aims to help participants on all sides formulate better arguments. The book is somewhat unusual for the debate because of the fact that its central purpose is not to argue for or against ID. I will not be attempting to persuade the reader that the cosmos is purposefully designed, or non-designed, or that proponents of ID or their critics are fools for rejecting obvious scientific truths. Where I offer critiques of various positions in the debate, I will also usually attempt to show how the position could be modified in a way that avoids the critique. Much of the study simply takes the form of systematic analysis of the debate, going over the central questions one by one to see what kind of insights emerge.

3 Coyne 2015, foreword.

Because the ideas of the ID movement are highly controversial, I contrast them to opposing views, mainly theistic evolutionism and naturalistic evolutionism. One cannot be fair to the debate by including only one viewpoint on the major issues. Accordingly, while preparing this study, I have read the arguments for each side as broadly as possible and have attempted to select the most crucial and most often repeated arguments for analysis. My hope is that persons of widely different persuasions reading this book can recognize that their own views are fairly presented and be stimulated in their thinking by the arguments I present.

The need for clarity and a balanced analysis has been stressed (for example) by philosophers Jeffrey Koperski and Del Ratzsch, who have called on scholars to analyse ID calmly to identify both the strengths and weaknesses of ID thought.[4] This is the central purpose of the present study: to understand the cognitive landscape of the debate and the structure of the ID debate. Of course, understanding any system of thought can also help one see its flaws more clearly. However, my personal hope is that this analysis will not just result in pointing out flaws in the various viewpoints but also build bridges between them to help develop the debate more into a dialogue.

The need for such an analysis is also revealed in the varied nature of the criticisms directed against ID. For example, philosophically, ID's design argument has been criticized both by arguing that the hypothesis of a designer is unfalsifiable and by arguing that ID's design argument has been falsified. To make matters even more complex, in theological critiques of ID, its susceptibility to falsification by future scientific discoveries is often seen as one of its greatest flaws. Some critics of ID argue that design is excluded from science on philosophical grounds, while others argue that naturalistic science is open even to supernatural explanations, if there is evidence. Some argue against ID from atheist premises, regarding the design argument as the best sort of evidence for God. Others argue against ID from theistic premises, believing it to lead to a mistaken view of the Creator. Some of ID's critics reject the possibility of all design arguments, while others defend broader cosmological design arguments themselves. Some critics even agree with ID that there are major problems in traditional Neo-Darwinian evolutionary theory, but they do not agree that intelligent design is any better as a scientific explanation for life's development. Rather, they argue for expanding the theory and searching for further natural explanations. This kind of disagreement on central issues leaves much room (and need) for a balanced theological and philosophical analysis of the movement's ideas.

Proponents of ID emphasize the scientific nature of their design argument. Nevertheless, the ID movement is not the first to make use of design arguments, or teleological arguments as they have been traditionally termed. These arguments 'focus upon finding and identifying various traces of the

4 Koperski 2008, Ratzsch 2001.

operation of a mind in nature's temporal and physical structures, behaviors and paths'.[5] In the tradition of natural theology, the existence of God is discussed in terms of what can be known based on 'natural reason' or 'natural revelation'.[6] Broadly speaking, natural theology speaks of knowledge of God available through human observation, memory and rational intuitions, as well as arguments based on them. Objections and defences of such arguments, and the general nature of religious rationality, have been extensively considered in the philosophy of religion, and I believe it is fruitful to relate the ID debate to this discussion.

The temptation of scientism

Defining scientism

I have titled the book *The Intelligent Design Debate and the Temptation of Scientism*. But what do I mean by scientism, and why is it a temptation that we should avoid? Usually, the term 'scientism' is understood as an epistemological claim, meaning a claim about the gathering of knowledge. For example, Alexander Rosenberg, who advocates scientism, argues that scientism 'is the conviction that the methods of science are the only reliable ways to secure knowledge of anything – Being scientistic just means treating science as our exclusive guide to reality, to nature – both our own nature and everything else's'.[7] Of course, the success of the natural sciences in providing understanding of nature and the importance of technology for our daily lives provide a good argument in favour of the general value of science. But does this mean that reliable knowledge and rationality is truly restricted to science? How could we build such an argument? To many authors, this kind of extension of the cultural authority of science seems like unwarranted scientific imperialism.[8]

As a European (Finnish) writer, I would be less troubled by scientism if we were to use the word 'science' in the way Germans use the term 'wissenschaft' to refer not only to the natural sciences but also to the humanities, to philosophy and also to theology. On this usage, science means simply the systematization of our thought and reasoning, whatever the field. Yet even with this broader usage, restricting knowledge and rational beliefs to science would still not be a credible position. This is because it still excludes even obviously

5 Ratzsch 2010.

6 Brooke 2002, 164.

7 Rosenberg 2011, 6–8.

8 I am indebted to Mikael Stenmark (2001) and Rik Peels (2015a) for their extensive analysis of various concepts of scientism. In practice, assumptions about reality often underlie the kind of epistemic scientism just described. In ontological scientism, it is assumed that only the kind of things that can be studied by the natural sciences exist. However, this does not have to be assumed by those holding to epistemic scientism: it could be that other things exist besides those that are discoverable by science, but we simply cannot have any knowledge of them.

rational everyday beliefs from the realm of rationality. The methods of science require strict conditions and typically aim at solving highly specialized problems. We cannot present scientific evidence even for such simple beliefs as 'my wife loves me' or 'I love my wife' (unless we adopt a very broad definition of 'science'). Now it is true that many of our everyday beliefs, such as 'I ate some bread for breakfast this morning' could in principle be corroborated by scientific inquiry (such as by investigating a sample of my blood), but this does not mean that we are not already justified in believing such things before scientific inquiry.

The problem with scientism is not that we love the natural sciences too much; I have no desire to argue against valuing science. Rather, the problem is that we undervalue the importance of philosophy, theology and everyday methods of reasoning. Actually, practicing the natural sciences itself requires a broader conception of rationality, allowing some reliability for rational beliefs through observation, memory, rational intuitions and so on. For example, in order to perform experiments, one has to be able to trust ordinary experiences like 'I see such and such through the microscope'. To function in the community of scientists, we need to trust in the existence of other minds, our ability to plan intentionally, the rationality of accumulating evidence and so on. Of course, the intersubjective testing of experience improves reliability, but that also does so only by assuming that experience is valuable. Therefore, it seems that if natural science is reliable, reliable knowledge and rational beliefs must also be possible outside the natural sciences.[9]

There are further broad problems with scientism. For example, it seems reasonable to understand the restriction of knowledge to science as a philosophical claim. However, in this case scientism appears to be self-refuting, because this philosophical claim is itself not the result of scientific research. So it seems that defences of scientism assume that there must be knowledge outside of science; otherwise scientism itself could not be defended. But if this one philosophical idea can be rational outside of the natural sciences, then why could not other philosophical ideas also be rational? It is true that natural science has been successful in gaining knowledge about many things, but this success can also be valued without assuming that science is the only way of gaining knowledge. Other fields could also employ evidence-based reasoning, even if they are very different from the natural sciences.[10]

9 See further, Peels 2015c.

10 One possible reply is that we do not need to understand scientism as a truth-claim about the value of science, but rather as a stance or a pragmatic program that one chooses to participate in (see for example Ladyman 2011). However, in this case scientism loses its teeth as an argument, because it will then become difficult to present persuasive reasons for adopting scientism, rather than some more inclusive understanding of rationality. See further, Peels 2015b and Stenmark 2001, 32–33.

Scientism in the context of the ID debate

Very few thinkers explicitly defend scientism generally or in the context of the debate over ID.[11] Proponents of ID themselves would balk at the suggestion that scientism is influencing their strategy or arguments; they aim to oppose scientism, not to defend it.[12] If you are a reader who is inclined to think that talking about scientism in religion and science discussions is a 'canard', like biologist Jerry Coyne argues,[13] I recommend that you read some of the good academic studies on scientism. For example, Mikael Stenmark's now classic study *Scientism: Science, Ethics and Religion* (2001), published in the same series as this book, contains good definitions, documentation and critique of various forms of scientism. Many other good studies of the matter are also available.[14] Furthermore, even if scientism were generally a 'canard', the concept is definitely relevant for the discussion on ID. The later chapters of this book will in any case critique the ways in which scientism adversely affects the debate over ID. These chapters will also more closely reveal what I think about the relationship of faith and reason generally.

To give the reader a general idea of what I am going to say, I believe the influence of scientism on the ID debate is implicitly visible in the overt focus on arguing over whether ID is part of the natural sciences or not, and in the undervaluing of arguments and forms of rationality that are not part of the natural sciences, such as philosophy and theology. Arguments based on the natural sciences are valued, while philosophical and theological arguments are often hidden or put in the sidelines on different sides of the debate. I agree that discussion of biological design arguments, for example, is very much affected by the theory of biological evolution, as well as by the empirical details of biological organisms. So in this sense discussing science is indeed crucial for the debate. However, what is often overlooked in the debate is that the overall question of whether nature is ultimately purposeful or not is not settled by just science or the debate over biological evolution. Traditionally, these types of arguments about the ultimate character of reality have reasonably been understood as primarily philosophical and theological questions, discussed as part of the philosophy of religion. Yet both atheistic critics of ID and proponents of ID often argue as if there can be no rational belief in the createdness of nature if science does not give us ground for such a belief. The philosophical and theological differences of the participants are important, and should be discussed more openly.

11 For some exception in the general discussion of the issue, see Ladyman 2011 and Rosenberg 2012.

12 See for example West (ed.) 2012. However, the collection criticizes scientism mostly in the form of moral scientism, rather than epistemic scientism, which I am concerned with. Again, for classification of different forms of scientism, see Stenmark 2001 and Peels 2015a.

13 Coyne 2015, chapter 4.

14 In addition to Stenmark's excellent book, see also for example Haack 2003 and 2013, Pigliucci 2013, De Ridder 2014a and Trigg 1993.

The structure of the argument

This book has ten chapters, which are designed to gradually lead the reader into understanding the debate over ID. The chapters are designed to be read in order, but are written so that the advanced reader can also read chapters in isolation. After this introductory chapter, Chapter 2 goes on to introduce the major players in the debate more closely. I analyse the relationship between ID, creationism, theistic evolutionism and naturalistic evolutionism. I argue that the discussion should also be linked to theological and philosophical discussion of theologies of nature and natural theology.

Chapters 3 and 4 then introduce the empirical debate over cosmology and biology, respectively, and show what kind of philosophical and theological disagreements emerge from these discussions. The material these chapters cover will introduce new readers to the debate on Intelligent Design, while hopefully also providing some new perspectives and food for thought to those readers who are already familiar with the debate.

Chapter 5 analyses the debate over the demarcation question: is ID a part of the natural sciences, and why or why not? Because of the ID movement's emphasis on the scientific nature of its design argument, and because of the political importance of the definition of science, much energy has been used to debate whether ID indeed fits under the definition of science. After classifying some answers to the question of definitions, I argue that the question is ultimately a side issue: if we don't accept scientism, what matters is whether ID is a good argument or not, not whether it is part of the natural sciences.

In Chapter 6, I move on to consider ID's relation to the project of natural theology more closely. Proponents of ID present a minimalistic understanding of the 'intelligent designer', though they believe that the designer can be identified as God based on non-scientific theological and philosophical reasons. Here both the possibility of this separation and the possibility of identification have been called into question by critics. I analyse this discussion. After this, I also analyse the idea that ID is a God of the gaps argument (which are abhorred in natural theology), rather than a limit question (which would make it a legitimate argument). I show what theological dangers we need to avoid, and argue that the empirical evidence is also theologically paramount in deciding whether something like ID's design argument is legitimate.

In Chapter 7, I consider general issues pertaining to design arguments. I begin by analysing the possibility of design arguments in light of thought experiments and then go on to discuss whether design beliefs are more properly understood as the product of intuitions or arguments. I argue that accounts of how we come to believe in design should do justice to the philosophical intuitions that these thought experiments reveal. In Chapter 8, I move on to consider the logic of design arguments in some detail, comparing different understandings of the logic and some objections to each argument. I argue that proponents of ID would do well to relate their argument to the broader arguments of natural theology.

Chapters 9 and 10 consider further theological issues of the debate. Both theistic evolutionists and proponents of ID have argued that the argumentation of the other side is theologically problematic. Theistic evolutionists have argued particularly that ID is a God of the gaps argument, and that it leads to difficulties with the problem of natural evil. Proponents of ID have argued that the theistic evolutionist's defence of the doctrine of creation is too weak and vague. In analysing these arguments, I show how proponents of ID need to formulate their arguments in order to respond to the problem of natural evil and how theistic evolutionists can respond to ID's critique. It is in its critique of theistic evolutionism that I believe ID comes closest to succumbing to temptation of scientism.

The breadth of this study is necessary to demonstrate how philosophical and theological ideas influence the discussion on ID and what their role is in relation to the empirical arguments. Based on my analysis of the arguments used in the discussion, I argue that there is no philosophical or theological 'silver bullet' that could by itself settle the discussion either for or against ID's design arguments. Though philosophical and theological reasons can and do influence our beliefs regarding the history of life, evolution and design, such considerations cannot allow us to wholly bypass discussion of the empirical evidence. Opinions about the designedness (and undesignedness) of the cosmos are in practice formed in a complex interplay of many influences, including empirical, philosophical, theological and psychological factors, among others.

On building bridges

The debate over ID and evolution tends to be viewed by both sides as an epic struggle between good and evil, between rationality and irrationality, between honest truth-seeking and ideological manipulation. It seems to be a general tendency of human beings to form tribes of like-minded people and to usually explain those beliefs that differ from our own as the result of some kind of cognitive error. Nevertheless, intellectual humility requires us to listen to and to attempt to understand even viewpoints that are very different from our own. Often dialogue with very different views can help us greatly refine our own views and help keep us honest.

I do accept the reality of good and evil, as well as of truth and error in the world. This means that I can appreciate the fact that usually one tribe indeed is more right than others. I also believe that we should pursue and value truth. So if we believe that in some debate one side has all the good arguments, and the other side is fully mistaken, there is no harm in stating that conclusion. What I am saying is that in my experience we often reach this kind of conclusion prematurely. In my experience, there are smart people on all sides of the ID debate. All sides of the argument also have strengths and weaknesses, and room for improvement and further research.

In stating this kind of view I of course risk being criticized by all sides of the debate. My attempts at building bridges between different views can be interpreted as being too lukewarm, when the reality of the battle between good and evil in the debate would rather require us to take a strong position. And in some cases, I will be taking strong positions in this study, particularly against scientism. But my overall feeling is that there has been too much polemics and too little listening in the debate over ID. In the contentious atmosphere of the debate, arguments and mischaracterizations that have been answered by the opposing side many times over keep being repeated, without acknowledging that any possible response even exists. It is unfortunate that the debate sometimes tends to resemble a cultural war much more than a real academic discussion.

2 Mapping the landscape of the debate

Even the history of ID is contentious, and narratives of it can be part of the political struggle for or against the movement. Many have connected ID with the creationist movement of the 20th century, noting similarities between the arguments used against Darwinian evolutionary biology. Proponents of ID themselves believe that their ideas have deeper roots in the tradition of design arguments stretching back to the philosophers of Antiquity, who already discussed whether nature is purposefully ordered by some kind of Creator or the product of the ultimately purposeless dynamic of chance and necessity. Proponents of ID see their efforts as the best contemporary defence of the idea of nature as a purposeful creation and believe that evolutionary biology represents a continuation of ancient belief in the ultimate mindlessness of nature. They also believe that these questions have great cultural significance. For instance, William Dembski has called the discussion over ID, 'the ground zero of the culture wars'.[1]

The purpose of this chapter is to map out some basic positions in the contemporary debate and to give the reader some idea of their roots and their general relationship to one another. To that end, I will begin in the first part of Chapter 2 by introducing the contemporary ID movement. In the second and third parts of the chapter I will then compare and contrast ID with various forms of creationism and theistic evolutionism and then introduce the atheistic understanding of evolution which ID aims to oppose. Finally, in the last part of the chapter I will link the debate over ID to the contemporary philosophical discussion on natural theology and chart out a basic position on science and faith which will help us approach the debate.

Intelligent Design's story

The ID movement's self-understanding

Though the idea of design has ancient roots, most consider the story of the ID movement to begin with Phillip E. Johnson, Professor Emeritus of Legal

1 See Dembski's foreword in Wiker (2002, 11).

Rhetoric from the University of Berkeley, California. On sabbatical in London in 1987, Johnson was looking for a new research topic, but inspiration was eluding him. Johnson had converted to Christianity in midlife after a divorce, and was now praying for a new direction for his life.[2] The purpose was finally found reading different perspectives on evolutionary biology: Richard Dawkins' book *The Blind Watchmaker* in which Dawkins argues that evolution reveals a universe fundamentally without purpose, and Michael Denton's *Evolution: A Theory in Crisis* in which Denton argues that evolution has failed to explain various features about life, and a return to the idea of design may be in order. Johnson explains, 'I read these books, and I guess almost immediately I thought, This is it. This is where it all comes down to, the understanding of creation'.[3] In the clash of different views about evolution and creation, Johnson had found an interesting and meaningful research topic.

In Johnson's opinion, Denton's arguments were clearly superior to Dawkins. Theologically, Johnson found profound meaning in the creation/evolution debate, coming to the opinion that our culture's views on origins will eventually determine our views also on 'all other questions of importance'.[4] Johnson began an intensive process of research and private discussion, and in 1991, just four years after reading Denton and Dawkins, Johnson's book *Darwin on Trial* was published. Other like-minded thinkers, such as mathematician-theologian William Dembski, biochemist Michael Behe, philosopher of science Stephen C. Meyer and others joined forces with Johnson, and the ID movement was born. Though the majority of scientists did not accept Johnson's arguments, to many regular U.S. citizens it appeared that here was a reasonable challenge to evolutionary biology and a credible defence of the ancient faith in creation. Though the movement remains the strongest in the United States, it has also gained international media attention and influence.

Despite the abundance of controversy over the origins and nature of the ID movement, both critics and defenders of ID at least agree that all of the major proponents of ID are at the present time connected in some way to the Center for Science and Culture of the Discovery Institute in Seattle, Washington. So, the Discovery Institute's definition of ID is a good place to begin:

> Intelligent design refers to a scientific research programme as well as a community of scientists, philosophers and other scholars who seek evidence of design in nature. The theory of intelligent design holds that certain features of the universe and of living things are best explained by an intelligent cause, not an undirected process such as natural selection. Through the study and analysis of a system's components, a design theorist is able to determine whether various natural structures are the product of chance,

2 The same basic details are accepted by both defenders and critics of the movement; see for example Woodward (2003, 29), Forrest and Gross (2004, 17), and Meyer (2006).

3 Stafford 1997.

4 P. Johnson 2000, 159.

> natural law, intelligent design, or some combination thereof. Such research is conducted by observing the types of information produced when intelligent agents act. Scientists then seek to find objects which have those same types of informational properties which we commonly know come from intelligence. Intelligent design has applied these scientific methods to detect design in irreducibly complex biological structures, the complex and specified information content in DNA, the life-sustaining physical architecture of the universe, and the geologically rapid origin of biological diversity in the fossil record during the Cambrian explosion approximately 530 million years ago.[5]

This definition emphasizes the ID movement's claimed intellectual and scientific nature. According to this definition, ID is three things: (1) a scientific research programme attempting to find evidence of design in nature; (2) a community (or movement) of scholars who participate in this research programme; and (3) a theory which holds that there is indeed evidence for intelligent design in nature. This theory is said to be based on the study and analysis of natural systems. Advocates of ID emphasize that their design argument rests on new scientific discoveries which provide evidence for design.[6]

The definition's distinction between the idea of evidence for design and the community known as the ID movement is useful. The idea that there is evidence for the operation of an intelligent mind in nature is far older and more popular than the ID movement itself. It is more popularly known as *the design argument* or the *teleological argument*, and it has been formulated in many ways over the centuries. This general idea finds support also outside the ID movement, even among many of its critics.

The design argument of the ID movement is distinctive in a few ways that make it controversial, and which make many supporters of the general idea of teleological arguments critical of ID. First, the critique of evolutionary explanations is a central part of ID's design arguments. According to ID supporter Thomas Woodward's analysis, the movement's story is about 'respected professors at prestigious secular universities—rising up and arguing that (1) Darwinism is woefully lacking factual support and is rather based on philosophical assumptions, and (2) empirical evidence, especially in molecular biology, now points compellingly to some sort of creative intelligence behind life'.[7] Woodward emphasizes the intellectual nature of the ID movement, just as the

5 I am quoting from the CSC's website at the time of this writing; see Discovery Institute (2015). Campbell et al. (2004, 33) provide a similar definition. Monton (2009a, 15–29) has some critical remarks about the matter.

6 Critics of ID have long complained that proponents of ID do most of their work simply in interpreting scientific data collected by others, rather than producing original new scientific research. In recent years the Discovery Institute has attempted to remedy this fault by sponsoring biochemical experiments through a separate institute called Biologic Institute.

7 Woodward 2003, 195.

previously quoted definition. The ID movement sees its critique of Darwinian evolutionary biology as a scientific dissent from a doctrine of evolution which does not fit the facts. Dissent from this doctrine is seen as the courageous and intellectually honest thing to do.[8] The movement's critique of Darwinism sets its design argument apart from views which seek to harmonize evolutionary biology and belief in creation and/or design. The majority of the scientific community accepts the viability of evolutionary biology, and this makes the scientists who are part of the ID movement a minority.[9]

ID's critique of methodological naturalism is also a distinctive mark of the movement's argumentation.[10] Methodological naturalism is understood in the movement as the idea that only 'natural', mechanistic and non-purposeful explanations are allowed in the natural sciences. ID's critique of methodological naturalism stems partly from a desire to challenge materialistic interpretations of natural science and build a new kind of natural science more consonant with religious belief in God as Creator. The issue is politically and theologically charged: it seems to violate typical understandings of the relationship of theology and science. Furthermore, the status of ID as science or non-science will determine whether it can be taught in public schools in the United States. Consequently, much has been written on whether ID is natural science or not.

ID as a cultural and religious movement

Though the previous definitions emphasize the scientific nature of the ID movement, other definitions reveal that the movement also has its theological side. For example, in Dembski's definition, 'Intelligent Design is three things: a scientific research programme that investigates the effects of intelligent causes; an intellectual movement that challenges Darwinism and its naturalistic legacy; and a way of understanding divine action'.[11] Here, 'a way of understanding divine action' reveals the importance of the theological side of ID. Woodward emphasizes the scientific motivations of Intelligent Design, but admits that its goal is also to open up both science and society for the 'serious consideration of the theistic perspective'.[12] Angus Menuge likewise argues that 'defenders of ID see themselves as revolutionaries who can build bridges between science and theology'.[13]

Though proponents of ID emphasize the scientific side of their motivations, many critics of the movement think the religious side is more important. For example, Barbara Forrest writes that 'in actuality, this "scientific" movement which seeks to permeate the American academic and cultural mainstream is

8 For examples of this, see, for example, Dembski, ed. (2004 and 2006).

9 See McGrath (2011, chapter 2) for the difficulties involved in using the term 'Darwinism'.

10 As noted by Beckwith (2003).

11 Dembski 1999a, 13.

12 Woodward 2003, 205.

13 Menuge 2004a, 48–49.

religious to its core'.[14] For Forrest, ID is not a scientific research programme, but a religious movement that is trying to gain power in American cultural and academic life. In her opinion, ID's so-called scientific arguments are just a smokescreen. Their arguments are not of any value scientifically, but represent reiterations of creationist arguments long since discredited by mainstream scientists. Robert Pennock also argues that 'the creation/evolution debate is only superficially about science. At its base, it is about religion and it is about philosophy'.[15]

I would not go quite as far as these critics. In the coming chapters, I will show that there are real disagreements about the state of natural science in the debate, and the empirical evidence is important for all sides of the debate. The empirical side of the discussion includes things like debates about the viability of various hypotheses of the origin of life, the possibility of evolving 'irreducibly complex' biochemical structures, what kind of values the constants of nature need in order to make life possible, is biological order machine-like and so on. Having read material from ID proponents and based on my interaction with some of the members of the movement, it is my feeling that they honestly believe in the strength of their empirical arguments. However, Pennock is right that the debate is definitely also about religion and philosophy.

Many secular critics of ID feel that ID's religious overtones are dangerous and believe that stopping ID is important for the preservation of Enlightenment values and a free secular society.[16] These secular critics of ID argue that the fact of evolution is so clearly established by the scientific evidence that any contrary opinions must be explained by non-rational factors, such as a fear of the religious and moral implications of evolutionary theory.[17] Here many critics of ID also have moral and political motivations: to safeguard the independence of the scientific process from religious considerations, to protect the secularity of society, to protect the teaching of evolutionary biology in schools and so on.[18]

Forrest's most important evidence of the movement's cultural agenda is the Discovery Institute's 'Wedge document': a plan sent to supporters which laid out a long-term plan for using ID as a means of affecting culture and opening up discussion on moral and religious values. The document was subsequently leaked and later also made available to the public by the Discovery Institute itself.

14 Forrest 2001, 30.

15 Pennock 2007, 309.

16 See, for example, Forrest and Gross (2004) and Shanks (2004, 244), who believe that ID is ultimately attempting to replace secular democracy with a theocracy. These ideas are quite sensational and go too far; see for example Numbers (2006, 382), and Discovery Institute (2005) for critical responses from different viewpoints.

17 Freeman and Herron (2007, 105) also argue against ID in this way in their textbook of evolutionary biology.

18 Forrest and Gross (2004) argue that the Discovery Institute is attempting to push the teaching of ID into schools; the Discovery Institute contends that its goals are merely to defend the academic freedom of teachers (Dewolf, West, Luskin and Witt 2006).

In the document, ID's scientific programme serves the cultural goal of preserving the cultural authority of Judeo-Christian values such as the value of human life.[19] While Forrest and her co-author Paul Gross present the 'Wedge Document' with the air of investigators uncovering a secret conspiracy, Menuge correctly points out that these cultural aims were already openly proclaimed by ID leaders such as Johnson long before the publication of the document.[20]

A balanced account of ID's motivations

The importance of religious, cultural and political motivations for ID's argumentation is a contentious issue. Both critics and defenders of ID accept that proponents of ID do have such motivations. Critics of ID tend to argue that these motivations distort the ID theorists' capability to evaluate scientific facts in a trustworthy manner. The point of the critics is not that morality in itself is a bad thing for a scientist to have. Some morality is essential to science. For example, scientists should value the scientific project, value truth, cooperate with other humans and be able to admit their mistakes.[21]

Stating that a scientist has moral motivations does not therefore imply that this scientist is not a good scientist. The argument of the critics is rather that the ID movement's specific moral and religious motivations are not congenial to science, because these moral and religious motivations are thought to direct the ID theorists away from the truth. It may be that some critics are influenced here by a fear of religion and their own conviction that religious claims about the world are false. Traditional Christian values at least should include valuing truth, and these values have historically also aided, rather than merely hindered, science.[22]

Defenders of ID indeed argue that seeking the truth is their primary moral motivation and that the religious and cultural importance of the issues merely give the movement additional moral energy to spend time studying and debating the issues. Thus Meyer argues that 'the theory of intelligent design generates both excitement and loathing because, in addition to providing a compelling explanation of scientific facts, it holds out the promise of help in integrating two things of supreme importance – science and faith – that have long been seen as at odds'.[23]

Though most of the ID literature emphasizes the importance of science and philosophy, the importance of morality and religious reasons for ID's critique

19 Forrest and Gross 2004, chapter 2; see also Shanks (2004, 244).

20 Menuge 2004a, 36; see also Discovery Institute (2003), Johnson (2000).

21 Stenmark 2004, chapter 3; see also chapters 8 and 9.

22 See Brooke (1991) and Harrison (2015) for two good historical accounts.

23 Meyer 2013, 513. Meyer also approvingly quotes Whitehead's statement: 'When we consider what religion is for mankind and what science is, it is no exaggeration to say that the future course of history depends upon the decision of this generation as to the relations between them' (Whitehead 1926, 260). Similarly, Woodward (2003).

of naturalism is also prominently present in several works. Johnson's works *Reason in the Balance* (1995) and *The Wedge of Truth* (2001) begin and end by emphasizing the religious and moral significance of the debate on evolution. For Johnson, the theistic creation story grounds belief in the purposiveness of our existence and the objectivity of morality, while naturalistic Darwinism undermines both.[24] In Johnson's strategy for changing culture, ID functions as a 'wedge of truth' which shows the baselessness of materialistic scientism and thus makes room for broader conceptions of rationality. This in turn will make it possible (Johnson hopes) for Western culture to return to belief in objective morality and to gain more credence for a theistic, Christian worldview.[25]

Now this moral vision can be reasonably criticized as overly dualistic. Theistic belief in ID and materialistic belief in Darwinian evolution are presented as the central competing alternatives, but this bypasses the possibility of theistic evolutionism and the fact that only a minority of naturalists choose to understand naturalism or evolutionary biology as the starting point of moral reasoning.[26] But leaving this aside, is the existence of religious or anti-religious motivations an argument for or against ID? I think not. In the history of science, theories and arguments have been proposed for a great variety of reasons, and clearly the evaluation of arguments is a separate matter from the motivation of those arguments. People, even scientists, are motivated by a multitude of factors, and moral and religious motivations are not necessarily in conflict with the motivation to search for the truth. Rather, moral and religious motivations can also often lead one to have a high regard for truth and to spend much time in ascertaining the truth about some matter.

It can be difficult to accept that different people could honestly and rationally come to a completely different conclusion about some matter. Studies have shown that humans generally have an unfortunate tendency to explain the opinions of those we disagree with by reference to non-rational reasons. For example, creationists tend to explain evolutionary beliefs by reference to the sinful nature of humans, causing us to ignore the clear evidences of the Creator, while evolutionists tend to explain scepticism of evolution as a result of religious or cognitive biases.[27]

The distinction between truth and rationality may be helpful here. If some view is not in accord with reality, then it will not be truthful. Believing in untrue things would be irrational for someone who has knowledge of all relevant facts and reasons correctly. But since none of us are gifted with divine omniscience, arguments for even false views can appear to be convincing from our finite and subjective perspectives. For example, belief in a geocentric universe was

24 Johnson 1995, 7.

25 Johnson 2001.

26 Mikael Stenmark (2001) has critiqued moral interpretations of science as scientism. A naturalist who rejects scientism could also reject such moral interpretations, and attempt to find other grounds for morality.

27 See Harman (2004) for a good overview of research on cognitive biases of this kind.

certainly rational for Medieval Europeans, though it was later overthrown by the heliocentric cosmology, which was again overthrown later.[28] Following this line of thought, even if we ourselves reject some view such as ID or Darwinian evolutionary biology as objectively false, it should be possible for us to believe that accepting these views may be subjectively rational for those who accept them. In a pluralistic society, it is important for us to attempt to understand the reasons others have for their beliefs and to engage in rational dialogue in order to learn from other perspectives and thus (hopefully) increase our chances of forming true beliefs and avoiding false ones.

ID and varieties of creationism

Controversy over ID's relationship to creationism

Even the history of ID is contentious, and narratives of it can be part of the political struggle for or against the movement. Many have connected ID with the creationist movement of the 20th century, noting similarities between the arguments used against Darwinian evolutionary biology. The ID movement's rise to publicity happened after the 1987 trial on the teaching of scientific creationism in public schools in the USA. The US Supreme Court ruled that teaching so-called creation science in public schools was a violation of the constitutional separation of church and state.

Around the same time, a new creationist textbook called *Of Pandas and People* was being prepared for use in the same public schools. Drafts of the textbook prior to the Supreme Court ruling used the word 'creationism', but it was replaced with the word 'intelligent design' in editions following the 1987 trial. Critics of ID such as Forrest and Gross also note that Johnson, the early visionary leader of the ID movement, is a professor of law, rather than a natural scientist. Here it seems possible to conclude that ID emerged into popularity at least in part as a legal strategy, not merely as an intellectual movement. This narrative of ID's origins has been used to connect the movement to creationism and to thus discredit ID by association.[29]

However, questions of historical causality are often quite difficult, and the needs of current political debates on ID should not lead us to construct overly simply caricatures of the movement. There are some factors calling for a more complex understanding of ID's origins. For instance, historically, the first versions of the contemporary ID movement's arguments indeed appeared already before the final trials on creationism, in the 1984 book *The Mystery of Life's Origin* by Charles Thaxton, Walter Bradley and Roger Olsen. Thus, while we may explain the increased popularity of these kinds of ideas as at least partially as a response to the legal situation, there must also be other factors at work.

28 See, for example, Hannam (2011, chapter 18).

29 Forrest and Gross 2004; see also Koperski (2005) and Dawes (2007) for critiques of this strategy.

If there really was a conspiracy to change to word 'creationism' into 'intelligent design', and if Johnson as the early visionary of ID was the author of this conspiracy, one should expect that he himself would have used the term 'intelligent design' consistently from the outset. But he did not. In Johnson's book *Darwin on Trial*, which for most marks the first public sign of the emerging ID movement, Johnson openly uses the term 'creationism' for his own view. However, Johnson's definition of the term is minimalistic. He states that he is only arguing for the existence of some kind of supernatural creator, without specifying much about the mechanism this creator may have used. Johnson allows that God could have created the species through evolution, as long as evolution was not understood as a purposeless process.[30] Later, the ID movement's design arguments would evolve to refer only to an intelligent designer instead of God, leaving the identification of the designer as God as a further theological philosophical question.

Karl Giberson and Donald Yerxa link ID with creationism in a more plausible, neutral way: the early ID proponents in the 1980s were dissatisfied with creationism already before the 1987 trial, and sought a way to break out of creationism's intellectual ghetto.[31] It seems credible to argue that the movement indeed gained more influence after the 1987 creationism trial gave additional reason for creationists to move away from the old approaches. However, ID's basic idea of presenting better and more minimalistic arguments in favour of belief in biological design was already present before the trial, and legal motivations were not the only factor in play.[32]

Though many of ID's high-profile leaders can also be characterized as creationists in a more traditional sense, it is also true that not all major ID proponents have such a background. Behe moved to ID from a theistic evolutionistic viewpoint rather than any variety of literalistic creationism. Some thinkers from an agnostic background, such as Denton and Berlinski have also been influential in the movement.[33] The simplistic accounts of the origins of the ID movement as a creationist legal strategy do not give enough attention to these thinkers.[34] Nevertheless, it remains correct that when its support is analysed demographically, ID no doubt has support in many of the same social circles (Evangelical Christians) that are also drawn to the 'scientific creationism' which was on trial in 1987.[35]

30 For example, Johnson (1993) and Dembski (1999a, 247–251). Forrest and Gross (2004, 273–283) also note the use of the word 'creationism' in early ID literature.

31 Giberson and Yerxa 2002, chapter 9.

32 Ratzsch (1996, 84–85) similarly identifies early ID theorists as 'upper tier' creationists trying to create more informed and scientific arguments for the creationist belief in the designedness of the order of nature.

33 Berlinski 2009. Woodward (2003, chapter 3) reports that most of the important people in the ID movement were influenced by Denton's 1986 book. Its effect on Johnson and Behe is particularly well known. Denton has later moved in the direction of Aristotelian deism (see Denton 1998).

34 Woodward 2003.

35 This is evidenced by the school education battles chronicled by Forrest and Gross (2004).

Defining creationism

History alone does not settle the question of the relationship of ID and creationism. Rather, the answer also depends on the definition of creationism. Broadly understood, creationism refers simply to the belief that some sort of creative intelligence was involved in the creation of the cosmos and life. For example, in his critique of ID, Niall Shanks argues that the design argument forms the core of creationism. On this broad definition, ID can clearly be classified as creationism. However, this definition also includes many theistic critics of ID (such as the biologist Kenneth Miller, who has even written textbooks teaching mainstream evolutionary biology) among the creationists. Consistent with his definition, Shanks does indeed call Miller a 'cosmological creationist' – but this is hardly in accordance with the common narrower use of the term.[36]

Historian David Sedley similarly classifies the thought of Socrates and Plato, as creationism in his important work *Creationism and Its Critics in Antiquity* (2007). Sedley defines creationism as 'the thesis that the world's structure can be adequately explained only by postulating at least one intelligent designer, a creator god'.[37] For Sedley, this is also the central issue that 'separates modern "creationists" from their Darwinian critics'.[38] Again, this definition is quite broad, since theistic evolutionists also qualify as creationists in this sense.

According to Robert Newman, creationism means simply belief in the doctrine of creation, according to which the world and everything in it has received its being from God, the Creator. Newman divides possible alternatives to creationism into four options: (1) atheism, which asserts that the world exists without gods; (2) pantheism, which asserts that the world is God; (3) panentheism, which asserts that the world is God's body; and (4) dualism, which says that matter is self-existent, but God has molded it.[39] While most ID theorists are creationists according to this definition, they would emphasize that their theory of design is at least theoretically also compatible with Newman's other options: atheism, pantheism, panentheism and dualism. Proponents of ID argue that their design argument does not identify the designer, so someone could in principle interpret the designer as an extraterrestrial alien or Plato's demiurge, for example. They argue that even an atheist could support ID, since the designer could also be a space alien. So on Newman's definition of 'creationism', ID is not identical to creationism, since it is also compatible with other positions. Rather, it is a minimalistic argument that does not determine the proponent's entire worldview.

There is one tension in ID's argumentation at this point: its cultural arguments presuppose a much more robust concept of a designer than merely a space alien or a deity from the Greek pantheon. ID's moral vision, which

36 Shanks 2004, 6, 234.

37 Sedley 2007, xvii.

38 Sedley 2007, xvii.

39 Newman 2001, 115.

I described previously, is clearly theistic. In order to fulfil its aims of changing culture, ID needs some way of linking its minimalistic understanding of the designer with this more robust theistic understanding. Later, I will be arguing that ID would greatly benefit at this point from the resources of theistic natural theologies and theologies of nature.

The definition of creationism can be further defined by specifying what is meant by creation. Does creation refer to God's maintaining the world in existence at every moment, the giving of existence sometime in the past, or both? In the contemporary discussion, varieties of creationism emerge particularly in relation to scientific investigations of origins. Three typical forms of creationism (as broadly understood) are literalistic (Young-Earth) creationism, progressive (Old-Earth) creationism and theistic evolutionism. Many proponents of ID use the term 'creationism' to refer only to Young-Earth creationism, and have laboured to distance ID from creationism as thus understood. For them, ID means only to the belief that the actions of an intelligent designer can in some way be recognized in the pattern of nature, while creationism makes much more specific claims.[40]

The central reason theistic evolutionism is typically separated from creationism is that creationism is understood to imply an opposition to mainstream evolutionary theory. However, none of the above definitions do justice to this feeling. Ratzsch's definition is the best in this regard. Ratzsch argues that in creationism, it is believed that 'whether or not God could have built evolutionary potentials into the creation, or could have brought about life and all its diversity by evolutionary means, he did not in fact do so. There are thus discontinuities in nature – e.g., non-life/life, reptile/mammal, animal/human – which cannot be crossed by purely natural means, each such discontinuity requiring separate supernatural creative action'.[41] I submit that this is what people typically have in mind when they use the term 'creationism' of ID. However, it is important to note that the use of the word 'creationism' varies greatly, and we must take care to define what we mean by the term. Because of the different uses of the term 'creationism', there is both substantial continuity and discontinuity between ID and the different varieties of creationism.

Literalistic creationism or *Young-Earth creationism* is the view that the Earth and all species of animals were miraculously created only 6,000–10,000 years ago. This view is based on a literal, historical interpretation of the biblical scriptures, which are understood as God's word about history, and an interpretation of the scientific evidence which seeks to harmonize science with this literalistic view. Thus science is argued to support belief in a Young-Earth, the reality of a global flood in Noah's time, the possibility of starlight to travel to the Earth from distant stars during the creation week and so on. These theories require extensive

---

40 Koperski (2003, 568) argues similarly that the term 'creationist' is often used pejoratively as a rhetorical tool against ID, rather than in a very precise fashion.

41 Ratzsch 1996, 12.

modifications of mainstream scientific physics, astronomy, geology, biology and history. Young-Earth creationism has not gained much ground in the scientific community, since the creationists' view about the literal understanding of the Bible as the guiding framework of the natural sciences is not widely shared.[42]

Some important ID proponents are Young-Earth creationists, such as the biologist Paul Nelson. However, Nelson reports that creationists of his sort are a minority among the movement's leading theorists.[43] Dembski and Denton have reported that their scepticism of evolution was influenced by the arguments of Young-Earth creationists, though they themselves accept mainstream estimates for the age of the cosmos and life on Earth.[44] There are indeed substantial similarities in the way these creationists and the ID movement criticize Darwinism both scientifically and morally.[45] However, while proponents of ID generally avoid bringing the Bible into the discussion on origins, and regard evidence of design as the central point, many in the Young-Earth camp consider the authority of the Bible to be the central issue.[46]

Progressive creationism (or *Old-Earth creationism*) accepts the old history of the Earth and the universe. The 'days' of the Genesis account of creation in ways which accommodates the long ages of natural history, and God's creating work, is believed to have occurred progressively over this time through numerous supernatural creative acts. Views on where such acts were required vary. Some progressive creationists believe that God acted to create the major kinds of animals, while others believe God intervened only in the origins of life and the origin of the human soul, for example. Progressive creationists can criticize the sufficiency of the Darwinian account of origins like literalistic creationists. Johnson can be classified as a progressive creationist, as can many others in the movement.[47]

Different understanding of theistic evolutionism

Theistic evolutionism or *evolutionary creationism* means the belief that God has used an evolutionary natural process to create the living species. Mainline Catholic and Protestant theology accepts the compatibility of evolutionary theory and the doctrine of creation. Theistic evolutionists want to take mainstream science

42 Numbers (2006) provides the most comprehensive discussion of creationism and its problems available; for another balanced discussion, see Ratzsch (1996).

43 Nelson 2002. The Finnish biotechnologist Matti Leisola, who is the editor of the ID journal *Bio-Complexity*, is another influential ID proponent who is sceptical of the old age of the Earth (Leisola 2013, chapter 8.1.).

44 Dembski 2005c, Denton 2004.

45 Forrest and Gross 2004.

46 YEC's do use the design argument, but they also concentrate much energy on their Flood Geology and on defending the authority of the early chapters of the book of Genesis, understood as literal history. See Numbers 2006 and Wieland 2002; the latter is a YEC critique of ID for its lack of such arguments.

47 Pennock 1999.

seriously when considering how we should interpret the text of Genesis, arguing that the main points of the text, when read in context, are quite compatible with evolutionary biology. Under the broad definitions of creationism, theistic evolutionism is also creationism, since it includes belief in a Creator. However, if we adopt a narrower definition where creationism requires belief in the miraculous activity of God within natural history, then most varieties of theistic evolutionism are not creationism.

Ian G. Barbour classifies theistic evolutionism broadly into three forms. On the first view (1), *God controls events that appear to be random.* On this view, the process of evolution is understood to be under God's control, though his supervision is not included in scientific theories of our origins. On the second view (2), *God designed a system of law and chance.* God set up the universe at the beginning in a way that makes evolution possible. On the third view (3), *God influences the events of evolutionary history without controlling them.* On this view, God is understood to give the world much freedom to evolve. God influences evolution through his love, but does not control it.[48] All of these theories are nuanced and complex proposals, which have results for our theories of divine action and our understanding of the problem of evil, among other things.

These three versions of theistic evolutionism are all united by their acceptance of mainstream Darwinian evolutionary theory. What is excluded is the possibility that a theistic evolutionist might accept parts of evolutionary theory (such as the idea of common descent) while rejecting others (such as the idea of natural selection as the mechanism driving evolutionary change). This type of theistic evolutionism is clearly not the same as literalistic creationism or progressive creationism, though it does not fit into Barbour's definition. However, it has also been historically quite common. Following the Darwinian revolution, the scientific community did not immediately reach a consensus that random mutation and natural selection were indeed the primary force driving evolution.[49] Some contemporary evolutionary biologists are again questioning the centrality of random mutation and selection in the evolutionary process.[50]

Within the ID movement, there is some acceptance of a fourth type (4) of theistic evolutionism, which I define as follows: *God controls the direction of evolution in a way that gives us scientific evidence of his design; non-teleological explanations are not sufficient even on the level of biology.* Behe is a theistic evolutionist in this sense. In his intellectual development, Behe moved from being a theistic evolutionist in the mainstream sense to this fourth category.[51] Behe accepts the doctrine of common descent as probably true, but does not believe that the Darwinian mechanism of mutation and selection can account for all of life's

48 Barbour, 1997; similarly, Giberson and Yerxa (2002, 172). Peters and Hewlett (2003) is a more throughout presentation of the different varieties of theistic evolutionism; see also Clark (2014, chapters 5–9).

49 Ruse 2003, Bowler 2009, 202–207.

50 See, for example, Pigliucci and Müller (2010).

51 See, for example, the arguments of Behe (2007a) and Behe's autobiographical essay, Behe (2006b). I will discuss ID's understanding of evolution further in Chapter 4.

evolution. Rather, he believes that explaining biological complexity requires references to design already on the level of biology. This type of theistic evolutionism includes critiques of evolutionary biology, and so comes closer to narrower definitions of creationism. Nevertheless, it is worlds apart from literalistic creationism.[52]

So, there are ID proponents who fit in each of the different major camps of creationism: literalistic creationism, progressive creationism and theistic evolutionism. If a broad definition of creationism as simply belief in some kind of Creator is used, ID qualifies as creationism. ID also qualifies as creationism under the more narrow definition, where creationism requires belief in a Creator and the rejection of the sufficiency of evolutionary explanations on the level of natural science. However, the variety of creationist views embraced by ID proponents shows that there is no necessary conceptual link between ID and any more specific creationist view, such as progressive creationism. ID's conception of creation is minimalistic and can be assimilated under a variety of broader frameworks. This makes ID distinct from any other view described here.

Because theistic evolutionism also seeks to defend the compatibility of science and theology, it might initially seem plausible that the ID movement would seek to ally with theistic evolutionism. Indeed, ID proponent Paul Nelson explains that ID is meant to be a 'big tent' to unite all those who believe that the order of nature is evidently designed. Nelson writes that 'under the canopy of design as an empirical possibility, however, any number of particular theories may also be possible, including traditional creationism, progressive (or "Old-Earth") creationism, and theistic evolution'.[53] This purpose of uniting those who believe in design and oppose a purely naturalistic understanding of the universe was also behind the ID conference 'Mere Creation' (1996). Questions about the method and timing of creation were seen as secondary to the basic idea of creation, which all Christians could accept.[54]

However, in practice ID proponents are deeply sceptical of the rationality of theistic evolutionism as a view. The ID blogs *Evolution News and Views* and *Uncommon Descent* frequently publish essays critical of theistic evolutionism and organizations which promote theistic evolutionism, such as BioLogos. Even an entire ID-friendly book is devoted purely to the critique of theistic evolutionism.[55] Nelson and the broader ID movement reject most forms of theistic evolutionism as highly problematic and incompatible with ID's vision. Dembski notes that while C.S. Lewis tried to defend only the essentials of

52 Pennock 1991, chapter 1; Scott (1999, 2004) and Ross (2005) all represent different attempts to map out the relationships between the varieties of creationism analysed in this chapter.

53 Nelson 2002.

54 Dembski (ed.) 1998. The title references the work of C.S. Lewis, who wanted to define the essence of Christian doctrine in a way acceptable to all Christians in his book *Mere Christianity* (Lewis 2001, originally published 1942–44).

55 Richards (ed.) 2010.

Christianity in his *Mere Christianity*, proponents of ID try to go further by developing their theory of creation so as to best oppose a purely naturalistic (and atheistic) understanding of the world. ID's vision is to unite all opponents of naturalistic evolutionism in defence of a minimalistic idea of design, *mere creation*. Those living inside ID's 'big tent' may disagree about particulars, but at least agree on the design argument and about opposing atheistic interpretations of science.[56]

In the opinion of many ID proponents, theistic evolutionism fails to properly challenge the atheistic understanding of the universe. Proponents of ID often explain theistic belief in evolution as a result of confining science to methodological naturalism and the desire of theists to gain the respect of materialists, rather than as a result of an open and honest engagement with the evidence. Theists who honestly believe that mainstream evolutionary biology contains good explanations for the evolution of life experience these kinds of explanations as offensive.

Some theistic evolutionists have also criticized ID in strong words, even as heretical or at least destructive to the Christian faith and dangerous for the harmony of science and religion. For example, with characteristic rhetorical vigour, theologian Conor Cunningham argues that ID leads away from the knowledge of the true God: 'the god of Intelligent Design' is one that orthodox Christians should find 'diabolic'.[57] In the coming chapters, I will nevertheless attempt to build some bridges between ID and theistic evolutionism.

ID's struggle against naturalism

Atheistic interpretations of evolution as an influence on ID

The Discovery Institute's definition emphasizes ID's project of presenting evidence of design in nature. However, ID has also been formed partly as a reaction against the perceived use of science as a weapon for atheism. For example, references to Dawkins appear prominently in many major ID works; recall also that Johnson came to his own views while reading Dawkins and Denton side by side.[58] In his famous book *The Blind Watchmaker: How the Evidence of Evolution Reveals a Universe Without a Designer* (1986), and in many subsequent works, Dawkins argues that the evolutionary biology reveals a cosmos without purpose, ruled over by uncaring chance and necessity rather than loving divine providence. Even if evolutionary biology does not rule

56 Dembski (ed.) 1998, 13–14.

57 Cunningham 2010, 280.

58 For example, Johnson (1991), Behe (2006a), Dembski (2001), Meyer (2010), Woodward (2003). Dembski has also stated that Dawkins was a central influence in his formulation of the concept of 'specified complexity' (Barham 2012).

out the existence of God, at least it makes it possible to 'be an intellectually fulfilled atheist'. Faith is left without grounds in the empirically studied world of the senses.

Dawkins' prominence in the ID proponent's works also reflects the public prominence of Dawkins' argumentation. Dawkins' *Blind Watchmaker* remains one of the most in-depth defences of the capability of evolution to explain the origin of complex biological adaptations like the human eye, and his arguments on this point are referenced even in some current textbooks of evolutionary biology.[59] Proponents of ID are therefore not unreasonable to refer to Dawkins' highly influential arguments on the central issue of the capability of the Darwinian mechanism to explain all of life's complexity without design, though there are also views of evolution which do not emphasize the mechanism of natural selection and random mutation as heavily.

Different strategies for responding to the challenge of naturalism

Some theistic evolutionists embrace the randomness of evolution posited by Dawkins and others, arguing that it represents a degree of freedom that the Creator has chosen to give nature. However, typically theistic evolutionists do not accept the broad idea of evolution as a completely purposeless process. According to theistic evolutionists, even though the mechanisms of random mutation and selection are sufficient explanations in the realm of biology, this still does not mean that the overall process could not be interpreted as purposeful in a broader, philosophical and theological context. For example, theistic evolutionists can argue that the Creator is necessary for upholding nature in existence and providing the background conditions of evolution.

This theistic interpretation indeed diverges from some interpretations of standard evolutionary biology, since evolutionary theory has commonly been argued to work without an overarching purpose. For example, Michael Ruse argues that 'it is absolutely central to Darwinian evolutionary theory that the course of evolution is contingent'.[60] However, as philosopher of biology Elliott Sober points out, it is not a necessary part of evolutionary theory that the 'random' mutations are not directed by God. The 'randomness' means simply that no physical cause is known to correlate mutations with the adaptive needs of the organisms and that mutations are statistically random. Nevertheless, as a statistical theory the theory of evolution does not, according to Sober, rule out the existence of higher variables. Under this understanding, thinking of evolution as an undirected or directed process is a philosophical interpretation of evolution, rather than a part of science as such.[61]

59 For example, Freeman and Herron (2007, 98–99).

60 Ruse 2012, 253.

61 Sober 2014; see further the discussion in Moritz (forthcoming).

This kind of philosophical interpretation and theological worldview-building is opposed to naturalistic philosophy. The meaning of the term 'naturalism' has no very precise meaning in modern philosophy – there are many varieties of naturalists. However, naturalists generally hold that our picture of the world should be based on science, and the function of philosophy is to support the work of building a scientific worldview. Accordingly, naturalists argue that there is no overarching purpose or goal for nature, and no mind beyond it. There can be many different ways of defending such a position: for example, one might argue that theological questions like the existence of God or the purposes of nature are beyond the reach of science, and that this means we cannot know anything about them. Alternatively, one might argue that the existence of God is in principle a question that we can investigate, but we have good evidence against his existence.[62]

In any case, naturalism is understood to centrally include the denial of the existence of God and divine purposes in nature. However, beyond this point, naturalism includes quite a broad variety of conceptions of what is 'natural'. A naturalistic definition of what exists might be that everything that exists is composed of the 'stuff described by chemists in the periodic table of the elements', though even more elementary levels can of course be studied.[63] However, this is still quite a vague description of what nature contains, especially as many naturalists allow for emergence of properties whose best description seems to be more than just chemistry, such as consciousness.[64]

In responding to the challenge of naturalistic evolution, the strategies of theistic evolutionists and defenders of ID are very different. Proponents of ID seek to primarily challenge naturalistic evolution as a scientific theory, arguing that a scientific worldview should actually include the idea of an intelligent designer and so become consonant with the doctrine of creation. In contrast, theistic evolutionists typically challenge naturalistic evolutionism on the level of philosophy and theology. They argue that as important as the natural sciences are, rationality is not restricted to natural science. Rather, both naturalism and theism are worldviews that go beyond the results of science, and we must use philosophical and theological arguments to differentiate between them. Theistic evolutionists do not want to refer to design in the context of the natural sciences, but many are happy to refer to the designedness of nature as part of a broader theological and philosophical understanding of the world.

62 Papineau 2009; see also Ritchie (2008) for an overview of varieties of naturalism. For some theistic attempts at defining naturalism, see Hardwick (1996, 5–6), Haught (2009, 247) and Goetz and Taliaferro (2008). I should note already here that this philosophical naturalism is distinct from methodological naturalism as a philosophical criterion of what counts as natural science. Whereas philosophical naturalism makes claims about reality, methodological naturalism only makes claims about what the proper domain of science is.

63 Drees 2006.

64 See further Ritchie (2008, chapter 6).

The possibility of natural theology

The challenge of fideism

Both proponents of ID and many theistic evolutionists aim to build consonance between religious belief and publicly available evidence, such as the natural sciences. This comes close to the traditional aims of natural theology, though a great difference between ID and mainstream natural theology is that the arguments of natural theology are not presented as part of the natural sciences. Both ID and natural theologians agree that it is important to build connections between religious beliefs and publicly available evidence, including the natural sciences. But does this kind of talk about evidence for religious truths make sense?

Religious *fideists* (from the Latin word *fides*, faith) emphasize the difference between evidential reasoning and religious beliefs. For example, D.Z. Phillips argues that seeing God as a hypothesis to explain the world is contrary to the actual nature of religious belief. Hypotheses are always uncertain, but for many believers God is their fundamental ground of being, an absolute certainty and not a hypothesis.[65] Though he is not a fideist by traditional definitions, Alvin Plantinga similarly argues that Christian belief does not originate in looking for explanations, but in the self-revelation of God: 'Believers in God do not ordinarily postulate that there is such a person, just as believers in other persons or material objects do not ordinarily postulate that there are such things'.[66] According to Plantinga, hypotheses are necessary for scientific theories, but Christians do not postulate God as an explanation, but receive knowledge of God through the action of the Holy Spirit.[67] In the way I use the term, fideism does not necessarily mean that religious beliefs are irrational, since rationality is not restricted to science. Rather, fideism argues simply that the rationality of religious beliefs should be compared more to the rationality of relationships, and to the rationality of a way of life, rather than to the rationality of a scientific theory. Here personal experiences and pragmatic considerations can also influence the rationality of religious beliefs.[68]

It seems to me that fideism captures something essential about religious beliefs. The origins of religious beliefs are complex and the process is for different for religious people, involving religious experience, community, tradition and so on. In the context of religious faith, treating God as a hypothesis can even seem impious, not fitting how we should relate to God as the ground of being. Nevertheless, it seems to me that though traditionally Christians have not presented belief in God as a scientific hypothesis, particular Christian

---

65 Phillips 1976; see also Koistinen (2000).

66 Plantinga 2000, 370.

67 Plantinga 2000.

68 For further explorations of this broad type of fideism, and the rationality of religious faith more generally, see Vainio (2010) and Stenmark (1995).

doctrines can still possess explanatory potential. Alister McGrath argues well that the Christian tradition contains explanations for the religious experiences of Christians. For example, we explain the experiences of the resurrected Jesus and the development of Christian belief in the resurrection as the result of a real resurrection. The doctrine of creation also has such explanatory potential in the eyes of many religious believers.[69]

Mikael Stenmark has provided an interesting metaphor for why a religious believer might consider it useful to engage in a theoretical discussion about evidence for the existence of God, even if belief in God is not primarily a hypothesis for the believer. Consider my belief that my wife loves me. This belief is grounded in my entire life experience with my wife, and my belief in it is not a hypothesis. Nevertheless, suppose that someone else does not believe that my wife loves me, or has doubts about her virtuous character. I could in principle discuss some evidences of this love, even though it will be difficult to convey the full grounds of my own beliefs. Similarly, Stenmark argues that a religious believer may discuss the evidence for God's existence, though the grounds for religious belief are broader.[70] Similarly, the reasons for belief discussed by Swinburne and other theistic philosophers (or the ID movement) can be discussed, even if religious belief itself is based on broader grounds.[71] Indeed, historically even most of those who classified as fideists have valued finding some sort of connections between Christianity and the broader culture.[72]

A brief history of natural theology

Though religious belief is clearly not limited to the arguments of natural theology, there has also been much support in the Christian tradition for the idea that some kind of publicly available evidence of the existence of a Creator exists. The standard biblical proof text for natural theology has long been Romans 1:20: 'For since the creation of the world God's invisible qualities – his eternal power and divine nature – have been clearly seen, being understood from what has been made, so that people are without excuse'. Acts 14:17 states that God 'has not left himself without testimony: He has shown kindness by giving you rain from heaven and crops in their seasons; he provides you with plenty of food and fills your hearts with joy'. These and other passages like them do not present arguments for the existence of God, but some idea of the common availability of knowledge of God, nevertheless, seems to be present.[73]

---

69 McGrath 2003, chapter 14.

70 Stenmark 1995, 325–327.

71 The parable is incomplete because natural theology is not just theoretical dialogue to convince others of the truth of some proposition. Rather, it is also the theoretical exploration and systematization of intuitions about the world and meditation before the mysteries of creation. McGrath (2008, chapter 11), for example, emphasizes natural theology's links to the theology of beauty and awe.

72 Vainio 2010.

73 For analyses of Biblical natural theology, see Barr (1993) and Rowland (2013).

Although some early Christians took a negative attitude to philosophy, many early Church Fathers, nevertheless, took a positive attitude to natural theology and valued connections between Christianity and Greek philosophy. Augustine writes that 'though the voices of the prophets were silent, the world itself, by its well-ordered changes and movements, and by the fair appearance of all visible things, bears a testimony of its own, both that it has been created, and also that it could not have been created save by God, whose greatness and beauty are unutterable and invisible'.[74] Here Augustine says that the order of the world is evidently created by God, and that this could be known even without the prophets. In many places the Church Fathers also support their views with philosophical arguments.[75] However, in their writings, faith and reason are arguably conceived as a holistic unity rather than making a sharp distinction between the deliverances of reason and the deliverances of faith.[76] In the Middle Ages, natural theology was developed further by theologians such as Anselm (1033–1109), Bonaventure (1221–74) and Thomas Aquinas (1225–74).[77] Many of the early scientific pioneers of modern science were also enthusiastic proponents of natural theology, particularly in Britain.[78]

The critiques of natural theology made in the 18th and 19th centuries are often still believed to be fatal to the whole enterprise, though they never caused natural theology to disappear. Since the renaissance of analytic philosophical theology starting from the 1960s, the demise of the philosophy of logical positivism (a historical predecessor of contemporary scientism) and the development of the field of science and religion, natural theology has also been making a comeback. The dispelling of the myth that 'science' and 'religion' have been historically in a state of war has also made it more interesting to discuss possible commonalities in the present day.[79]

In the contemporary discussion, natural theology has many defenders, and many ways of answering or bypassing the traditional critiques have been developed.[80] Even prominent university presses are publishing large tomes on natural theology like the *Blackwell Companion to Natural Theology* (2011) and the *Oxford Handbook of Natural Theology* (2013). The design argument is only one of several theistic arguments that continue to be defended. For example, the cosmological argument portrays God as the necessary ground of our contingent being.

---

74 *De civitate dei*, XI, 4.

75 Irenaeus, *Against Heresies*, II: 1–9; Gregory of Nyssa, *On the Soul and Resurrection*, chapter 1; Augustine, *On Free Will*, 2.12.33. I have found these examples through Swinburne (2004b, 536).

76 McGrath 2001, chapter 6.

77 See further Hall (2013) and Feser (2008).

78 Brooke 1991; see also McGrath (2009b).

79 For good works on the historical relationship of science and religion, I recommend Brooke (1991), Ferngren, ed. (2002) and Harrison (2015). For general introductions to the field of science and religion, I recommend Southgate, ed. (2011), McGrath (2010) and Russell (2008).

80 Prominent defenders and critics of natural theology agree that the Humean and Kantian critiques are no longer convincing without substantial modification, if even then. For example, see the evaluations of Swinburne (2004a, 2011a, 2011b) and Philipse (2012).

Many of the theistic arguments are metaphysical and not dependent on the very specific empirical details studied by the natural sciences in the same way that the ID movement's design arguments are. The new formulations of traditional theistic arguments have not persuaded everyone, but discussion of them is very much alive, and it is difficult to dismiss them as irrational, even though the arguments are not scientific.[81]

Defending the possibility of a moderate natural theology

Whereas many critiques of natural theology assume that the project fails if there is any way to deny the conclusions of the theistic arguments, modern natural theologians typically argue that there can be good evidence in favour of the existence of God, even if not all are persuaded. It does indeed seem too stringent to demand that any useful natural theology must provide certain and deductive proof of God's existence, whereby all who hear the proof will be thoroughly convinced. Very few things in philosophy can be known with such certainty.[82] Thus Richard Swinburne, perhaps the best-known contemporary natural theologian, argues in his work, *The Existence of God*, only to the conclusion that the probability of theism being true is over 50 per cent after considering several cumulative arguments which each raise the probability by some amount. Swinburne himself believes that the probabilities are much higher, and the arguments from religious experience in particular raise them further.[83]

Once we reject scientism, it seems clear to me that the philosophical arguments of natural theology deserve serious consideration, and that natural theology can be formulated in a way that takes the best points of the fideistic critique into account.[84] For some readers, the term 'natural theology' may cause aversion because some forms of natural theology have not taken the complex nature of religious rationality into account properly. However, even if we reject natural theology for this reason, the same kind of arguments can also be valued in theologies of nature.[85] Whereas natural theology seeks to speak of God based on human reason and experience and attempts to build discussion based on premises as broadly acceptable as possible, theologies of nature begin the interpretation of nature from within a religious tradition such as Christianity. Dialogue with the natural sciences can then allow Christian believers to find that the empirical order of nature resonates with their prior religious beliefs.

81 See, for example, Swinburne (2004a), Spitzer (2010), Evans (2010), Mackie (1982) and Philipse (2012).

82 Plantinga 1990 [1967], ix–x.

83 Swinburne 2004.

84 For one analysis of the relevance of the concept of 'evidence' for theology, see Dougherty (forthcoming); see also the other articles in the book. McGrath (2001) also provides a well-reasoned general defense of the relevance of empirical studies for theology. Denys Turner (2004) attempts to reconcile apophatic theology and natural theology; I will also have something to say about this is Chapter 6.

85 The distinction between natural theologies and theologies of nature is based on the work of Barbour (1997, 100).

Theologies of nature do not seek to establish the existence of God through any supposed neutral starting point. However, they can also still value traditional theistic arguments like the design argument as a way of demonstrating how a theistic interpretation of nature can work. In a way, theologies of nature present an interesting compromise between the insights of fideism and natural theology.[86]

I believe that dialogue across worldviews increases our chances of correcting errors in our own viewpoints. This is also a weighty reason to value connections or 'resonance' (as McGrath terms it) between theology and publicly available evidence, including the natural sciences. So, I will not be rejecting the general quest for dialogue between theology and the natural sciences, which the ID movement also attempts to do in its own way, nor will I be rejecting the general theological idea of natural revelation, nor the general idea of design arguments. However, acceptance of these general ideas does not necessarily lead to embracing the particular arguments that ID makes, and much of the contemporary theology and science community has indeed rejected ID's arguments. Rather, we must ask the further question of what kind of arguments are most fruitful for such dialogue between the natural sciences and theology.

Summary

Intelligent Design is a movement and an idea. The basic idea that nature provides some kind of evidence of an intelligent creator has ancient roots and is even shared by many theistic critics of ID; ID's defence of the idea is controversial because of its emphasis on the scientific nature of the design argument, and also because of its critique of evolutionary biology. This critique brings ID into a continuum with what have been known as 'creationist' views. However, there are many definitions of 'creationism', and the term does not capture the minimalistic nature of ID's argument.

Though ID's design argument is minimalistic, its cultural goals are far broader. Thought proponents of ID emphasize the scientific nature of their argument, they also openly declare that their intent is to transform broader culture through creating a form of science that (they believe) is more congenial to a theistic vision of reality than mainstream evolutionary biology. In this, ID opposes most forms of theistic evolutionism, since theistic evolutionists challenge atheistic philosophical interpretations of evolution, but leave evolution as a scientific theory intact. ID's interpretation of the consequences of accepting

86 The precise border between natural theologies and theologies of nature can be difficult to determine (Padgett 2004, Runehov 2010). For instance, McGrath is a theologian of nature by the definitions I have used in the main text, but he himself calls his enterprise natural theology. Both theologians of nature and natural theologians can also refer to the same evidence, such as cosmic fine-tuning, as supporting religious belief. For example, compare Robin Collins' (2012) and McGrath's (2009) uses of the fine-tuning evidence.

evolutionary biology is much closer to those of many atheists than the understanding of the theistic evolutionists.

In theology, attempts to find connections between theology and publicly available evidence have usually been investigated as part of natural theology. The general idea of presenting reasons for belief and seeking to create dialogue between theology and the natural sciences is appealing, though one should be careful not to reduce religious rationality to something like a science. For me, acceptance of this kind of general idea means being open to theistic arguments, of which the design argument is one. But it still needs to be evaluated whether some way of arguing for such connections (like ID) is fruitful or not. While proponents of ID have sought to distance their arguments from traditional philosophical natural theology, the resources of the theology and science community and the fruits of hundreds of years of discussion on natural theology would surely be helpful for bringing the discussion on ID forward.

3 The cosmological debate

The basic idea that nature must have properties which allow for the existence of complex life seems to be as true as the fact of our existence. At the everyday level, this can be seen in the way human life depends on the environment. Life operates in a complex ecosystem which is itself dependent on antecedent conditions: soil must have nutrients that allow the growth of plants, water must be present, as must air and light. Water, wind and fire have been used to power our economies and technology and the phenomena of astronomy have allowed the creation of calendars.

Traditionally many theists have believed that these and other environmental factors were in fact designed for our benefit and are not just accidentally useful. A design argument to this effect was already formulated by the Jewish philosopher Philo (20 BC–40 AD), who argued that the cosmos can be compared to a house which has been built to accommodate people. According to Philo, just as we would immediately see that a well-built house has an architect, so we should also see the cosmos as designed. In both cases, Philo sees the apparent teleology as a sign of purposive design.[1]

In the contemporary discussion, many have argued that this kind of design argument is only strengthened by the progress of science. As noted, the debate over ID definitely has its scientific side in cosmology and biology. In cosmology, proponents of ID argue that the cosmos is fine-tuned for the existence of complex life, and for scientific discoverability. At this point proponents of ID are not particularly original, though they do make some new contributions to the debate. Indeed, the best fine-tuning arguments have been formulated by philosophers outside the movement, such as Richard Swinburne and Robin Collins.

The ID movement is rightly known best for its biological arguments, and proponents of ID emphasize the biological case for design much more than the cosmological one. For example, Behe writes that 'by 'intelligent design' I mean to imply design beyond the laws of nature. That is, taking the laws of nature as given, are there other reasons for concluding that life and its component

1 *Legum Allegoriae* III, 32, 98–99. Hurlbutt 1985, 8. See also Barrow and Tipler 1986, chapter 2.

systems have been intentionally arranged?'[2] Johnson admits that naturalistic evolution leaves room for a Creator who set up naturalistic processes to do the 'work of creation'. However, for him this is not enough: 'If God stayed in that realm beyond the reach of scientific investigation, and allowed an apparently blind materialistic evolutionary process to do all the work of creation, then it would have to be said that God furnished us with a world of excuses for unbelief and idolatry'.[3] The implication is that mere fine-tuning does not provide enough evidence of a *theistic* God who has been active in natural history, as opposed to the God of *deism*, who merely set things up at the beginning. Proponents of ID want to argue that there is evidence of design beyond the laws and basic properties of nature.

However, cosmological design arguments are also important for the ID movement. The fine-tuning argument is also present in the ID literature from the beginning. The early collections of ID articles, 'Mere Creation' (1998) and 'The Creation Hypothesis' (1994) included chapters on fine-tuning and the cosmic design argument. The later ID books *The Privileged Planet* (2004) and *A Meaningful World* (2006) even focus on cosmic design arguments. Many ID proponents use the discussion on fine-tuning as background for their own biological arguments.[4] Johnson himself sometimes gives very broad formulations of the grounds of design beliefs, such as the following: 'reality is simply too rational and beautiful ever to be forced into the narrow categories that materialism can comprehend'.[5]

Later in this book, I will compare the relative virtues of different approaches to design arguments. But the point of this chapter is to introduce the cosmological debate and to reveal some of the philosophical and theological assumptions that go into interpreting nature's order as either purposefully created or non-purposeful. I will begin with the empirical data in the first two sections of this chapter, and then go on to discuss its interpretation in the last two sections.

Fine-tuning for the existence of complex life

The basics of fine-tuning

The fine-tuning design argument is based on the observation that the laws of nature allow for the existence of complex life. The 'weak anthropic principle', popularized by John Barrow and Frank Tipler, states that 'the observed values of all physical and cosmological quantities are not equally probable but they take on values restricted by the requirement that there exist sites where

2 Behe 2001a, 696. Behe has not been totally consistent in this definition. At other times he writes as though believing in cosmic design is enough to make someone a believer in 'intelligent design'; see Behe (1999a).

3 Johnson 1993b.

4 Moreland (ed.) 1994, Dembski (ed.) 1998, Gonzales and Richards 2004, Wiker and Witt 2006.

5 P. Johnson 2000, 152, similarly also, for example, Dembski and Wells (2008, 30).

carbon-based life can evolve and by the requirement that the Universe be old enough for it to have already done so'.[6] It is further argued that the requirements for the existence of complex life in our cosmos are quite exact, and not likely if the values are random. It appears if the constants of nature were slightly different, the evolution and continued existence of complex life would be impossible. In the discussion concerning fine-tuning, the use of the term 'fine-tuning' is not typically understood to assume that there is a designer. The idea is rather that the laws of nature are balanced between extremes and are just right to allow for the existence of life. ID proponents Guillermo Gonzales and Jay Richards illustrate this with the analogy of a universe-creating machine. The machine contains a dial for each law and constant of nature. All of the different variables have to be set just right for life to be possible. The conditions required for life are stringent, and it seems that 'if we were just to pick these values at random, we would almost never find a combination compatible with life or anything like it'.[7]

There are many examples of fine-tuning in the scientific literature, and few critics of the fine-tuning argument question the fine-tuning of the cosmos for life.[8] Cosmologists and physicists with very different worldviews – such as Martin Rees,[9] Paul Davies[10] and Stephen Hawking[11] – acknowledge the reality of fine-tuning. In light of this quite broad consensus, Collins seems to be right to argue that while some examples have been shown to be poor in the course of time, most have stood the test of time. It thus seems unlikely that the majority of the examples of fine-tuning will be shown to be scientifically incorrect.[12]

The evidence for fine-tuning can be broadly classified into four types. First (1), the general existence and properties of the laws and forces of nature are important. For example, all of the four basic forces have to exist. Second (2), the relative strengths of the basic forces of nature must be such that they allow life to exist. Third (3), the starting conditions of the cosmos must be appropriate, with the proper arrangement of matter and anti-matter. Fourth (4), the properties of the elements which are consequences of the previous three factors must allow for life: life needs suitable 'building blocks'.[13]

In the general literature about fine-tuning, a common example of this fitness of the laws of nature for life comes from the fine-tuning of the four basic forces of nature. These examples fall into the first and second category, and

6 Barrow and Tipler 1986, 16. ID proponents Gonzales and Richards simplify the principle as follows: 'we should expect to observe conditions, however unusual, compatible with or even necessary for our existence as observers' (Gonzales and Richards 2004, 136.)
7 Gonzales and Richards 2004, 197.
8 Stenger (2006, 2011) is a prominent exception to this trend.
9 Rees 2000.
10 Davies 1992, chapter 4; Davies 2006.
11 Hawking and Mlodinow 2010.
12 R. Collins 2003.
13 See also the classification in R. Collins (2012).

are commonly used by proponents of ID.[14] The strengths of gravity, electromagnetism, the strong nuclear force and the weak nuclear force must be in right proportion to each other. The strong nuclear force holds the protons and neutrons of the atomic nuclei together, offsetting the natural repulsion between positively charged protons. With a weaker strong nuclear force, we would have much fewer elements, missing many of those crucial to life. The lighter elements would also be radioactive to the extent of making life impossible. If the gravitational force were weaker, the expansion after the Big Bang would have been too rapid and clumps of matter like stars and galaxies could not have formed. If it were stronger, the universe would have collapsed in on itself. In order for complex life to be possible, all of the fundamental forces need to exist, and they need to have values which are suitable for life.[15]

The problem of evaluating likelihoods

One problem for the argument stems from evaluating the probability of the fine-tuning. In accounts of fine-tuning, scientists commonly present astronomically small probabilities for the facts of fine-tuning. For example, Roger Penrose calculates that the 'Creator's aim' must have been able to hit a bull's-eye that is the size of one part in 10^10^123:

> This is an extraordinary figure. One could not possibly even write the number down in full, in the ordinary denary notation: it would be '1' followed by 10^123 successive '0's! Even if we were to write a '0' on each separate proton and on each separate neutron in the entire universe – and we could throw in all the other particles as well for good measure – we should fall far short of writing down the figure needed.[16]

On the understanding that evaluations of probability are based on our knowledge of the causal processes which operate in a given situation, these kinds of calculations should be impossible, since evaluating the likelihood of the values would require background knowledge of the natural processes which could have generated these values. However, since we do not know any natural processes which are at a deeper level than the data used in the cosmic design argument, we cannot give a statistical probability to the values. This has been called the 'normalization problem'.[17]

Several different responses to this problem are available, however. For example, Collins has argued that the argument only requires the evaluation of *epistemic*

---

14 For example, Gonzales and Richards (2004, 201–205), Denton (1998), Behe (2007a, chapter 10) and Meyer (1999c).

15 Leslie 1989, 2–6; R. Collins 2003, 183–190.

16 Penrose 2002 [1989], 445–446.

17 See, for example, McGrew, McGrew and Vestrup (2003) and Manson (2009).

likelihoods (understood as what we have grounds to expect based on some hypothesis) instead of *physical* likelihoods (what is in actual physical reality likely or necessary). Our inability to evaluate physical likelihoods does not mean that we cannot evaluate epistemic likelihoods. The procedure for calculating the likelihoods of the constants of nature is similar to the process for creating a null hypothesis in statistics. We simply assume that the range can vary and that the different possibilities are all equally possible. This is a standard way of operating in many cases. For example, if we try to calculate the probability of a given dice roll, we simply assume that results are equally probable, even though the result is actually determined by factors like the force of the throw and the position of the dice. Similarly, Collins argues that it is not unreasonable to calculate some epistemic probabilities for the constants of nature and to use these to compare design-based explanation to random chance.[18]

Fine-tuning for discoverability

The intelligibility of the cosmos

The data used in cosmic design arguments is not limited to the fine-tuning of the cosmos, however. The cosmic design argument also appeals to the general rationality of the cosmos. Albert Einstein famously said that 'the most incomprehensible thing about the universe is that it is comprehensible'.[19] In the broader discussion on fine-tuning, this argument has been developed by philosophers like John Leslie, Richard Swinburne and Robin Collins.[20] Within ID, the argument has been taken up particularly by Michael Denton, Benjamin Wiker, Jonathan Witt, Guillermo Gonzales and Jay Richards.[21]

The design argument based on the rationality of the cosmos is not based just on the general intelligibility of the cosmos. Rather, particular features of the order of nature are argued to be fine-tuned so as to make nature comprehensible and amenable to scientific discovery. Thus the possibility of natural science and the development of technology are upheld alongside the possibility of complex life as another outcome of fine-tuning. Proponents of ID argue that such features of the universe are surprising and in need of explanation.

As one example of such an empirical argument, Gonzales and Richards argue that there exists a correlation between the conditions that allow for habitability and the conditions that allow for scientific discovery. They argue that only a very small section of the universe is habitable, and (surprisingly) it is this same section which also allows for scientific discovery. The features which are

18 R. Collins 2005a, 179; 2012, 226–252. The possibility of fine-tuning arguments against the normalization problem is defended with a different strategy by Koperski (2005).

19 Quoted in Wiker and Witt 2006, 237.

20 Leslie 1989, 58–61; Swinburne 2004a, chapter 8, R. Collins 2005a.

21 Denton 1998, Wiker and Witt 2006, Gonzales and Richards 2004.

fine-tuned for life are, according to this analysis, simultaneously fine-tuned for discovery.[22]

Another example comes from the properties of the Earth's atmosphere. The atmosphere contains elements like oxygen, which are highly beneficial for life and technology. Oxygen is reactive and can thus provide energy for larger living organisms as well as the fires of technology. It protects us from solar radiation in the form of ozone. Simultaneously, our atmosphere also allows for the visible spectrum of light to pass through it. Here our atmosphere is different from many other planets which have a dense cloud covering at all times. Many gases do not allow for the passage of light. Thus the Earth's atmosphere is simultaneously beneficial to life and allows for scientific discovery, unlike the atmospheres of other known planets.[23]

A related argument is based on the effectiveness of mathematics in scientific theories about the universe. According to Wiker and Witt, for scientists, 'the greatest and most peculiar intellectual exhilaration occurs when they find that the order of mathematics illuminates the order of reality'.[24] Mathematics is a human language, which is nevertheless highly applicable to the study of nature. The possibility to formulate the basic laws of physics in simple mathematical language has been highly conducive for the development of natural science. Highly theoretical developments in mathematical theory which have been studied simply for the sake of developing the system in a logically consistent way have turned out to be highly useful in studies of nature.[25] This pattern is not an invention of the ID theorists. Eugene Wigner's classic 1960 paper 'The Unreasonable Effectiveness of Mathematics in the Natural Sciences' is another well-known argument. Wigner marvels that many highly esoteric and at first useless theories of mathematics have later turned out to be essential for the progress of natural science: 'the miracle of the appropriateness of the language of mathematics for the formulation of the laws of physics is a wonderful gift which we neither understand nor deserve'.[26]

Discoverability and mystery

Wiker and Witt admit that the progress of science has been a long and arduous journey of discovery. No matter how far we probe, we encounter ever further mysteries. Our best scientific theories turn out to be just approximations from which we can proceed to more accurate theories. For Wiker and Witt, this nevertheless does not provide counterevidence to the claim that the universe is intelligible. This is because on each level of increasing understanding, our

22 Gonzales and Richards 2004.

23 Gonzales and Richards 2004, chapter 4. Similarly Behe 2007a, 208–209; Denton 1998, 21–46; Wiker and Witt 2006.

24 Wiker and Witt 2006, 103.

25 Wiker and Witt 2006.

26 Wigner (1960), discussed in the ID movement by Dembski (1999b) while reviewing Steiner (1999).

models of reality still work and allow us to proceed deeper into understanding nature.[27]

The argument that nature is fine-tuned for discoverability is not as widely accepted as the argument that nature is fine-tuned for the existence of complex life. Certainly the majority of scientists do agree that nature can be understood and studied. However, it could also be argued that many current theories of physics, such as quantum mechanics, are counter-intuitive and are only understood by a handful of brilliant physicists. So clearly there is mystery to nature, not merely intelligibility, even though the possibility to even formulate theories like quantum theory can still be understood as examples of the amenability of the cosmos to scientific study. To the high-level physicists talking about the intelligibility of the cosmos, it does not imply that the cosmos needs to be equally understood by all.[28]

However, Wiker and Witt interpret the simultaneous mysteriousness and intelligibility of nature as a strength of the design argument. Using the periodic table as one example, they argue that the order of nature is built in a way that makes it possible for us to proceed to an ever deeper understanding of nature: 'The universe, and our privileged place in it, proves not only meaningful; the cup of its meaning continually overflows into mystery and wonder. The universe is crafted to condescend to our capacities as a teacher to a student and to draw us patiently upward; and the superabundance of intelligibility is a sign that it was made by a mind that far exceeds the merely human'.[29] Wiker and Witt argue that if the universe was intelligible without being mysterious and open to ever deeper understanding, we would be left with a lesser appreciation of its Creator. Their argument attempts to go beyond the conclusion that there is an intelligent designer to the conclusion that this designer possesses the attribute of ingenuity. Here the design argument almost approaches the tone of worship: Wiker and Witt revel in the magnanimity of the unidentified 'intelligent designer'.

Wiker and Witt also bring the concept of beauty into their analysis of fine-tuning as something that complements our appreciation of how special the order of nature is. They argue that the true meaningfulness of fine-tuning can only be seen when we consider the marvellous beauty and plurality of complex life which fine-tuning makes possible. 'The chemical elements themselves (made possible by fundamental, cosmological fine-tuning) point toward living things, carrying in their very structures extraordinary and exact chemical potentialities beautifully designed for actualization in the biological world'.[30] This fine-tuning helps us appreciate the surface beauty of the world: 'a rose is most meaningful to us when we understand it as a kind of dramatic culmination,

27 Wiker and Witt 2006.

28 See for example Barrow 2002.

29 Wiker and Witt 2006, 245.

30 Wiker and Witt 2006, 223.

one possible only because all these layers of complexity are integrated by and toward the whole, brought into harmony in and by the living form itself'.[31] Similarly, Gonzales and Richards note that the need for an explanation for fine-tuning becomes more clear if we share the assumption that a 'fine-tuned habitable universe has an intrinsic value that an uninhabitable one would lack'.[32] Here ID's cosmic design arguments are clearly influenced by considerations of value and beauty which go beyond the movement's usual minimalistic understanding of the argument and move towards a more robust theological understanding of the designer.

Design arguments and critiques

The basics of the argument

Though some squabbling about the basic facts of fine-tuning can be done, the more controversial part is the interpretation of this data. Within theistic natural theology, cosmological design arguments have typically been formulated as inferences to the best explanation. I will analyse the logic of such arguments more closely in Chapter 8; for now it suffices to understand that the data to be explained is the fine-tuning of the cosmos for life (given the stringent requirements for building life) and the rationality of the cosmos. The hypothesis that this order is created by a theistic God is thought to be a far likelier explanation than any naturalistic explanation, particularly random chance. Usually, the reason given is that God is good and has the motive to create life and order and the ability to order the cosmos in a fine-tuned manner.[33]

Some ID proponents have referred to the formulations used by Collins and Swinburne approvingly.[34] However, because these formulations are openly theistic, they are in tension with the ID movement's strategy of not identifying the intelligent designer as the good God of theism. To be consistent, the ID movement needs to provide a cosmic design argument for an unidentified designer. This inference would also be an inference to the best explanation, though here the hypothesis lacks the support of broader theistic philosophical arguments which Swinburne and Collins believe are essential to the argument.

Collins himself does provide an alternative way of stating the argument that is more congenial to ID's minimalistic design hypothesis. Collins writes in an earlier formulation: 'In the case of the fine-tuning, we already know that minds often produce fine-tuned devices, such as Swiss watches. Postulating God – a "supermind" – as the explanation of the fine-tuning, therefore, is a natural

---

31 Wiker and Witt 2006, 242.

32 Gonzales and Richards 2004, 300. Similarly, Ratzsch (2001).

33 Collins 2005a, 179; Collins 2012; similarly, Swinburne (2004a, chapter 8).

34 For example, Meyer (1998).

extrapolation from of what we already observe minds to do'.[35] In this inference, the motives of the Creator do not do the explanatory work. Rather, this inference relies on the idea that design just is a good explanation for certain types of order, even if the motives of the designer remain unknown.

The formulations of the cosmic design argument reveal the importance of contrasting design with naturalistic explanations. It is argued that the rational order of the cosmos has something that is explained better by a design hypothesis than by any naturalistic alternative – and perhaps even that some things about the cosmos cannot be explained at all on the naturalistic picture.

There are four main naturalistic responses to the fine-tuning argument. First (1), there are naturalistic alternative explanations for the order of the cosmos. In effect, these explanations are allies of the design argument, because they at least admit that there is something to be explained about the laws of nature. Second (2), the problem of natural evil is used as counterevidence to the fine-tuning. Perhaps the cosmos is not so fine-tuned after all, it is argued. Third (3), it is argued that it is possible to just accept the existence of the cosmos as a brute fact and deny the rationality of seeking any further explanations. Fourth (4), the explanatory power of the design argument is criticized. It is argued that it is better to state that one does not know the explanation than to posit that design is the explanation for fine-tuning.

Natural explanations for fine-tuning

Collins divides naturalistic explanations for fine-tuning into atheistic one-universe models and atheistic many-universes models.[36] In one-universe models, it is hypothesized that the fine-tuning can be explained by referring to some physical explanation beyond the known laws of nature. For example, perhaps the values of the constants of nature can ultimately be explained without reference to design based on some even more foundational scientific theory, such as string theory.[37] Though such theories are not yet fully fleshed out, multiverse hypotheses provide another common way to explain fine-tuning.[38] The idea is that there may be an infinite or at least enormously large amount of universes, with varying constants of nature and natural laws.[39] The weak anthropic principle is then used to explain why we find ourselves in a world with laws of nature that can sustain our existence. We simply could not live and observe a world which did not allow for our existence, so it is unsurprising that we live in a part

35 R. Collins 2005b, 661.

36 R. Collins 2005a, 184–185. These critiques thus typically admit the existence of fine-tuning beneficial to life. For further discussion of the distinction between different uses of the word 'probability' in fine-tuning arguments, see Monton (2006, 407–413).

37 For example, Greene (2005).

38 For example, Dawkins (2006a).

39 Rees 2003.

of the multiverse which allows for life.[40] In this scenario, if the universe appears designed to us, this is only because of this selection effect, which ensures that we will only ever observe a fine-tuned universe. However, the vast majority of universes may well be hostile to life.[41]

A common way of arguing for the explanatory superiority of design is based on how well supported each hypothesis is by our background knowledge. Many argue that multiverse hypotheses are simply *ad hoc* to explain the data. To avoid this critique, it needs to be argued that there is independent rationality for believing in the multiverse. For example, some interpretations of inflationary theory and quantum mechanics require a multiverse; some theists also embrace the multiverse.[42] In response, proponents of design arguments can still argue that the reasons for accepting models involving a multiverse are weak without appealing to the need to explain fine-tuning. Or one might argue that the theistic hypothesis at least is less *ad hoc* than the multiverse hypothesis, since it was formulated and strongly believed already prior to the discovery of fine-tuning.[43] Using this strategy would require the ID movement to give up its minimalistic design argument, however, and engage in a more robust theistic natural theology.

In a way, naturalistic explanations for fine-tuning are congenial to design arguments, since they at least admit that there is something to be explained in the order of the universe. Proponents of the multiverse hypothesis agree that it is not satisfactory to just argue that the universe is a brute fact. Leonard Susskind puts the point as follows:

> Our own universe is an extraordinary place that appears to be fantastically well designed for our own existence. This specialness is not something that we can attribute to lucky accidents, which is far too unlikely. The apparent coincidences cry out for an explanation. – But [design] is an intellectually unsatisfying, if emotionally comforting, explanation. Left unanswered are: who designed the designer, by what mechanism the designer intervenes to guide evolution, whether the designer violates the Laws of Physics to accomplish its goals, and whether the designer is subject to the laws of quantum mechanics.[44]

40 John Leslie's example of a firing squad is often used to show that the anthropic principle does not by itself explain the fine-tuning. (See Leslie 1989, 13–15.)

41 Dawkins 2006a.

42 For more on these, see Rees 2003, Susskind 2006a; see also Cleaver (forthcoming).

43 R. Collins 2012, 205–209. A further way of arguing that theism has a higher background probability is to argue that theism is a simpler explanation than the multiverse (See Swinburne 2004c, 305–306). In response to this, it has been argued that naturalism, nevertheless, has a simpler ontological economy, since it posits fewer kinds of entities. (Dawes 2009, chapter 7) Here the debate is again strongly influenced by our philosophy of mind and our general ontological views.

44 Susskind 2006a, 343.

In Susskind's analysis, the multiverse hypothesis is a better explanation than the design hypothesis, because the design hypothesis leaves unanswered questions. However, the basic admission of the need of an explanation leaves the door open for natural theologians and ID proponents to answer these questions, and to argue that design actually explains the data better.

The problem of good and the problem of evil

The goodness of the universe we inhabit is relevant for evaluating the explanatory power of the design argument against naturalistic hypotheses. In the multiverse hypothesis, the explanation for why we find ourselves in a habitable universe is that otherwise we could not be alive at all. However, this hypothesis only explains fine-tuning that is absolutely necessary for life. Defenders of the design argument can well claim that the fine-tuning we observe extends well beyond that needed for survival. For example, the rationality of the cosmos and its amenability to discovery does not seem to be predicted at all by the multiverse hypothesis, but is explained by design.[45]

Within the ID movement, Behe argues similarly that the amount of different biological forms possible and the amount of purposeful biological complexity in the universe are also not predicted by the multiverse hypothesis, but are explained by design.[46] Denton argues that the multiverse hypothesis also does not explain the evolution of our abilities for art, music and philosophy, which are unnecessary for our survival.[47] Here the concept of fine-tuning used in the ID literature is quite broad, encompassing many varieties of 'natural good': the beauty, rational orderliness and the useful arrangements of the natural world as a problem for atheism. This is another example where the ID movement seems to move between a minimalistic and a more robust conception of the designer.

When the evidence of fine-tuning is stated as a problem of natural good, the relevance of the problem of natural evil – the second naturalistic objection to cosmic design arguments – becomes clear. Defenders of the design argument claim that the fine-tuning of our universe is in excess of that needed for survival, and that this is not explained by the multiverse hypothesis. In this they seem to be correct: the multiverse hypothesis does not explain these other features of the cosmos. The best available response of the multiverse proponent is instead to shift to the attack and to argue that the theistic hypothesis also does not explain all of the features of the cosmos, particularly the existence of natural evil. The point is made eloquently by the character Philo in Hume's *Dialogues Concerning Natural Religion*, comparing the universe to a poorly built house where tenants live in suffering. Philo argues that the bad outweighs the good in our universe, and that this provides evidence against the claim that the

45 Leslie 1989, 58–61; Swinburne 2004a, chapter 8.

46 Behe 2007a, 223.

47 Denton 1998.

Creator is good. At least it may be argued that while the multiverse hypothesis does not explain everything about nature, neither does theism.[48] By this point, the discussion of the proper interpretation of scientific facts has become openly theological and philosophical, and finding the best explanation already requires consideration of our entire worldview.

Level-shifting and the need for explanations

Combining design and natural explanations?

The previous discussion has treated naturalistic explanations and design as competing explanations for the same data. On this understanding, both attempt to explain the natural laws, constants and conditions of the cosmos, and the question is simple: which one does it better? However, though interesting for the purposes of argument, this way of stating the question does contain a problem. As several proponents of design arguments have stated, the naturalistic explanations do not always seem to be able to answer the question that the theists are asking. Thus it can be argued that design and naturalistic explanation operate on different levels.

For example, consider atheistic one-universe explanations for the fine-tuning. As stated, these rely on finding a fundamental natural mechanism that has the properties needed to produce our fine-tuned universe deterministically. However, as Collins notes, this appears to only move the problem of fine-tuning, since this fundamental natural mechanism would then have to be fine-tuned itself, or it could not produce such a specific outcome. If the question of the origin of fine-tuning was reasonable in the case of our cosmos, then it appears that it should also be reasonable in the case of this fundamental physical mechanism.[49] Thus a proponent of cosmic design arguments can always argue that the designer works on a different level than the laws of physics.

A similar strategy is also available in the case of multiverse hypotheses. Proposed multiverse hypotheses typically require precisely fine-tuned laws of nature to generate the universes and their varying natural constants. The multiverse hypothesis does not explain the existence of the fine-tuning required for a multiverse capable of generating life-supporting conditions. Because of this, Collins argues that the multiverse hypothesis only moves the problem back and does not eliminate the evidence for the designer.[50]

Ratzsch calls this type of defence of the design argument 'level-shifting', identifying both plausible and implausible examples of level-shifting. On the

48 *Dialogues*, chapters X and XI.

49 Collins 2012, 256–262; see also Collins (2005a, 184–185). Collins argues that this holds for restricted multiverse hypotheses where the amount of universes is not infinite and eternally existing, not for unrestricted multiverses where all logically possible worlds exist.

50 Collins 2005, 185; see also Cleaver (forthcoming).

one hand, suppose that an elderly uncle dies in suspicious circumstances, and relatives suspect the niece killed the uncle. Police investigations, however, reveal a natural cause for the death: the uncle's medication was mixed up. The relatives can plausibly claim that the niece killed the uncle by mixing up his medication, thus moving their design-explanation up one level. Here the natural explanation does not eliminate the evidence for design. On the other hand, suppose that crop circles (which some UFO enthusiasts suppose are produced by aliens) are proven with video evidence to be made by humans. A UFO enthusiast could respond to this alternative explanation by claiming that the aliens must be mind-controlling the humans. However, here level-shifting is clearly implausible.[51] The central factor separating plausible and implausible level-shifting in these examples seems to be whether the natural explanation eliminates the reason why the design hypothesis was made in the first place.

Is level-shifting then a plausible strategy in responding to naturalistic counter-arguments in the case of fine-tuning? I would argue that it is, insofar as the naturalistic hypothesis does not eliminate the evidence of design, but only moves it back one level. This is just what Collins argues: proposed naturalistic explanations for fine-tuning themselves require fine-tuning to work.

The cosmos as a brute fact

As a response to level-shifting design arguments, the third naturalistic response to design arguments is relevant: perhaps we should simply stop looking for explanations beyond the ultimate theory of physics or the multiverse, rather than seeking an explanation for them. Perhaps an ultimate theory of physics is not even needed – one could also say that the laws and constants of nature we now know provide the natural stopping point for seeking explanations. In this response, the existence of our universe is understood as simply a brute fact about reality which we must leave without explanation. So, this line of argument does not even attempt to present an explanation for the properties of natural explanations. Rather, the question is about the legitimacy of the design inference and what the proper stopping point for seeking explanations is.

The idea that we should not seek explanations for the order of nature is perhaps best defended with an old Humean argument. In *Dialogues*, Philo argues that if we can accept the mind of a designer as the stopping point, we can just as well accept the material world as the stopping point to avoid the conclusion of design.[52]

The answer of classical theism to this problem has been that God is capable of being the foundation of reality in a way different from contingent natural laws. Theists can well argue that it is always reasonable to seek further explanations and understanding, until no more can possibly be found. In the case

51 Ratzsch and Koperski 2015; see Glass (2012b) for further analysis of this type of argumentation.
52 *Dialogues*, chapter II.

of natural order, we can find a further explanation in divine design. However, because of the properties which this divine creator has, we cannot possibly find any further explanation for God. Thus a divine creator arguably forms a more natural stopping point for explanations than the order of nature. This conclusion becomes stronger if we accept the cosmological argument, which infers that contingent beings have their origins in the absolute, necessary being – God. On this understanding of the divine nature, it does not make sense to ask where God came from, though it does make sense to ask such questions of any contingent being or composite of contingent parts, such as the universe.[53]

The above response is credible for theists. The ID movement, however, claims that its design argument is credible without assuming prior belief in God. Thus it needs another strategy for responding to the 'who made the designer' objection. One possible strategy is to argue that evoking the further question of where the designer came from does nothing to invalidate the logic of the design argument as such. The design argument can explain fine-tuning even if it evokes some further questions. Proponents of ID can appeal to the history of science, where new explanatory factors have frequently been proposed without knowing what explains these new factors. If design is thought to have explanatory value at all, it can be argued that there is no reason not to accept the design hypothesis merely because this then creates additional questions.[54] Here the fourth and final naturalistic objection – that design is not explanatory – is relevant and seems to be the one the whole case for rejecting cosmic design arguments ultimately hangs upon. This is a philosophical objection, not a scientific one, and so the importance of philosophy for the debate is revealed once again.

I have already argued that the ID movement sees evidence for cosmic design as providing one reason for seeking evidence for design from biology, as well. Here the ID movement's rationale is inverse to that of many naturalists, who argue that the evidence from evolutionary biology increases our confidence of finding naturalistic explanations for cosmic design, as well. Dawkins, for example, argues that the success of Darwinism in explaining the appearance of design in biology makes it rational for us to seek such explanations for cosmic order, as well.[55] The idea here is that the progress of science demonstrates the replacement of intentional explanations with reductionistic and non-purposeful explanations. Any appeal to design is seen as a 'God of the gaps' argument based on our ignorance of the natural causes which are in fact the only necessary explanation. Stenger argues that 'the fine-tuning argument and other recent intelligent design-arguments are modern versions of God-of-the-gaps reasoning, in which God is deemed necessary whenever science has not fully explained some phenomenon'.[56]

53 See, for example, Feser 2008, Hart 2013, Turner 2004.

54 Leslie 1989, chapter 5; Lennox 2007, 62–64.

55 Dawkins 2006a.

56 Stenger 2006, 184.

As noted, for some naturalists, confidence in the successes of naturalistic reductionism extends not just to the evidence for cosmic design but also into explaining our own consciousness. Here the evaluation of the design argument even depends on our understanding of the philosophy of mind. If design is not the kind of highly detailed, law-like and mathematical explanation as those preferred in the natural sciences, it is argued that even ignorance of the true explanation will typically (always?) be better than invoking a designer. If taken too far, this line of argument will come close to scientism, since it seems to assume that only the type of explanations that are valid in the natural sciences can ever possess true explanatory power. In order to avoid the charge of scientism, the criticism needs to be made in a way that allows for the in principle possibility of design arguments.

Summary

Cosmic design arguments are based on fine-tuning of the cosmos for the existence of complex life, and the amenability of the cosmos to scientific understanding. For proponents of ID these are evidence of the existence of an intelligent designer, whereas in traditional theistic design, arguments speak of evidence for the existence of a good God. However, proponents of ID also sometimes slip into formulations of the argument referencing the beauty and plenitude of the created order, which are more in line with openly theistic design arguments.

Though some squabbles can be had about the precise facts and numbers of fine-tuning, the more important controversy is to be had over the interpretation of the data. Here the discussion quickly gets philosophical and even theological: when is it legitimate to search for explanations at all? What kind of explanations count as good ones? Is the existence of good and evil in the cosmos better in harmony with theism or naturalism? When we scratch the surface of the controversy over ID, the arguments on all sides are ultimately dependent on what we think about such philosophical and theological questions.

4 The biological debate

When philosophers Daniel Dennett and Alvin Plantinga debated on the relationship of science and religion in 2009, one of the questions addressed in the debate was Plantinga's view that ID might explain the origin of life and the evolution of biological forms better than evolutionary biology. Dennett argued in response that if ID's challenge to evolutionary biology indeed was credible, then the mainstream scientific community should have already accepted its validity. Dennett is aware that proponents of ID have their own explanation for this state of affairs – they argue that philosophical and ideological considerations lead scientists to be prejudiced against ID. However, Dennett contends that the more credible explanation for the majority opinion of scientists is simply that ID is mistaken and evolutionary biology has the best theories around.[1]

For many philosophers and theologians, the agreement of the mainstream scientific community on the veracity of evolutionary biology is already sufficient reason to accept the theory, and to be sceptical of ID. Here the philosophical discussion of the epistemology of testimony is relevant.[2] Most of our justified beliefs come through trusting in the testimony of others. Particularly when faced with issues that are unfamiliar to ourselves, we are quite reasonable to trust those who spent a great deal of time researching those same issues, and have thus become experts in that field. This is simply typically the best way to maximize our amount of true beliefs and minimize our amount of false beliefs. Therefore, it seems reasonable to argue that the agreement of most biological scientists about evolution does give us a good *prima facie* reason to be sceptical of ID's challenge to evolutionary biology.

However, I do not think the testimony of the majority of biological scientists should lead us philosophers and theologians to dismiss ID without giving it a hearing, particularly in an academic study of ID like the present one. Though questions of the natural sciences can be difficult for laypersons, it is still desirable to gain further understanding of the issues and not merely rely on the word

1 Dennett and Plantinga 2011, 12–15; 32–33.

2 See, for example, Lackey and Sosa (2006), Zagzebski (2012). I have written much more on social epistemology in the context of the ID debate in Kojonen (2015).

of authorities. Defenders of evolutionary biology do not generally believe that the evidences of the theory are all that difficult to understand, which is evidenced by the existence of so many popular-level books on the subject. With numerous books already out on the ID debate, it is also possible to compare and contrast the arguments of ID proponents with those of evolutionists and to see whether relevant points have been answered.

Having read through many critiques of ID and delved into evolutionary research literature, I have noticed that many of the critics actually agree with ID on a number of points, though they disagree about ID's overall thesis. For example, many scientists have written about the appearance of design in biology, and the use of teleological (purposeful, goal-oriented) language is prevalent in biology. There is also discussion within evolutionary biology about ways in which the theory needs to be expanded beyond the traditional ideas criticized by ID, and the current mysteriousness of the origin of life is generally admitted. I have also found that philosophical and theological arguments against ID play an important role in its rejection, in addition to purely scientific arguments in favour of evolution. This all makes me interested in digging a bit deeper and listening to what different sides of the controversy have to say.

In this chapter, I will analyse the ID movement's biological design argument and the discussion on evolution. The goal of the chapter is to understand the structure of ID's argumentation. I fear that readers who are hoping me to take a strong position either for or against ID will be disappointed by the chapter, since I will deliberately be refraining from doing so. There are already many books available advocating strongly for or against ID's biological arguments. Here my goal will rather be to provide a more balanced treatment of the debate than has usually been done, analysing points and counterpoints made by each side. Again, I will attempt to identify common points and build bridges between ID and its critics. I will begin with some details about various forms of biological teleology in the first section of the chapter and then go on to analyse the debate about evolution in some detail in the following two sections. This will help show the importance of philosophical and theological ideas in the final section of the chapter.

Biological 'machinery' and 'information'

The language of design in biology

The writings of both critics and defenders of ID are full of wonder at the order of nature. These feelings can be seen quite well in two formative books that have influenced the ID movement: Dawkins' *The Blind Watchmaker* (1989), and Denton's *Evolution: A Theory in Crisis* (1987). Dawkins describes biology as 'the study of complex things that appear to have been designed for a purpose',[3]

3 Dawkins 1991, 1.

arguing that it is an intuitively compelling argument to interpret structures like the human eye or the complex echolocation system of bats as designed structures. Denton's perhaps most rhetorically forceful passages come when he discussed the complexity of the living cell, comparing its precise functions to a gigantic automated city operated by robots.[4] But the authors differ in their explanations of biology.

The use of teleological (purposeful, goal-oriented) language remains widespread in the biology. Even though organisms are natural entities, it has proven difficult to understand these self-organizing, self-nourishing entities without such language. The purpose of the heart seems to be to pump blood, the purpose of lungs seems to be to breathe air and so on, all of the organs working together to keep the animal alive. This teleological language used to be understood in a literal manner as the purposeful creation of God. But it continues to be used in contemporary biology, without references to God, so there has been some searching for more neutral descriptions of biology. In this way, talk of purposeful complexity and teleology has often been replaced by terms like 'adaptation', 'functional complexity' or 'teleonomy'.[5]

In a way, Darwinian evolutionary biology and ID are allies in their use of teleological descriptions of biology. Ruse argues that Darwinian evolutionary biology was initially created partly to explain the appearance of this kind of teleology and to show how it can be explained by natural factors. But if teleology were not real, there would be no need to postulate the Darwinian mechanism of natural selection to explain such adaptations.[6] Recently, cognitive scientists have argued that the use of such descriptions is based on our intuitive processes utilizing teleological explanations. However, it is also based on the features of biological organisms. I believe our cognitive processes have good reason to identify biological structures as teleological, regardless of what ultimately explains this teleology.[7]

Though evolutionary biologists and proponents of ID agree that there is something to be explained in nature, it may be that there is some difference in the way this order is described. The central examples of biological order used in the ID movement's design arguments are examples of (1) functional, apparently purposeful complexity and (2) biological information. The argument based on biological purposeful complexity has been most developed by Michael Behe, and the argument from information has been developed by William Dembski and Stephen Meyer. But the elucidation of what exactly is meant by biological 'functions' and biological 'information' is a thorny problem.

4 Denton 1986, 328–329; see also Denton 1998; 2013.

5 In the philosophy of biology, these are often recognized merely as new names for teleology. Aristotle himself did not argue that teleology has to be purposeful or conscious, so the desire to avoid talk of conscious purposiveness does not require abandoning the term. See, for example, Walsh (2008), Melander (1997) and Ariew (2002) for accounts of teleological language.

6 Ruse 2003.

7 But see the discussion in De Cruz and De Smedt (2015, chapter 4).

Biological 'machinery'

In general terms, even something as simple as the colour of fur can be a biological adaptation and an example of functional order. While traditional design arguments were based on the visible anatomical features of organisms, much of ID's argumentation is based on 'biochemical machines' only visible with advanced instruments. According to Behe, 'it was once expected that the basis of life would be exceedingly simple. That expectation has been smashed. Vision, motion, and other biological functions have proven to be no less sophisticated than television cameras and automobiles'.[8] Behe calls these objects 'machines': 'The cumulating results show with piercing clarity that life is based on machines – machines made of molecules!'[9] In *Darwin's Black Box* (1996), Behe uses five different molecular machines as examples of structures that he argues are difficult to explain by referring to Darwinian evolution and that instead require design. His examples are ciliar motors, the blood clotting system, the cellular transportation systems, the immune system and the system for the biosynthesis of the energy molecule AMP.[10]

For Behe, design is 'purposeful arrangement of parts', and this definition applies equally well to man-made artefacts and biological machines.[11] He argues that the strength of the design argument is 'quantitative and depends on the evidence; the more parts, and the more intricate and sophisticated the function, the stronger is our conclusion of design'.[12] For Behe, biochemical 'irreducibly complex' machines exemplify this definition of design particularly well. He argues that the strength of the design argument is probabilistic and gets stronger when there is more purposeful complexity, because it becomes progressively more difficult to explain in any way other than design.

Massimo Pigliucci, Peter Boudry and some other ID critics have argued that proponents of ID use this kind of machine-like language in a more literalistic fashion than naturalistic biologists. According to Pigliucci and Boudry, the usefulness of the metaphor can be seen, for example, in the way the concept of the human heart as a pump was important for William Harvey's (1578–1657) discoveries about blood circulation.[13] However, biological structures should not be thought of literally as machines, since the metaphor may be misleading in some respects. For example, man-made machines cannot reproduce and so cannot evolve. Pigliucci and Boudry argue that the machine metaphor should be abandoned or at least used with great care, because it leads too easily to

8 Behe 2006a, x.

9 Behe 2006a, 4.

10 Behe's descriptions of these systems have generally been regarded as accurate, though his understanding of the plausibility of evolutionary scenarios has been criticized. See, for example, Perakh (2004, 118–119) and Orr (1997).

11 Behe 2006a, 193.

12 Behe 2006a, 256.

13 Pigliucci and Boudry 2011, 3.

inferring that biological machines must be designed.[14] The criticisms is that using the term 'machine' creates rhetorical force for design arguments by overlooking the substantial differences between biology and man-made machines.

As Pigliucci and Boudry also acknowledge, Behe is in good company in using terms like 'machines' of biochemistry. For example, writing in the journal *Cell*, biologist Bruce Alberts explains that these objects are called machines because 'like machines invented by humans to deal efficiently with the macroscopic world, these protein assemblies contain highly coordinated moving parts', and because terminology used in engineering has proven to be useful in biology.[15] Here, the definition of a machine is simply a system composed of several coordinated moving parts, and this definition encompasses both human machines and biochemical machines as machines. Like Behe's definition of irreducible complexity, Alberts' definition of a machine references systems which require the coordination of several interacting parts. It seems to me that the definition of machinery used here encompasses both man-made and natural machines. Used in this way, the term itself does not require that the machine must have a designer. Rather, design is simply one possible explanation for such machinery.[16]

So, while Pigliucci and Boudry may be correct that the term 'machine' creates rhetorical force for ID's argument, at least the use of the term need not be dishonest or assume the conclusion of the argument. Behe himself argues that his definition is simply based on appearances and our ability to recognize functions in biology. Identifying functions does not require reference to the designer's purposes. Rather, '*the function of the system we must look at is the one that requires* the greatest amount of the system's internal complexity. *The function of a system is determined from the system's internal logic: the function is not necessarily the same thing as the purpose to which the designer wished to apply the system*'.[17] He then explains this appearance of teleology as a result of the unknown purposes of an intelligent designer.[18] In the end, I do not see any major difference between how Behe and mainstream biologists write about functions in biology. The controversy here is more about whether ID is a good potential explanation of the data or the best explanation of it, rather than about whether biological structures are amazingly complex and functional.

Biological information

The situation is similar in the case of biological information, which forms the other main basis for ID's biological design arguments. For example, Meyer has argued that the genetic information in DNA is a 'signature in the cell', strong

14 Pigliucci and Boudry 2010. For similar views, see Shanks (2004).

15 Alberts 1998, 291. Quoted in Pigliucci and (2010, 6); Dembski (2002a, 247) also quotes Alberts approvingly.

16 Behe 2006a, 265.

17 Behe 2006a, 196.

18 Ariew (2002, 8) has identified ID's argument as an argument for the existence of Platonic extrinsic teleology on the basis of Aristotelian immanent teleology.

evidence of intelligent design in biology.[19] Dembski has also developed ID as a theory of information, where the information present in biology is best explained by supposing that mind, rather than matter, is fundamental.[20] Again, as with functionality, some concept of information is generally thought to be essential to modern biology. The genetic information of DNA is needed for all of the vital functions of life, since organisms need it to produce all of the proteins they need for their molecular machinery and various tasks. Developmental biology is just beginning to unravel the secrets of animal development, but there is research on genetic regulatory networks and epigenetic information (hereditary information residing outside the DNA) which govern the development of the biological form of animals, such as the growth of a human embryo into an adult.[21]

As with talk of biological machines, Meyer and Dembski can certainly claim wide support for their understanding of biological genetic and epigenetic information as a masterful code. However, since the science of bio-informatics is quite new, there is still quite a bit of controversy over what is meant by that elusive term 'information' in biology. Philosopher of biology Peter Godfrey-Smith has criticized ID on this basis. Godfrey-Smith differentiates three main ways the term 'information' is used in biology:

> (1) The description of whole-organism phenotypic traits (including complex behavioural traits) as specified or coded for by information contained in the genes);
> (2) The treatment of many causal processes within cells, and perhaps of the whole-organism developmental sequence, in terms of the execution of a *programme* stored in the genes;
> (3) The idea that genes themselves, for the purpose of evolutionary theorizing, should be seen as, in some sense, 'made' of information. From this point of view, information becomes a fundamental ingredient in the biological world.[22]

According to Godfrey-Smith, the first of these theses is the most well founded, but it remains very reasonable to question the other two. Godfrey-Smith agrees that on the level of DNA, a limited sort of semantic information is required to encode for proteins, as Meyer argues. However, Godfrey-Smith goes on to argue that this information is, nevertheless, far less robust than that produced by humans. So, as with the term 'machine', the criticism is that the ID movement is using the 'information' without realizing the differences between biological information and human-produced information.[23]

---

19 Meyer 2009.

20 See particularly Dembski (2014), published in the same series as the present study.

21 See, for example, Noble (2008) and Noble (2013) for popular accounts of this change.

22 Godfrey-Smith 2007, 103–104.

23 Godfrey-Smith 2007, 110. See also Yockey (2005) for an account of information in biology that accepts quite a strong definition of information but is nevertheless critical of ID. Denis Noble (2008) and other expanders of the modern synthesis also argue that the focus on genes is misplaced.

Here it seems clear that our understanding of information does have an impact on the strength of ID's argument. The stronger the analogy between human-produced information and biological information, the stronger the design argument becomes, particularly if it can also be argued that information is something irreducible to physics and chemistry. However, the argument will not completely defeated, even if the analogy is not this strong. Information is at least an example of functionality in biology and so can function as another example of the appearance of teleology in biology. The central matter in the debate over ID and evolution is then the interpretation and explanation of this functional complexity.

Functional complexity is not the only evidence that needs to be taken into account when comparing theories about biology, however. Evolutionary biology also attempts to explain (and according to most scientists, succeeds in explaining) a wide variety of other facts, which I will get to in a moment. But here I should already note that the problems of natural evil and bad design also affect evaluations of design versus evolution. While the theistic and atheistic defenders of evolutionary biology are full of wonder at the complexity of nature, they also argue that nature contains a great deal of bad design, which counts against ID. The same contrast is already present in Darwin's though. On the one hand, Darwin felt that there was 'grandeur' in his view of life and obviously felt love, rather than disgust, for the natural world.[24] On the other hand, he thought that the facts of nature favoured a view where God did not assume direct responsibility for biological design, writing that 'I cannot persuade myself that a beneficent and omnipotent God would have designedly created the Ichneumonidae with the express intention of their feeding within the living bodies of caterpillars or that a cat should play with mice'.[25]

This has been an important response to ID from the beginning and is repeated in both theistic and atheistic critiques. For example, reviewing Johnson's *Darwin on Trial for Nature*, biologist David L. Hull asks: 'What kind of God can one infer from the sort of phenomena epitomized by the species on Darwin's Galapagos Islands? The evolutionary process is rife with happenstance, contingency, incredible waste, death, pain and horror. – The God of the Galapagos is careless, wasteful, indifferent, almost diabolical. He is certainly not the sort of God to whom anyone would be inclined to pray'.[26] The problem of natural evil is so important for the debate that I will devote Chapter 9 entirely to it. Here I just want to note how theological and philosophical judgments often lurk behind different interpretations of nature.

Teleology is in the entire structure of the organisms, not merely in the genes. Meyer's newer work (2013, chapters 13 and 14) shows that he is cognizant of these new developments.

24 Darwin 2009 [1859], 360.

25 Darwin 2012 [1860]. Desmond and Moore (1991, 622–637) argue Darwin evolved in his religious views from a theist into an agnostic. Even as an agnostic, he wavered between belief and unbelief.

26 Hull 1991.

Understanding evolutionary biology

As I've noted, descriptions of biology and positive arguments for design form only part of the ID literature. Much of the literature is instead devoted to critiquing naturalistic explanations for the origin of biological forms. Here it will be important to understand what exactly we mean by Darwinian evolutionary biology and what parts of the theory ID theorists accept and reject.

The basic components of evolution

Ernst Mayr, one of the 20th century's leading evolutionary biologists, divides Darwinian evolutionary theory into five distinct parts. First (1), there is the general thesis of evolution as such. This states the changeability of species as opposed to a constant, unchanging world. Second (2), there is common descent, the thesis that all different branches of animal species share a common ancestor. Third (3), there is the thesis of gradualness, which states that species change by small, successive and cumulative mutations. Thus there are no big 'jumps' in evolution where a completely new form of animal is formed through just one mutation. Fourth (4), there is the thesis of populational speciation, which states that new species can emerge from existing populations through changes. Fifth (5), there is natural selection working on random mutations – the Darwinian mechanism for explaining evolutionary adaptations.[27] As Mayr argues, it is in principle possible to accept just parts of Darwinian evolutionary theory. For example, many of Darwin's contemporaries did not accept natural selection as the mechanism of evolutionary change, but accepted the thesis of common descent.[28]

There is a broad variety of different views within modern evolutionary biology, as well. Recent discussion on evolutionary theory has complicated the picture. For example, there has been discussion of evo-devo, neutral evolution, endosymbiosis, neo-Lamarckian epigenetic evolution, punctuated equilibrium and even 'natural genetic engineering' as complementary mechanisms to Darwinian natural selection. Here there is room for debate: some evolutionary biologists regard these merely as supplements to the traditional Neo-Darwinian synthesis, while others, such as the proponents of the 'Third way of evolution', see these as large revisions and expansions of evolutionary biology.[29] However, natural selection still typically plays a pivotal role in explaining complex biological adaptations, such as the systems described by the ID movement. Even recent

27 Mayr 2002, 94–95.

28 Mayr 2002, 95. See also Bowler (2009, chapters 6 and 7), particularly pages 196–199.

29 See, for example, Laland et al. (2014), Shapiro (2011) and Pigliucci and Müller (2010). Cunningham (2010), Cobb (2008) and Noble (2013) also emphasize the breadth and continuing development of evolutionary biology.

biology textbooks still reference Dawkins' arguments in *The Blind Watchmaker* as a good, popular presentation of the issues in evolving complex adaptations.[30]

Evolutionary biologist Mark Ridley summarizes four main lines of evidence for Darwinian evolutionary theory.[31] First (1), small-scale changes in organisms can be directly observed. It is then extrapolated that past changes in organisms can be explained through the same evolutionary mechanisms observed in the present. Second (2), the similarities of living things can be explained by the proposition that they are descended with modification from a common ancestor. Such similarities can be seen both in the appearance (phenotype) and the genetic structure (genotype) of organisms. The classification of living things into different species and classes by pre-Darwinian biologists was historically necessary for the emergence of Darwinian theory. It then became possible to argue (for example) that all different cats were descended from the same cat-like ancestors, all mammals from the same ancestors and so on.[32] Third (3), the geological evidence demonstrates that past forms of life were different from those that now live, which fits well with the supposition of descent with modification. Fourth (4), evolutionary biology acts as a unifying theory for all of biology and helps explain many details which would otherwise be unexplained. Theodosius Dobzhansky's famous statement 'nothing in biology makes sense except in the light of evolution' succinctly expresses this fourth idea.[33] Now, over 150 years after the publication of Darwin's *Origin of Species*, there is truly a massive amount of biological research using evolution as this kind of overall organizing idea.

Dobzhansky and contemporary evolutionary biologists admit that not all details about how evolution happens have been worked out, but argue that this should not stop us from accepting the general picture given by the theory as correct. The logic of the inference to the best explanation does not demand that all questions related to a theory, such as evolution, are resolved before it can be affirmed as a clearly better explanation than any rival hypothesis.[34]

The focus of ID's critique

The ID movement's critique of evolutionary biology is mostly aimed at the sufficiency of the Darwinian mechanism for explaining the origin of complex functional order in life (part 5 in Mayr's division above). As John G. West puts it, 'intelligent design is simply the effort to investigate empirically whether

30 For example Freeman and Herron 2007, 98–99, Ridley 2004, 70. Even Fodor and Piatelli-Palmarini (2011, chapter 8) recognize in their critique of Neo-Darwinian theory that this is the strongest argument in favour of the importance of natural selection.

31 Ridley 2004, 66.

32 See Bowler (2009, chapter 3) for this history. See also Freeman and Herron (2007), Dawkins (2009) and Coyne (2009) for presentations of the evidence for common descent.

33 Dobzhansky 1974.

34 Lipton 2004, Sober 2008.

the exquisitely coordinated features we find throughout nature are the result of an intelligent cause rather than a blind and undirected process like natural selection'.[35] All of the ID movement's main thinkers similarly affirm the compatibility of common descent and ID's biological design arguments. This theme is already present in Johnson's *Darwin on Trial*,[36] and continues in later ID works. Dembski, for example, argues that 'intelligent design is also fully compatible with large-scale evolution over the course of natural history, all the way up to what biologists refer to as "common descent" (i.e., the full genealogical interconnectedness of all organisms.)'[37] The general reason for the acceptance of common descent as a possibility is that common descent is not perceived to provide any explanation for biological adaptations by itself. Therefore proponents of ID do not perceive it as a competitor to design as an explanation.

However, in addition to Denton, Behe is the only major proponent of ID who has actually professed belief in common descent as the best explanation of the similarities of living beings and who restricts his critique to naturalistic mechanisms of evolution. All of the other major proponents of ID do recognize Behe's position as coherent and as part of ID. However, most of them also criticize common descent extensively. This critique is clearly a major part of ID literature and is also prominently present in ID textbooks like *The Design of Life* (2007) by Dembski and Jonathan Wells.[38] Nevertheless, the major ID theorists do not consider the critique of common descent a necessary, core part of ID's project or its design argument. Therefore I will leave discussion of the first four parts of Mayr's thesis aside and focus on the central question of natural selection as the mechanism driving the evolution of new functional structures.[39]

Microevolution and macroevolution

Proponents of ID admit the powers of naturalistic evolutionary mechanisms in explaining minor changes, but do not accept them as a sufficient explanation for all of life's complexity. In other terms, at issue is the extrapolation from microevolution to macroevolution.[40] According to Johnson, 'If empiricism were the primary value at stake, Darwinism would long ago have been limited to microevolution, where it would have no important theological or philosophical

35 Gauger, Axe and Luskin 2012, 11.

36 Johnson 1993, 4.

37 Dembski 2001.

38 Wells' (2002a and 2002b) critiques of standard evidences for common descent are among the deepest in the ID movement.

39 Though many sources (for example Mayr 2002, Bowler 2009) argue that the idea of common descent was historically acceptable without accepting the other parts of Darwinian evolutionary theory such as gradualism and natural selection, Korthof (2005) argues that there is tension between Behe's acceptance of common descent and his rejection of the Darwinian mechanism as the explanation for macroevolution.

40 The distinction is also common in creationism. See Ratzsch 1996, 86–90. For an example within ID, see Dembski and Wells 2007, 102–104.

implications'.[41] In the ID movement's terminology, microevolution is 'small-scale genetic and structural changes in organisms', whereas macroevolution means large-scale genetic and structural changes, 'leading to new and higher level of complexity'.[42] In the *Edge of Evolution* (2007), Behe attempts to determine the limits of Darwinian evolutionary mechanisms and concludes that Darwinian evolution is likely possible beyond the species level and the limits of Darwinian mechanisms are somewhere on the levels of animal genera, families and orders. For proponents of ID, the boundaries of the system of classification are not what limit the possibilities of the Darwinian mechanisms. Rather, the argument is that though this mechanism can explain some features of life, there are many features which it cannot explain. Thus Behe writes that 'the major architectural features of life – molecular machinery, cells, genetic circuitry, and probably more – are purposely designed. But the architectural constraints leave spandrels that can be filled with Darwinian adaptations'.[43]

The issue of microevolution versus macroevolution is also discussed in mainstream philosophy of biology. For example, philosopher of biology David Sepkoski (who is by no means a proponent of ID) formulates the basic question in the move from micro- to macroevolution as follows: 'Do major taxonomical groups represent real, ontologically distinct entities with their own emergent properties and are the factors that govern their development discontinuous with the mechanisms that produce variation and fitness among individuals?'[44] In the typical usage of the terms in Neo-Darwinian biology, macroevolution has been understood as the same process as microevolution, only on a larger scale. In this understanding, there is no qualitative difference between microevolution and macroevolution. Rather, if there is a sufficient amount of time, microevolution is argued to lead to macroevolution without the need for further mechanisms. This is still perhaps the most common opinion particularly in popular presentations of evolutionary biology, and even theistic evolutionism.[45] However, as Sepkoski shows, there are also many evolutionists who argue that other mechanisms are required as well.[46]

Some of the arguments of these biologists are also referenced by proponents of ID. For example, Meyer references research in developmental biology and genetic regulatory networks. Following eminent geneticist Eric H. Davidson

41 Johnson 1993, 118.

42 Dembski and Wells 2007, 315–6. Unfortunately there are several different ways of making the distinction between microevolution and macroevolution, leading to misunderstandings. In the standard terminology of evolutionary biology, microevolution refers to the evolutionary change within the species, while macroevolution refers to evolutionary change above the species level. However, the biological species line (meaning a reproductively isolated population) can be crossed without changes that proponents of ID would term macroevolution (Dembski and Wells 2009, chapter 4).

43 Behe 2007a, 202.

44 Sepkoski 2008, 212.

45 See, for example, Giberson and Collins (2011, 44). But see Cunningham (2010).

46 Sepkoski 2008, 213–216.

and others, Meyer argues that the evolution of new proteins is not sufficient to produce new animal body plans, because the information required for developing new animal forms resides in complex genetic regulatory networks and even in structures outside the DNA.[47] Davidson argues that different types of changes are needed for macroevolution: 'contrary to classical evolutionary theory, the processes that drive the small changes observed as species diverge cannot be taken as models for the evolution of the body plans of animals'.[48] He also draws the conclusion that traditional evolutionary biology needs to be supplemented in light of these discoveries.

The usefulness of these quotes for ID is weakened by the fact that Davidson himself (who knows his own results best) argues that these findings should lead only to a modification of evolutionary theory and the continued scientific research of the processes behind macroevolution, not rejecting the naturalistic understanding of evolution. Though modern organisms may indeed be incapable of undergoing macroevolution because their development requires such finely tuned genetic regulatory networks, perhaps ancient organisms were more amenable to change. But even in this case, the basic point remains. If Davidson is right about genetic regulatory networks, most evolutionary changes we observe in the present day would not result in changes to the organism's fundamental body plans, even if many of these changes were accumulated over large amounts of time. So, there appears to be basis for distinguishing between micro-and macroevolution as somewhat different processes.[49]

Proponents of ID have many other arguments against the credibility of explaining macroevolution by reference to Darwinian mechanisms. For example, they argue that most mutations do not increase functional information, that the demands of protein evolution are too stringent for unguided evolution, and that the claimed sudden appearance of forms in the fossil record (particularly during the Cambrian explosion) are problematic for gradual evolutionary explanations. The mystery of the origin of life also looms large in the ID literature.[50] Going deep into this discussion would take a large book in itself. As an illustration of the debate, I will nevertheless analyse ID's most celebrated and criticized argument against evolution: Behe's argument from irreducible complexity (IC).[51] Analysing this example is also an interesting way to gauge

---

47 Meyer 2013, chapters 13 and 14.

48 Meyer (2013, 269) quotes Davidson (2006, 195) as well as Davidson 2011, 35–36.

49 Davidson (2011, 40) himself infers that ancient regulatory networks must have been different, and not yet solidified in a way that prevents evolution. In response to Meyer, Marshall (2013) similarly argues that the biological forms were easier to mutate in the past.

50 Recall that the first book of the ID movement was *The Mystery of Life's Origin* (1992 [1984]) by Charles Thaxton, Walter Bradley and Roger Olsen. Meyer (2009) also focuses on the origin of life.

51 Both friendly and hostile sources identify irreducible complexity (IC) as ID's most central argument, particularly in the 1990s. See, for example, Shanks (2004, 160) and Woodward (2003, 155). Discussions of the argument from irreducible complexity take much space in many sources both for and against ID. For examples, see Dembski (2002a, chapter 5), Shanks (2003, chapter 5), Dawkins (2006a, 144–150) and Kenneth Miller (2002, chapter 5). It is also the standard argument discussed

the strength of each position since we can safely assume that there has been sufficient time for development of sufficient critiques and counter-critiques since Behe's argument became well known already in 1996.[52]

Irreducible complexity?

Dawkins' defence of evolution as the background of the critique

In order to understand Behe's argument from irreducible complexity, I return to Dawkins' argument from *The Blind Watchmaker* (1989), since it provides the backdrop to Behe's argument. Dawkins argues that it is highly rational to believe in the capacities of the process of mutation and natural selection to explain even complex structures. Consider the evolution of the mammalian eye, a highly complex structure that was already used as an example of design by Paley.[53] Dawkins argues that evolution may have started with a small light-sensitive patch on the skin. When mutations improving the capability for vision appeared, they were beneficial and thus contributed to the fitness of the organism. Natural selection preserved these mutations and accumulated them. Over a long period of time, argues Dawkins, the modern eye was evolved. Dawkins presents the central questions behind this evolutionary explanation as follows:

1. Could the human eye have arisen directly from no eye at all, in a single step?
2. Could the human eye have arisen directly from something slightly different from itself, something that we may call X?
3. Is there a continuous series of Xs connecting the modern human eye to a state with no eye at all?
4. Considering each member of the series of hypothetical Xs connecting the human eye to no eye at all, is it plausible that every one of them was made available by random mutation of its predecessor?
5. Considering each member of the series of Xs connecting the human eye to no eye at all, is it plausible that every one of them worked sufficiently well that it assisted the survival and production of the animals concerned?[54]

by philosophers of religion when presenting ID. See, for example, Nagasawa (2010, part II) and Swinburne (2004a, appendix).

52 Moreover, the argument from irreducible complexity has predecessors that were already responded to in the literature of evolutionary biology prior to Behe's book. Denton (1986, 90–91) makes a similar argument from 'integrated complexity', which he traces back to biologist Jean Cuvier (1796–1832). Denton also uses the bacterial flagellum as one example of biological complexity which Darwinian evolutionary theory fails to explain (Denton 1986, 224–225). Forrest and Gross (2004) find similarities in Behe's argument to creationist Ariel Roth's argumentation (for example Roth 2001, 86–87).

53 *Natural Theology*, chapter III.

54 Dawkins 1991, 77–81.

Dawkins' answer to the first question is negative: explaining the emergence of new complex organs through large random mutations is too improbable to believe. Dawkins answers the remaining four questions in the affirmative, however.

Behe regards the example of eye as misleading, because the small steps described by Dawkins are actually extremely large on the biochemical level. According to Behe, there is no such thing as a 'simple' light-sensitive cell. Rather, the biochemical basis of vision is highly complex, an irreducibly complex cascade of proteins.[55] So, explaining the evolution of the eye in Dawkins' manner is, for Behe, akin to explaining the production of a stereo set by saying that you just first need a CD player, then add loudspeakers and so on. The small leaps described by Dawkins are, for Behe, giant leaps between canyons.[56]

Behe's argument from irreducible complexity is directed against the fifth point of Dawkins' argument: the plausibility that all mutations necessary for the evolution of the current form are useful. With his argument, Behe is attempting to answer Darwin's challenge, as set out in *On the Origin of Species*: 'If it could be demonstrated that any complex organ existed, which could not possibly have been formed by numerous, successive, slight modifications, my theory would absolutely break down. But I can find out no such case'.[57] If some biological organ could not be developed through the mechanism of natural selection and mutation, then evolutionary theory's claim to explain life's order would be jeopardized. Behe argues that 'irreducibly complex' machines in cells satisfy Darwin's challenge.[58]

Behe assumes that each mutation in the evolutionary series has to be useful or at least neutral in order for natural selection to help generate new biological structures. Otherwise, natural selection will act against its preservation. The basic idea is common in explanations of evolution: As 'Third Way' proponent Denis Noble states, if we compare the design of an organism to an aircraft, evolution must modify and improve the aircraft without foresight while the aircraft is in flight and all systems are in use.[59] The basic idea of Behe's argument is that this sort of useful modification and building up of irreducibly complex structures is highly improbable, or even impossible for undirected evolution.

As I have pointed out, Behe claims that his argument is 'quantitative and depends on the evidence; the more parts, and the more intricate and

55 Behe 2006a, 38.

56 Behe 2006a, 22.

57 Darwin 2008 [1859], chapter VI. The basic idea remains part of the mainstream of current mainstream evolutionary theory. As Coyne (2007) puts the point: 'It is indeed true that natural selection cannot build any feature in which intermediate steps do not confer a net benefit on the organism'. Like Darwin, Coyne argues that the existence of any such feature has not been demonstrated, and that even complex features can evolve through indirect routes.

58 Behe 2006a, 36. See also Behe (2001b, 2003 and 2004a).

59 Noble 2008, 109.

sophisticated the function, the stronger is our conclusion of design'.[60] Behe also means his argument to be cumulative: the more of such intricate systems there are, the more difficult it becomes (he argues) to believe that indirect Darwinian pathways for all of them exist.[61] Behe has further written of the interdependence of irreducibly complex systems as an amplification of the probabilistic difficulties: if such a system will not work without the presence of another similar system, then the evolution of this system can no longer be treated as an isolated evolutionary problem. The probabilistic nature of Behe's argument also makes it easier to understand why Behe has not been fazed by critics showing why evolving irreducible complexity is in principle possible. Something that is in principle possible may in practice still be probabilistically nearly impossible, depending on the details.[62]

Irreducible complexity as an obstacle to evolution?

According to Behe, an irreducibly complex system is 'a single system composed of several well-matched, interacting parts that contribute to the basic function, wherein the removal of any one of the parts causes the system to effectively cease functioning'.[63] He argues that there are multiple irreducibly complex structures in cells. His basis for this is both empirical and conceptual. First, biochemical experiments can be used to test the necessity of the parts of biochemical machines. If the functioning of the system ceases when a part is removed, this part can be judged essential for the functioning of the system. Second, upon understanding how a system works, we can determine that certain parts are crucial for its operation. Behe argues that a system for swimming, for example, requires a minimum of three parts: a paddle, a motor and a part connecting the two. These parts also have to be fine-tuned to fit each other, or 'well-matched', as Behe defines.[64]

In the discussion on ID, the bacterial flagellum has emerged as the most often used example of biological irreducible complexity. The flagellum, according to Behe, is an outboard motor which propels bacteria forward. Behe argues that the flagellum requires tens of parts to function.[65] Additionally, he argues that the flagellum is part of a network of interlinked irreducibly complex machines, so that the construction of the flagellum also depends on the existence of other irreducibly complex machines working together. For Behe, this interdependence of irreducibly complex structures makes it yet more improbable to explain these structures in a Neo-Darwinian way.[66]

60 Behe 2006a, 256.
61 Behe 2007a, 93–95, appendix C.
62 For example, Behe (2001a).
63 Behe 2006a, 39.
64 Behe 2006a.
65 For example, Behe (2004a).
66 Behe 2007a, chapter 5.

Some problems with Behe's initial definition of irreducible complexity have emerged in the discussion. The definition of irreducible complexity assumes that all of the parts of a system are necessary for its function, but in practice no biological system is like this. For example, many parts of the bacterial flagellum are unnecessary for its functioning. Behe himself does admit already in *Darwin's Black Box* that not all of the parts of his systems are necessary, and the functions of all parts are not even known. Moreover, he recognizes that a given function can be fulfilled by several different kinds of systems. However, for Behe, this does not mean that we cannot identify many of the parts of a given system as crucial for the functioning of that system.[67] So, Behe's definitions needs to be expanded to apply only to the irreducible core of the system – there can be additional parts which make the system more robust and which can be removed without necessarily losing the function.[68] It seems to me that such an amendment is possible, though this then may present difficulties in identifying the irreducible core of natural systems.[69] The more important critique is based on the possibility of evolving such systems in spite of irreducible complexity.

The possibility of evolutionary pathways

Behe argues that irreducible complexity is a barrier to 'direct evolutionary pathways'. By direct evolution, Behe means evolution which works by improving some existing function step by step, as in Dawkins' depiction of the evolution of the eye, where each modification results in a slight increase of vision. A direct evolutionary pathway means the evolution of a system from humble origins by small improvements in the system's 'core function'. Irreducible complexity is, for Behe, impossible to evolve in this way, because the core function of the system emerges only after all of the necessary parts are in place. Natural selection, however, cannot select for a function that emerges only after all of the parts are in place. The system thus cannot be evolved by small beneficial steps through a direct evolutionary pathway. For example, the bacterial flagellum cannot have evolved from a simpler system for moving the bacterium.[70] Instead, its evolution is – according to Behe – better explained by the actions of an intelligent designer who can arrange parts to fulfil some future end.[71]

Most of Behe's critics have admitted that the argument works against direct evolutionary pathways, but have still considered indirect evolutionary pathways possible.[72] Behe's argument is that the parts of an irreducibly complex system

67 Behe 2006a, 39, 72–73; chapter 3. Miller (2002, 141) critiques Behe without noting these qualifications.

68 Dembski 2002a, 285.

69 Draper 2002.

70 Behe 2006a, 39.

71 Behe 2006a, 36–39.

72 For example, Miller (2002, 132–136), Orr (1996); see also Thornhill and Ussery (2000); one exception to the general trend is Draper (2002).

would not have the function of the system and so would not be selected by natural selection. However, this does not mean that they could not have had some other function and then only later been transformed into parts of the newly formed, irreducibly complex system. The evolutionary history of Behe's irreducibly complex systems, such as the bacterial flagellum, could be very complex, with similar parts serving in many slightly different systems with different functions. This is how evolutionists have typically explained the evolution of complex anatomical structures, such as the evolution of hands from feet, or the evolution of wings.[73] The adaptation of an existing biological structure for a new function is called evolutionary co-option.

The evaluation of these kinds of evolutionary scenarios is typically done by comparing the existing system and its parts to other systems. For example, the modern bacterial flagellum doubles as a secretory system, and so the metaphor of a motor does not succeed in describing all of its functions. Many of the parts of the flagellum are also similar to parts in use elsewhere. For example, Miller argues that an important part of the bacterial flagellum is similar to the type III secretory system also found in bacteria, and other critics have argued that homological parts are known for around 90 per cent of the parts of the flagellum. Homological parts can also be found for other systems Behe describes. It can thus be argued that we already have at least the beginnings of plausible evolutionary histories for many of Behe's irreducibly complex systems.[74]

This co-option argument has been the most popular response to Behe's argument from irreducible complexity.[75] The idea of the argument is that the precursors of irreducibly complex machines had other functions, and thus natural selection preserved them. Serendipitously, the parts initially useful in other machines were also useful for the construction of current irreducibly complex machines. However, few critics have noted that Behe himself considers the co-option answer in *Darwin's Black Box* and presents another version of his irreducible complexity – an argument against it.

Behe's fallback argument from irreducible complexity

Directly after presenting his argument against the direct evolution of irreducible complexity, Behe argues as follows:

> Even if a system is irreducibly complex (and thus cannot have been evolved directly), however, one cannot definitively rule out the possibility

73 Gishlick 2006, 71.

74 Miller 2002, 85–87; Sarkar 2007, chapter 6; see also Musgrave (2006), Matzke (2006) and Venema (2012) for more detailed explanations. Whether such explanations already exist in the literature assumed great importance in the Dover trial; see Jones (2005, 78), Nagasawa (2010, part II) and Dewolf et al. (2006).

75 For example, Miller (2002, 151), Dawkins (2006a, 143–146), Coyne (1996, 227) and Kitcher (2007, 89). Other explanations have also been proposed, which Behe has been quite active in debating; see, for example, Behe (2001a).

> of an indirect, circuitous route. As the complexity of an interacting system increases, though, the likelihood of such an indirect route drops precipitously. And as the number of unexplained, irreducibly complex biological systems increases, our confidence that Darwin's criterion of failure has been met skyrockets toward the maximum that science allows.[76]

Here Behe is admitting the point of his critics already in the course of stating his original argument. Irreducible complexity can in principle evolve through an indirect route, by which Behe means the co-option account. However, Behe argues that as the complexity of the system increases, the probability of such evolutionary accounts decreases to extremely low. Behe's argument against Darwinian evolution is thus probabilistic, just as his argument for design is also probabilistic. In Behe's argument, as the amount of apparently purposeful, irreducible complexity increases, so the probability of design goes up and the probability of naturalism goes down.

In describing molecular motors, cilia, as irreducibly complex, Behe himself considers the possibility of co-option: 'So an evolutionary story for the cilium must envision a circuitous route, perhaps adapting parts that were originally used for other purposes'.[77] Like his critics, Behe argues this by referring to homology: it is clear that proteins similar to the parts of the motor are used in cells to serve other functions. Behe speculates that perhaps the building of the motor could proceed by adapting these parts first into some simple system serving an unknown function and then add further parts until we come to the ciliar motor. Behe's scenario is exactly like the co-option arguments used by many of his critics. So, Behe admits that the literature contains many examples of homology in biochemical systems, but claims that mere similarity does not prove the viability of evolutionary mechanisms, particularly when the similarities are distant.[78]

Behe argues this based on the functional requirements of proteins for a specific machine: the protein parts of irreducibly complex machines have to be 'well-matched' to fit the other protein parts of that same machine, attaching itself automatically only to those proteins and not to any others. Because irreducibly complex machines need to be a seamless whole before functioning, the requirements for proteins are, according to Behe, quite strict. Actually, the prior functions of the parts will naturally make them poorly fitting to serve in the new system.[79] Behe concludes that 'analogous parts playing other roles in other systems cannot relieve the irreducible complexity of the new system; the focus simply shifts from "making" the components to "modifying" them'.[80]

---

76 Behe 2006a, 40.
77 Behe 2006a, 66.
78 Behe 2006a, 175–176; Behe 2001a, 686.
79 Behe 2006a, 66; 2007, appendix A.
80 Behe 2006a, 112–113.

One of Behe's critics, biologist Allen Orr, surprisingly makes largely the same criticisms as Behe against the co-option scenario: 'we might think that some of the parts of an irreducibly complex system evolved step by step for some other purpose and were then recruited wholesale to a new function. But this is also unlikely. You may as well hope that half your car's transmission will suddenly help out in the airbag department. Such things might happen very, very rarely, but they surely do not offer a general solution to irreducible complexity'.[81] This is essentially the same as Behe's own response. Orr's own solution is that irreducibly complex systems have been evolved from more complex, but not irreducibly complex systems; a solution that Behe finds a conceptual possibility, but requests evidence that it has actually happened.[82]

ID proponent Angus Menuge has developed Behe's argument against indirect evolution into more systematic form. Menuge elucidates five conditions which have to be fulfilled in order to evolve an irreducibly complex structure: (1) Availability: parts fitting to build the irreducibly complex machine have to be available in the cell. (2) Synchronization: the parts of the machine must be available at the same point in time. (3) Localization: the parts must be moved to the same part of the cell, where they can be assembled into a whole. (4) Coordination: the parts have to be fitted together in the correct order. Having the right sort of parts is not enough, if they are not also assembled in a functional order. (5) Interface compatibility: the parts have to be precisely compatible and capable of acting together. Menuge sees the fulfilment of these conditions as unrealistic, just as Behe does. Behe's responses to the co-option argument focus on conditions (4) and (5).[83]

Disappointingly, the existence of this critique against the possibility of indirect evolution is not usually noted and responded to by Behe's critics. Two exceptions to this trend are Niall Shanks and Paul Draper. Shanks only cites Behe's idea briefly, dismissing it simply as a statement of Behe's feelings of incredulity, not commenting on the arguments that Behe presents in its favour.[84] The fragmentariness of Behe's argument may be partly to blame for the lack of attention his argument has received. Behe does not state his argument against indirect evolution concisely, but elaborates on it further only as he analyses his examples of irreducible complexity in more detail. Behe has further developed this argument in his later works. Within the ID movement, the existence of Behe's argument has been more widely recognized, however.[85]

Is the problem of modifying and assembling the components of irreducibly complex biochemical machines difficult for Darwinian evolution? Draper's critique of the argument against indirect routes focuses on the crucial point: Behe needs to show that the parts of an irreducibly complex system indeed

81 Orr 1997.

82 Behe 2001a.

83 Menuge 2004b, 104–105. Some similar conditions are elucidated by Dembski (2004b, chapter 4).

84 Shanks 2004, 162; Draper 2002.

85 For example. Dembski 2004b.

need to be fairly tightly well-matched. If less finely tuned parts will do, then adapting parts from other systems will pose much less difficulty for evolution.[86] Here Behe's argument depends on the details of how proteins work and on the ID movement's arguments about the difficulty of protein evolution. In recent years, such arguments have surged in popularity in the ID literature. For example, following other estimates in the literature and based on their own biochemical experiments, biochemists Douglas Axe and Ann Gauger have argued that functional protein folds are extremely rare and transitions even between homologous proteins are difficult. If this is correct, then Behe's response to the co-option argument seems strong. If Axe and Gauger are wrong and transitions between homologous proteins are easy, as some critics argue, then Behe's response to the co-option argument is greatly weakened. Behe himself has referenced Axe's calculations in this way.[87]

Other critiques of ID and defences of evolution also apply indirectly to the problem of irreducible complexity. For example, critics argue that: (1) homologies of the parts of 'irreducibly complex' systems are just the sort of evidence one would expect on the co-option account; (2) more detailed evolutionary histories of many biochemical systems are beginning to be written, including for many of Behe's systems; and (3) evolutionary histories written on the larger anatomical level are supported with paleontological evidence. In biochemistry, finding such explanations may be more difficult due to the lack of fossils. These arguments do provide indirect evidence in support of the evolution of irreducible complexity, and they cannot be lightly dismissed. However, they also do not provide a direct answer to ID's arguments against indirect evolutionary routes, and so proponents of ID are left requesting more evidence.

How to explain the unexplained?

The existence of the unexplained

Whether the evolutionary origins of Behe's examples of irreducible complexity remain a mystery or not, it seems that all sides acknowledge that there are still unsolved mysteries within biology. It is not difficult to find acknowledgements of this in the discussion on ID even from some critics of ID. For example, atheist Johnjoe McFadden explains one difficulty as follows:

> The basic problem is that the complexity of biochemical pathways (unlike the eye) do not appear reducible. For instance, one of the cell's essential

86 Draper 2002.

87 Behe 2007a, 248n15. For discussion on the protein specificity argument from the ID side, see Axe (2004, 2010a, 2010b, 2011, 2012), Behe (2007a, appendix C), Gauger and Axe (2011), Gauger, Axe and Luskin (2012), Gauger (2012) and Meyer (2013, chapter 10). For defences of the evolvability of proteins, see Wood (2011), Myers (2011) and Matzke (2013), as well as Carroll, Ortlund and Thornton (2011). Meyer (2013) also discusses protein evolution extensively.

> biochemical molecules is AMP (adenosine monophosphate), the precursor of ATP (the energy carrying molecule), which also finds its way into DNA, RNA and many other cellular components. AMP is made from ribose-5-phosphate, but the transformation involves thirteen independent steps involving twelve different enzymes. . . . Each of the twelve enzymes involved in this pathway is absolutely essential for the biosynthesis of AMP. Darwinian evolution would require this complex system to have evolved from something simpler. But, unlike the eye, we cannot find the relics of simpler works. Half or a quarter or a twelfth of the pathway does not generate any AMP or indeed anything else of value to the cell. It appears that the entire sequence of enzymes is needed to make any AMP. But without viable stepping stones, how can an entire complex system have evolved through Darwinian natural selection?[88]

Here McFadden's idea is very similar to Behe's argument from irreducible complexity: it is difficult to understand how the complex molecular system required for the production of AMP could have evolved, since the parts do not appear to have any use otherwise, and since AMP seems essential for life. McFadden argues that this presents a very difficult, even unsolvable problem for current conceptions of Darwinian evolution and motivates transitioning into a new 'quantum' understanding of evolution. Cellular biologist Franklin Harold similarly argues that 'there are presently no detailed Darwinian accounts of the evolution of any biochemical or cellular system, only a variety of wishful speculations'. However, 'we should reject, as a matter of principle, the substitution of intelligent design for the dialogue of chance and necessity'.[89]

As I have argued, the literature does seem to contain at least some beginnings of accounts for biochemical evolution. However, Harold's point is still interesting. Let us suppose that such detailed accounts are indeed missing to a large degree, and we are confronted with mysterious structures in biology. Would this then give us grounds for accepting ID?

Harold's own approach at this point is to rely on philosophical principles to justify the rejection of ID. Such philosophical critiques are used in the majority of critiques against ID, even in textbooks of evolutionary biology. For example, Freeman and Herron argue that appealing to design is simply unallowed in science, and so science should always look for natural explanations for biology.[90] Though the estimates of proponents of ID and their critics differ on the severity of unsolved problems within evolutionary biology, both agree that evolutionary biology is still an incomplete science. Whereas critics of ID argue that these are minor anomalies that are likely to be solved by future research, proponents of ID argue that the progress of science has only made the problems

88 McFadden 2000, 76. Quoted in Cunningham (2010, 277–278).

89 Harold 2001, 205.

90 Freeman and Herron 2007, 102.

facing naturalistic theories worse. In order to justify continued belief in the causal powers of evolutionary mechanisms, ID proponents ask for exact details of how the evolutionary transitions in question could have happened before believing in the possibility of macroevolution through naturalistic mechanisms.

Here a critic could well go on a counterattack: proponents of ID do not require similar exact details about the nature and *modus operandi* of the designer before believing in intelligent design as the best explanation. So, the demands proponents of ID make of Darwinian explanations seem perhaps more stringent than the demands they make of design-based explanations. Perhaps this could be justified by the difference of design-based explanations from the mechanistic explanations typically favoured in the natural sciences: proponents of ID argue that we already know from our experience that intelligent designers can produce such systems, whereas we do not know from our experience that undirected natural causes can do the same. The demand for details is a demand for the demonstration that undirected natural causes indeed do have sufficient causal powers for the task. But for many critics of ID, appealing to the differences between design-based explanations and other explanations merely shows the emptiness of design as an explanation.

Examples of philosophical arguments for evolution and against ID

Jerry Coyne's defence of Darwinian evolutionary biology shows the way philosophical arguments are often used in the debate. Coyne argues that we can be sure that mechanism of selection and mutation explains complex adaptations partly because the only alternative – creationism, including intelligent design – is so clearly a bad explanation. Coyne's arguments are that: (1) ID is unscientific, because it is untestable; (2) ID is a 'God of the gaps' argument; (3) ID can explain potentially any feature of nature, and thus explains nothing; and (4) the burden of proof is not on naturalists to provide a step-by-step demonstration of how complex systems can evolve, but rather on critics who should demonstrate that the step-by-step evolution of some complex system is impossible.[91]

Coyne's case does not rest only on these philosophical arguments, because he goes on to explain empirical evidence for the evolution of complex adaptations (using the evidences from homology and the evolution of the eye, for example). Nevertheless, Coyne's philosophical arguments certainly seem to affect the level of certainty he has regarding natural selection as the mechanism of evolution.

Dawkins has even stronger confidence in philosophical and metaphysical arguments against creationism. Dawkins does begin *The Blind Watchmaker* with apparently affirming that design could in principle be the best explanation of biology. At first Dawkins appears to rely on evolutionary biology as the central critique of design arguments and affirms that prior to the advent of Darwinian theory, design was an intuitively very plausible explanation for biological

91 Coyne 2009, 136–143.

complexity. The progress of science was required to drive out the gods from the realm of rationality.[92]

However, on closer examination, it becomes clear that philosophical reasons also weight strongly in Dawkins' mind: the rules of rationality would strongly mitigate against the design argument and belief in God even without the existence of good evolutionary explanations for life. At the end of *The Blind Watchmaker* Dawkins considers the question of how the origin of life should be explained and argues on philosophical grounds that even random chance is a better explanation for the origin of life than supernatural design. He states outright that even if (contrary to the actual world) there was no evidence for evolution, Dawkins would prefer to wait for a naturalistic explanation, rather than believe in design. This is because, for Dawkins, the purpose of explanation is to understand the complex by referring to something less complex, and in this the God hypothesis fails.[93] Many critics have thus remarked that given Dawkins' philosophy of what scientific, rational explanations are, something like Darwinian evolution would have to be the most rational explanation even on purely *a priori* grounds and such philosophical arguments have a large bearing for what Dawkins believes about nature.[94]

This kind of very strong metaphysical preference for evolutionary explanations of biology has also been criticized by evolutionary biologists and many theists who accept evolution simply as the best scientific theory. The presence of many theistic and apparently honest scientists who believe there is good evidence for Darwinian evolution is a problem for the ID movement's argument that evolution is accepted only because of philosophical prejudice. But it is nevertheless true that often these theists have additional reasons to disbelieve in ID because of their model of divine action. In their minds, ID is a philosophically and theologically false 'God of the gaps' argument. I will have much more to say about this in the coming chapters.

Theological and philosophical presuppositions are also important for proponents of ID, and this will become clearer as I analyse the logical structure of their design argument more closely. For example, if our background beliefs include the design of life as a live possibility, believing that events like the origin of life may have resulted from the activity of a designer should be less difficult than for someone whose background position is closer to Dawkins. And if our background beliefs even include the idea that evolution and creation are incompatible or poorly compatible ideas, then we already have theological reasons to be sceptical of evolutionary biology. These kinds of metaphysical ideas cannot help but influence the high probability many proponents of ID give to

92 Dawkins 1999, chapter 1; similarly Dawkins 2006, chapter 1.

93 Dawkins 1991, chapter 6. This argument is a condensed version of what would later become Dawkins' 'main argument' in *The God Delusion*: the improbability of the God argument (Dawkins 2006, chapter 4).

94 For example, Orr (2007), Plantinga (2007); for a more in-depth critique see Glass (2012a).

their design hypothesis. Those theists who accept in principle the compatibility of evolution and design have much less reason to be sceptical of evolutionary biology.

Previously in this chapter I have already remarked that evolutionary biology is a well-established and widely accepted scientific theory, and ID would require large changes to it. Philosopher of science Jeffrey Koperski argues that conservatism in theory choice weighs against ID: 'Many biologists acknowledge that neo-Darwinism has serious anomalies. – Even if orthodox neo-Darwinism collapses, design is not the only alternative. More importantly, the rivals are more conservative vis-á-vis the reigning theory'.[95] There is no avoiding the fact that after 150 years of what many consider to be highly fruitful research, evolutionary explanations are the reigning paradigm and the 'default option' for explaining biology in the scientific community. So if the anomalies can be solved by expansions and modifications of the current theory, most scientists also have good scientific reasons to prefer that. But this hope of salvaging the theory is just what ID denies.

At least in this situation where the biological evidence is still incomplete, it seems that many supporters and critics of evolutionary theory are quite reasonable to feel that philosophical and theological arguments are important for the issue. My point here is not that it is illegitimate to such arguments (as long as they are good arguments). This would be a form of scientism, since it would assume that only scientific arguments are important in deciding what a rational person ought to think. Rather, I believe we should openly recognize that the debate about biology has its theological and philosophical side. We need not be ashamed to admit that our views are not based just on science, and that we find philosophical and theological considerations valuable.

Summary

Proponents of ID seek to defend the idea that the laws of nature are designed, but they also argue that the designedness of nature is also manifest in biological organisms in a way that goes beyond what the natural laws themselves could produce. Talk of biological 'machinery' and biological 'information' are essentially ways to restate the old idea that nature contains goal-directed order in today's scientific language. Defenders and critics of ID agree that biology bears the appearance of teleology, but disagree on whether biology requires explanation by reference to a purposeful designer. Despite general agreement on the existence of something like teleology in nature, opinions differ on the degree of perfection or imperfection nature exhibits.

ID formulates its biological design arguments in competition with the mainstream Darwinian theory of biological evolution. ID's central aim is to criticize the sufficiency of the mechanism of random mutation and natural selection

95 Koperski 2015, 218.

for producing the kind of order found in biological organisms. Contemporary evolutionary biologists have also defended many different understandings of evolution, and some agree that a distinction between micro- and macroevolution needs to be made. This is also the kind of view of evolution that I myself am more drawn to.

ID's arguments are about mysteries or anomalies within evolutionary biology, and not all of the arguments have been answered in the debate. Mysteries in biology remain, so we need to ask what kind of mysteries (if any) would allow us to conclude that natural explanations likely do not exist, or that the grounds for a design inference are more weighty than the ground for just waiting for the discovery of a natural explanation. Here philosophical and even theological arguments quickly become important for participants of the debate as they begin to argue over matters such as the definition of science, the desirable criteria of explanations, the God of the gaps and the problem of evil. Some have a strong metaphysical view favouring evolutionary explanations, just as some others have a strong preference for rejecting evolution.

5 Intelligent Design as science or pseudoscience

In the discussion of cosmological and biological design arguments, one chief objection to ID's design-based explanations has been that they are not scientific. Much energy has been used to discuss criteria of science like methodological naturalism, testability, fruitfulness, detailed predictions and so on. In part, the prominence of the theme is based on the political situation and the debate over whether it is permissible to teach creationism or ID in public schools in the United States of America.

The legal strategy for combating the teaching of creationism in the United States was designed around methodological naturalism as a requirement of real science. Against the efforts of creationists to portray 'creation science' and evolution as competing scientific theories, it was argued that no theory which appeals to supernatural entities can possibly be science, already by definition. The definition of science has even been called 'the philosophical question' in the controversy over creation and evolution, implying that this question is philosophically more important than (for example) evaluating the merits of the design argument or understanding whether the fundamental character of reality is purposeful or purposeless.[1]

Practical reasons also influence ID's insistence on the scientific nature of its design arguments. As noted, the movement desires cultural influence and public impact. The movement recognizes the immense cultural authority of 'science' and wants to reclaim it from naturalists. In challenging the sufficiency of the scientific theory of evolution and naturalistic philosophy in the public arena, they want to say that their critique and their alternative are also scientific. However, ID's main arguments against methodological naturalism are based on their understanding of the nature of science, and their belief that methodological naturalism unduly restricts science as a search for true explanations, rather than merely a search for naturalistic explanations.

In this chapter, I will analyse the controversy over ID and the definition of science. In the first section I will look at ID's critique of methodological naturalism and several ways in which methodological naturalism has been defended

1 Pennock and Ruse (eds) 2009.

against this critique. I then move on to consider several possible defences and formulations of methodological naturalism. I argue that intellectually responsible defences of methodological naturalism will not allow us to dismiss the consideration of the more interesting questions in the debate, such as the evaluation of ID's arguments. In the third section of the chapter, I discuss other ways of differentiating between science and non-science, and argue that the definition of science is not the central philosophical question of the debate, unless we accept some kind of scientism – or unless we care most about influencing public education than the core philosophical questions of the debate.

Methodological naturalism and ID's critique

The historical background of methodological naturalism

Methodological naturalism has historical roots extending far beyond current political controversies. Methodologically naturalistic science can be broadly construed as a project of understanding the structure of the universe in terms of natural causes. It always looks for natural explanations, laws and mechanisms, rather than resorting to supernatural explanations of any phenomena. As Ronald Numbers argues, this broad approach has Christian and even medieval roots. Even in the middle ages, natural philosophy was guided by a 'preference for natural explanations over divine mysteries' when dealing with natural phenomena.[2] It was thought that God had created a rational world, whose structure was open to human investigation. Explaining things by reference to God's mysterious will was not the default position of the natural philosophers; rather, they wanted to understand the natural processes which God had created. Similarly, many contemporary theists also restrict natural science to the study of natural causes and adopt methodological naturalism.

The importance of methodological naturalism for the debate over ID is inherited from the discussion over whether creationism could qualify as part or science or not. In the 1987 trial over the teaching of creationism, five main criteria of science were defined: (1) science is guided by natural law; (2) it explains by reference to natural law; (3) it is testable against the empirical world; (4) its conclusions are tentative; and (5) it is falsifiable.[3] In defining science as restricted to non-supernatural factors, the courts followed the testimony of philosopher of science Michael Ruse, who had argued in his testimony that 'any reliance on a supernatural force, a Creator intervening in a natural world by supernatural process, is necessarily not science'.[4]

After the trial, much critical discussion has ensued about these criteria, and some critics of creationism also argued that they were not philosophically

---

2 Numbers 2003, 266. Similarly, Bishop (2013) and Halvorson (2014).
3 Overton 2009 [1981].
4 Ruse 2009 [1981], 272.

rigorous, and that it is the definition of science as a complex philosophical question that cannot be decided by courts of law. Philosopher of science Larry Laudan in particular argued that though the banning of creationism was desirable, the criteria used to demarcate between science and pseudoscience in the trial were problematic. Laudan argued that scientific creationism contains much that is testable – and which has been tested and found false. Rather than being excluded from science *a priori*, creationism should rather be treated as a bad scientific theory, Laudan argued. However, this was not sufficient for the legal strategy against creationism or ID: in order for them to be barred from schools, ID and creationism have to be non-science, not merely bad science.[5]

In the same collection of articles, *But Is It Science*, philosopher Philip Quinn even argues that while there are good arguments against creationism, these may be too complex, and so 'there may well be circumstances in which only the bad effective argument will work against them in the political or legal arenas. If there are, then I think, though I come to this conclusion reluctantly, it is morally permissible for us to use the bad effective argument'.[6] As Bradley Monton has commented, this strategy is unfortunate. We should seek for the truth and reject bad arguments, even if they are expedient.[7] To that end, I will go on to consider some critiques and defences of methodological naturalism.

ID's designer and the critique of methodological naturalism

Methodological naturalism was used as a weapon against creationism, and so it has also been used as an argument against understanding ID as part of the natural sciences. To defend the scientific nature of their argumentation, proponents of ID have responded by criticizing methodological naturalism. As I pointed out in Chapters 3 and 4, proponents of ID argue that cosmology and biology provide data which point to purposeful design as the explanation. The structure of the argument is often aimed to show that the design argument utilizes the best methods used in historical science, such as the inference to the best explanation. Proponents of ID argue that their design argument is analogous to forensic sciences, archaeology and the search for extraterrestrial intelligence (SETI), and as such should also be accepted as scientific.[8]

It is somewhat curious why methodological naturalism should be an issue in the debate, since as noted, proponents of ID typically insist that their designer does not have to be supernatural. While Johnson's early argumentation in *Darwin on Trial* critiqued the way methodological naturalism bars supernatural

5 Pennock and Ruse 2009.

6 Quinn 2009, 398.

7 Monton 2009b.

8 For example, Meyer (2009) proceeds by arguing that the same type of reasoning used to decipher the structure of DNA also works for reasoning that the origin of life was an intelligently designed event. Meyer (1999a, 1999b) similarly argues that ID fulfills the same criteria of science as evolutionary biology, other than methodological naturalism.

design from science,[9] later ID writings have emphasized that design can be detected without knowing anything about whether the designer is supernatural or not, and without reliance on prior religious beliefs.[10] The idea that ID does not require supernaturalism is common in the ID literature. Dembski, Behe and Meyer all emphasize that ID does not violate the rule against supernatural agents, because ID's designer is not identified as supernatural, and indeed the question of the designer's identity cannot be settled by the scientific evidence.[11]

One way in which methodological naturalism could be relevant is if it is very difficult to avoid the conclusion that the designer must be somehow supernatural. The question of the designer's identity arises immediately, and the religious interpretation is a plausible one. (I will come back to these issues in Chapter 6). But the ID movement insists that it is cogent to separate the design argument and the identification of the designer as a supernatural identity. The movement criticizes methodological naturalism rather because it understands the restriction to bar all kinds of intelligent causes from the natural sciences, not merely supernatural ones.

Proponents of ID even agree that the natural sciences are predominantly a search for natural causes. For example, Behe argues that even if supernatural designers were allowed in science, 'the fear of the supernatural popping up everywhere in science is vastly overblown. If my graduate student came into my office and said that the angel of death killed her bacterial culture, I would be disinclined to believe her'.[12] According to Behe, belief in a rational, understandable, law-bound universe is not threatened by belief in a Creator, but is something that religion and science can agree on.[13] However, Behe argues that science should be a search for truth, and it should also allow design as an explanation when that is warranted by the evidence: 'I count as "scientific" any conclusion that relies heavily and exclusively on detailed physical evidence, plus standard logic. No relying on holy books or prophetic dreams. Just the data about nature that is publicly available in journals and books, plus standard modes of reasoning'.[14] For ID, the debate is about the freedom of science to follow the evidence, and methodological naturalism is understood to be an obstacle to the search for truth.

The freedom of science and the freedom of the creator

The critique of methodological naturalism has been a hallmark of ID's argumentation from the beginning. Johnson argued already in his *Darwin on Trial* that the naturalistic ground rules of science have led to a far too positive view of

9 Johnson 1993, chapter nine.
10 See Luskin 2008 for one ID proponent's overview of the ID's views.
11 Meyer 2009, 428–430; Dembski 2004a, chapter 25; Behe 2006a, 251.
12 Behe 2006a, 241.
13 Behe 2006a, 241.
14 Behe 2007a, 233. Similarly, Monton (2009a, 62).

the powers of Darwinian evolution. According to Johnson, defenders of naturalism 'enforce rules of procedure that preclude opposing points of view'.[15] Johnson argues that methodological naturalism actually assumes a philosophical, naturalistic understanding of the world. Science must be understood as a search for the truth. If methodologically naturalistic science only searches for natural explanations, then this must be because it is assumes that only naturalistic explanations are true. Otherwise it would make no sense to restrict the search for truth to merely naturalistic explanations, Johnson argues.

In this way, Johnson argues that methodological naturalism is not actually religiously neutral at all. In contrast to methodological naturalism, Johnson proposed an alternative 'theistic realist' framework for science. This theistic realism would be an open investigation of nature, allowing that God has created nature in an orderly fashion to be studied scientifically. In natural history, God could have used evolutionary mechanisms, or he could have acted miraculously. Johnson has a strong theological preference for any option which allows us to have evidence of divine action in history. However, neither evolution nor creationism is to be barred from science on *a priori* grounds (as Johnson believes is done in methodological naturalism), but only on the basis of empirical investigation.[16]

Johnson's emphasis on the independence of God from the world and his ability to create any sort of world is reminiscent of the medieval debates on the logic of 'possible worlds'.[17] Pierre Duhem dates the beginning of the scientific revolution as 7 March 1277, when a set of theses of Aristotelian physics was condemned as wrongfully imposing limits on God's omnipotence. Duhem argued that this led to the rise of empirical science, because now Christians could not discover how God had created the world based just on philosophical first principles but had to rely on empirical observations and experiments.[18] This type of theistic background assumption can also be identified in many of the founders of modern science, such as Francis Bacon and Isaac Newton, and it is commonly referred to in the theology and science discussion.[19] Johnson's novel argument is to apply this reasoning also to the creation/evolution debate.

Later proponents of ID typically do not emphasize the aforementioned theological framework in just the same way. Though the idea of theistic science has found other defenders, mostly the ID literature does not discuss theistic realism as the alternative framework to methodological naturalism. Rather, the proponents of ID generally argue only that the foundational assumptions of

15 Johnson 1993, 118.

16 Johnson 1995, appendix. See Plantinga (1991) for Plantinga's initial defense of theistic science; see also Moreland (1994) for another defense of theistic science that has likely influenced Johnson here, as Moreland's article is based on a presentation at an ID-friendly conference. See, for example, Stenmark (2004, chapter 9) for a critique of theistic science and a defense of scientific neutrality. The issues are further discussed also by Ratzsch (2004) and Labody (2015).

17 Knuuttila 1993.

18 Koons 2003, 80.

19 For example, Clark (2014, chapter 3).

science do not require that no intelligent designers have acted in history. The assumption remains the same as in Johnson's argument: it could be that design is actually the true explanation of the development of biological species.

This is argued to be a serious possibility that should not be dismissed *a priori* from scientific consideration but should be allowed to compete with non-purposeful explanations. Suppose that the actions of an intelligent creator are in reality responsible for the origin of life and much of its development, and that there are real 'gaps' in the capabilities of natural processes nature. In this case, reliance purely on the results of methodologically naturalistic science would produce a false picture of the history of life, because it could not even in principle recognize this being's role and the really existing limits of naturalistic processes. In such a case, science would lead us away from the truth. Proponents of ID argue that this can be avoided by giving up methodological naturalism.[20]

Defending methodological naturalism

The ID movement's critique of methodological naturalism generally assumes that methodological naturalism means an *a priori* restriction barring the use of supernatural or teleological explanations from the natural sciences. Proponents of ID generally also operate on the premise that methodological naturalism is not credible in any traditional theistic framework, because theism allows that God could have acted in natural history. However, in the literature responding to the ID movement, there are different strategies for defending methodological naturalism, not all of which are vulnerable to ID's critique.

Strong methodological naturalism

In its critiques of methodological naturalism, ID mainly criticizes methodological naturalism as an *a priori* restriction on what kinds of explanations are allowed in science. This kind of strong form of methodological naturalism does indeed exist, and it has indeed been a central part of the legal strategy against creationism and ID. For instance, Ruse, whose testimony was pivotal in the creationism trial of 1987, defines methodological naturalism as the claim that 'any reliance on a supernatural force, a Creator intervening in a natural world by supernatural process, is necessarily not science'.[21] This means that excluding design from the natural sciences is not done only after evaluating the evidence, but based on the definition of science and based on logic. Sometimes critics of ID have stated this outright very strongly: 'even if all the data point to an intelligent designer, such an hypothesis is excluded from science because it is not

20 This ID-friendly argument is developed further in Monton (2009a, chapter 2); see also Ratzsch (2002). For one of the responses which note the critique based on such theological possibilities, see Halvorson (2014).

21 Ruse 2009 [1981], 272.

naturalistic. Of course the scientist, as an individual, is free to embrace a reality that transcends naturalism'.[22] On this understanding, science is simply by definition a search for natural explanations. Science is concerned with understanding the natural causal structure of the cosmos, and its methods are unsuited for discussing theological and philosophical questions, such as whether nature is ultimately purposeful or not.

Proponents of ID argue that this kind of strong methodological naturalism can only be defended if we assume that there are in reality no intelligent or supernatural causes acting in nature. Otherwise it would be misleading. This is indeed one possible way of defending strong methodological naturalism. If we assume that nature is all there is, or at least that God has no effect on the world, then there should not be any need to consider supernatural explanations within science (or anywhere else really). However, this cannot be the only way to defend methodological naturalism, since it was initially formulated in a theistic framework. Furthermore, philosophical naturalism or deism are not obviously true worldviews, nor are they universally accepted by scientists. So this kind of defence of methodological naturalism would not be persuasive for all.[23] Furthermore, in order to defend philosophical naturalism in a dialogue with other views, the non-existence of a God who acts in history cannot be simply assumed, but must be argued. And part of this process should also involve the detailed examination of arguments for design, such as those presented in natural theology and ID.

Theological defences of strong methodological naturalism

However, methodological naturalism can also be defended theologically. For example, John Haught argues that theologies of nature can incorporate the findings of natural science, but that it would be mistaken to use design as an explanation on the same level as natural science functions. According to Haught, theological accounts of nature are rather concerned with the ultimate character of reality, rather than operating on the level of scientific theories: 'theology would have the role of ultimate explanation in an extended hierarchy of explanations that includes, and does not in any way compete with, scientific accounts'.[24] This type of hierarchical understanding of the relationship of different disciplines is very common in the theology and science community: each discipline is understood to have its own territory, to which its methods are best suited. While there can be overlap and dialogue between the disciplines, investigating questions of natural science with the methods of the humanities or theology is not likely to be fruitful. Rather, references to supernatural design should take place outside the sciences, in theology and philosophy. And so,

22 Todd 1999.

23 See, for example, Larmer (2003).

24 Haught 2008, 35.

methodological naturalism within the natural sciences could be quite justified also for theists.[25]

Does this defence evade ID's critique of methodological naturalism? Suppose that it were indeed a true fact about the world that God created life through a miracle and that the origin of life would have been impossible otherwise. Suppose further that we can construct a good argument showing that design is the most credible explanation for the origin of life. Would it then be problematic to exclude design from science and instead say that some objectively very unlikely naturalistic hypothesis is the best scientific explanation for the origin of life? It could well be that the created reality does not respect the boundaries of scientific disciplines as they are understood in the theology and science community model.[26]

In my judgement, the aforementioned form of methodological naturalism can avoid this criticism, as long as we do not adopt scientism. We do not have to assume that the general criteria for good explanations are exactly the same as the criteria for good scientific explanations. If we do not restrict rationality to the natural sciences, then it is completely fine that often the best explanation for some phenomenon will lie outside the range of the natural sciences. Psychological and theological explanations, for example, might be best studied by methods outside the natural sciences. If we respect the idea that there are valid disciplines other than the natural sciences, then each question should belong to the domain of the discipline that can best study the question, though often a question might require input from several different disciplines. On this kind of understanding, the inability of the natural sciences to refer to personal explanations is no more problematic than the inability of psychologists to study quantum mechanics.[27]

However, one problem (or benefit, depending on your viewpoint) of this defence of methodological naturalism is that it does not allow us to bypass discussion of ID's arguments. This is because there is no *a priori* criterion for determining where the precise limits of the disciplines are and what kind of methods are best suited for studying which question. Rather, the boundaries of disciplines have been historically fluid and changing. The proper domains of each discipline have not been written for us in an infallible holy revelation, but must be decided as we go, based on our previous experience of what kinds of methods work in answering these particular kinds of questions. So, we could in principle discover that the origin of life, for example, is better explained when we use methods of design detection, such as those used in archaeology or SETI, rather than the methods we normally use in methodologically naturalistic biological research. So, even though this kind of methodological naturalism allows us to banish ID from the natural sciences, this does not mean stopping ID's arguments altogether.

25 Russell 2008, introduction.

26 Monton (2013, 46) argues this point eloquently.

27 This is also Halvorson's (2014) defense of methodological naturalism.

Here the discussion comes down to how good the arguments for various views are, and in the end cannot be settled simply by reference to the traditional boundaries of disciplines (as valuable as these are). If we think that biological problems are properly a realm where strong methodological naturalism applies, we have to present arguments for why we think this is so. These arguments will have to show why it is likely that we will find naturalistic explanations for all biological problems, and why things like ID's critiques fail to overturn these naturalistic explanations. So, approaching some problem as an issue best suited to study by methodologically naturalistic natural sciences should not be a dogmatically held position, but a working assumption and the result of the evaluation of our knowledge of that problem.

The strong form of methodological naturalism outlined above holds that the natural sciences are by definition a search for natural causes. I have argued that this is not a problematic position, as long as it is not coupled with scientism, where rationality and the possibility for knowledge about the natural world are restricted to the natural sciences. Together with scientism, methodological naturalism would indeed be the kind of ideological position that ID proponents criticize, because this would mean that the entire possibility of design-like explanations is barred from consideration. In order to be defensible, methodologically naturalistic science must in principle be able to have boundaries, outside of which other methods and disciplines are the better source of true beliefs. If ID proponents were to adopt this understanding, they could well present ID more as a way of challenging the mainstream understanding of where these boundaries lie, rather than as a violation of methodological naturalism as such.

Moderate methodological naturalism

In the debate over ID, not all who defend methodological naturalism have understood it as an *a priori* restriction against intelligent causes in the natural sciences. Rather, some have argued that the natural sciences are in principle open to creationist and design-based explanations, if the evidence is good. On this understanding, methodological naturalism merely means a preference for natural, non-teleological explanations, rather than an absolute exclusion of them from the sciences. ID's exclusion from the natural sciences is based on the failure of its arguments, rather than on definitions. For example, Phillip Kitcher argues that ID does qualify as science, and that even methodologically naturalistic science can be open to evidence of design. However, he goes on to argue that ID is bad 18th-century science which has been superseded and refuted by the developments of science after that.[28] Niall Shanks similarly argues that 'the methodological naturalist will not simply rule hypotheses about supernatural causes out of court'.[29]

28 Kitcher 2007.

29 Shanks 2004, 141–142. Similarly, Sarkar (2011) also favours criticizing Intelligent Design based on its lack of scientific content rather than demarcation criteria.

Methodological naturalists of this type (which I will now term 'moderate methodological naturalism') can maintain a critical openness to design arguments within science, while nevertheless favouring natural explanations. This type of methodological naturalism avoids the central point of the ID's critique, because it does not rule out the question of design based purely on *a priori* criteria before considering the evidence and the quality of the arguments. Proponents of ID could also themselves be classified as moderate methodological naturalists, since they also believe that science is predominantly in the business of studying the operation of natural, unintelligent causes. Moderate methodological naturalism can allow for defending or rejecting ID based on what the evidence supports.

In contrast to proponents of ID, some adopt moderate methodological naturalism for the purpose of arguing against theological claims with the authority of science. If theological claims were a part of science, then scientific methods would be suitable for evaluating – and rejecting – theology. Thus ID critics Maarten Boudry, Stefaan Blancke and Johan Braeckman argue that there are many ideas about the supernatural that scientific results could in principle corroborate or contradict: 'not only in the life sciences, but also in other domains of inquiry, paranormal researchers and sceptics have investigated extraordinary claims which, if corroborated, would substantiate the existence of immaterial and supernatural entities' such as ghosts and extra-sensory perception.[30] According to Boudry, Blancke and Braeckman, sceptics who restrict science from evaluating supernatural explanations give up their most powerful weapon in the fight against superstition and nonsense. It is important to be able to say that we can scientifically test and falsify some such claims. However, this also means admitting that science could in principle also corroborate them.

On the difficulties of defining science

Some problems of demarcation criteria

There have also been attempts to refer to criteria other than methodological naturalism in order to show that ID is not science. However, the question of demarcation is notoriously difficult and unsolved. As philosopher Yujin Nagasawa notes, 'it is much more difficult to show that intelligent design is not science as to show that it has not been established as a good viable scientific theory'.[31] It is difficult to find a criterion which could be used to definitely rule out design-based explanation from biology. For example, suppose that only observable entities can be referenced in scientific theories. Because the 'intelligent designer' has not been observed, ID would then not be a part of science. But this is problematic, because the natural sciences typically allow for indirect

30 Boudry, Blancke and Braeckman 2012, 1159.

31 Nagasawa 2010, 97–101. Similarly, also Haack (2013). On testability, see also Sober (2011, 369–373).

observation and theories, which allows scientific status for the Big Bang theory, belief in electrons and so on. Or consider falsifiability as a criterion of science. One problem is that the core of theories can seldom be falsified directly: theories can often be amended to explain anomalies, and tests require the addition of auxiliary hypotheses to the theory. Ratzsch argues that even a hypothesis of supernatural design can have such testable parts, though the designer's existence cannot be falsified directly.[32]

Discussion of various demarcation criteria has shown that it is very difficult to formulate a strict boundary between science and pseudoscience. However, this difficulty does not show that we cannot say anything about what makes the quality of a scientific theory good or bad. Evaluating the virtues of scientific explanations or the values of science instead of absolute criteria seems a more promising approach. Testability (including predictive power), coherence with existing scientific theory, fruitfulness in opening up further avenues of research, simplicity and other criteria allow us to judge the scientific quality of competing theories and research programs.[33] Using scientific virtues as criteria of judging the best explanation, one could (for example) argue that naturalistic theories of natural history are scientifically more virtuous than the competing research program of ID. It is also possible to argue that though there are problems with naturalistic understandings of the world, ID represents a larger revision of science than these anomalies require.[34] Thus, even if design were admitted as a possible part of science, one could continue to argue against it. In contrast, proponents of ID can claim that their design argument provides a more virtuous scientific explanation of the data than naturalistic explanations.

Personal explanations and science

Another fruitful way to evaluate ID's scientific status would be to ask what disciplines it has most analogies with. Is it with the natural sciences or perhaps more with the humanities, philosophy or theology? Even if drawing absolute boundaries between science and pseudoscience, or between various disciplines of science is difficult, we can still usually quite naturally think that some questions are more suited to the methods of the humanities and others more to the methods of the natural sciences. ID makes use of personal explanations, which are quite different from those typically used in the natural sciences. For example, Collins argues that scientific explanations typically possess *scientific tractability*: they are highly detailed, with references to laws, mechanisms and the minutest details of the systems being investigated. Science also does not provide

32 Ratzsch 2001, chapters 7–11. See also Koperski 2008 and Sober 2011.

33 The criteria for the best scientific explanation are controversial, and are of course linked to the question of what is the best explanation in general. See also Niiniluoto (2002, chapter 6.1) who differentiates between institutional and pragmatic criteria for measuring the success of science.

34 Koperski 2008.

explanations for everything – for example, it is difficult to specify a mechanism explaining why gravity works the way it does. However, in general, an attempt is made for investigating natural phenomena in detail.[35]

By contrast, explanations by reference to intentionality do not include this level of mechanical detail. Theistic intentional explanations typically do not involve any specification about the mechanism by which God creates the laws of nature, for example. Indeed no such mechanism needs to be given, since according to the hypothesis God can bring about any result he chooses without any need for intermediate second causes. Both theistic natural theology and ID require that intentional activity as a cause itself possesses some explanatory power, even without specification of any particular mechanistic process the designer worked through.

Furthermore, while intentional explanations seem to work on a different level than mechanistic explanations, this does not mean that they have no explanatory power.[36] Like natural theologians, ID proponent Meyer also references the example of human design as one basis of this claim. In the case of humans, we cannot yet specify how our consciousness and will influence the molecules of our bodies, but we nevertheless believe that our consciousness has an effect in the world, and that references to human design can be explanatory. In addition, we can typically detect that something is designed by humans without being able to specify how these humans do so.[37] We could also state that in all explanations there comes a point where we reach the level of basic causal powers and are unable to specify further intermediate mechanisms.[38]

This does show that design can be explanatory even without precise knowledge of mechanisms. However, in the case of human designers, we do typically have at least some idea of how the designed objects were produced (or how they could have been produced) in practice. The possibility to investigate such details further is a good thing for the hypothesis, though it is not unconceivable that a hypothesis could not have explanatory power even if further details about the cause cannot yet be investigated. If personal explanation is indeed explanatory, it is not necessarily a fatal flaw for it that personal explanations are different from mechanistic explanations. Even a vague hypothesis could in principle be the most plausible one and could provide us with valuable knowledge. Following Aristotle, it could be argued that there may be great value in even a glimpse of 'celestial things': 'half glimpse of persons we love is more delightful than an accurate view of other things'.[39] But such glimpses are quite different from what are usually considered to be scientific theories. If ID were to be admitted as natural science, at least we would have to argue that this would be a quite

35 R. Collins 2006.

36 Dawes 2009, appendix.

37 Meyer 2013, 392–398.

38 There is reason to think that the demand for intermediate mechanisms should not be absolute; see, for example, Dawes (2009, 51–53).

39 Aristotle, *Parts of Animals*, 644b32–35 Quoted in Zagzebski (2012, chapter 9).

different type of science, applying methods of design detection to subjects that have traditionally been the domain of the natural sciences.

Because of ID's combination of methods from the natural sciences and the humanities, it may be too restrictive to think of ID simply as either part of the natural sciences, or as pseudoscience. Rather, one could believe that part of ID's argument is part of the natural sciences, part some other kind of science and part that is better characterized as philosophical. For example, Collins argues that the difficulty of developing the basic idea of an intelligent designer into a detailed scientific theory makes it disanalogous with the best scientific theories. Thus it is better thought of as a philosophical idea than a scientific theory. However, Collins goes on to argue that the idea of a designer could still function as a background assumption of a 'metascientific' research program of intelligent design. This research program could then include many parts (for example, the question of the exact limits of Darwinian evolutionary mechanisms) which can be investigated scientifically and others which are better characterized as philosophical arguments (such as the design argument).[40]

Words have socially agreed upon meanings. If the generally agreed on meaning of the words 'natural science' excludes design-based ideas, then that means that ID is not natural science as a semantic matter. However, socially agreed upon meanings do change over time and over cultures, and current meanings of the words have their own complex history. For example, continental Europeans usually also define the humanities as 'sciences', whereas Anglo-American thinkers are more likely to mean only the natural sciences with the term. In any case, definitions cannot settle the questions that form the more substantive content of the debate.[41] If we were to accept scientism, then the definition of science would indeed be the central philosophical question of the discussion on ID. But we can recognize the immense success of the natural sciences without believing that science is the only reliable way to gain knowledge, or even that scientific theories are in every case better or more reliable than common experience, theology or philosophy.[42] Because of this, the quality of the arguments for different points of view is the crucial thing to be analysed, rather than the status of these arguments as science or non-science.[43]

Different reasons for rejecting ID

Related to the discussion on methodological naturalism, Gregory Dawes makes a useful distinction between 'in principle' and 'in practice' reasons for rejecting

40 Collins 2006.

41 Keener (2011, 189) argues the same for the discussion on miracles.

42 See further Ratzsch (2009b) and Stenmark (2001).

43 In practice many arguments used to claim that ID is unscientific can be formulated as arguments that ID lacks some explanatory virtue. In this way they could still be useful as critiques of ID. For example, the idea that ID is not science because design is not a good scientific explanation may imply that design is not a good explanation in any other sense, either.

theistic explanations. 'In principle' reasons would be reasons for excluding theistic explanations from ever being good explanations (within science or otherwise) and 'in practice' reasons are based on the actual successfulness of theistic explanations. If theistic explanation and design can never be acceptable explanations, then natural explanations are the only acceptable game in town not only within science but also outside of science. However, if theistic explanations are good, then it can be rational to believe in them, whether they are scientific or not.[44]

In my analysis of strong and moderate methodological naturalism, I have argued that defending methodological naturalism against ID's critique cannot be done in a way that allows us to bypass considering ID's arguments entirely. Under both strong and moderate forms of methodological naturalism, we need to be able to argue that phenomena like the origin and evolution of life are likely to be best explained on the level of the natural sciences without invoking designers.

This type of rejection of *a priori* arguments against ID is also implicit in all accounts in which the rise of Darwinian evolutionary theory is seen as the central reason why biological design arguments can now be rejected. For example, cosmologist Sean M. Carroll writes that 'A few centuries ago, for example, it would have been completely reasonable to observe the complexity and subtlety exhibited in the workings of biological creatures, and conclude that such intricacy could not possibly have arisen by chance, but must instead be attributed to the plan of the Creator. The advent of Darwin's theory of evolution, featuring descent with modification and natural selection, provided a mechanism by which such apparently improbable configurations could have arisen via innumerable gradual changes'.[45] This implies that without Darwinian evolutionary biology, design would still be the best explanation for biological order. This assumes that design possesses at least some rationality as an explanation and cannot be dismissed on *a priori* grounds just by invoking the definition of science. At the very least, we need to argue that the generally agreed upon boundaries of scientific disciplines reflect the historical success of certain methods in answering certain types of questions.

Summary

In the debate over ID, much energy has been used to debate whether ID can qualify as natural science or not. I identified several different ways to exclude ID from science. Strong methodological naturalism requires that theistic

---

44 Dawes (2009, chapter 1). Petri Ylikoski (2001, 51) argues well that demarcation questions are also generally somewhat uninteresting when compared to the question of evaluating explanations: 'it is unclear why we should raise the issue of demarcation at all. An appeal to virtus dormitiva is a bad explanation outside science as well. We should be analyzing what makes explanations good in general. There are good explanations that are not scientific, and there are bad scientific explanations'.

45 Carroll 2003, 631.

explanations will in principle always lack some essential characteristic that is required of scientific explanations. Moderate methodological naturalists can admit that design-based explanations can in principle possess explanatory power even within issues normally studied by natural science, but argue that these cases are exceptional or non-existent. Defining 'natural science' in a universally valid way has proven to be a highly difficult philosophical problem. It is much easier to argue that an idea like ID is bad science than to argue that it is not science at all. Comparing ideas to other, readily accepted scientific theories can also help draw out some differences between ID and what is usually understood natural science.

However, once we reject scientism, we should realize that there are also questions that are better studied by methods other than those typically used in the natural sciences. For example, methods of design detection are important in studying human culture and artefacts. The precise boundaries within disciplines are best based on our experience of what kinds of methods actually work in increasing understanding in each area. There is no *a priori* way to determine that methods of design detection could not in principle also provide the most understanding in problems like the origin of life. The superiority of methodologically naturalistic science in investigating these problems needs to be argued, rather than assumed *a priori*. Because of this, methodological naturalism will not ultimately allow us to avoid giving ID a hearing, if ID's arguments are otherwise good.

It is my belief that the overt focus on the demarcation question in the debate reflects the cultural influence of scientism. Science has enormous cultural authority, and proponents of ID wish to be able to claim it for their ideas. But in the long term, it would perhaps be more prudent to also question the undervaluing of non-scientific ideas in our broader culture. If the problematic nature of scientism became more widely known, perhaps proponents and critics of ID would feel less pressure to argue about the definition of science and could instead concentrate on more interesting questions, such as the evaluation of the arguments themselves. The quality of our arguments and the reliability of our conclusions is far more important than the labels we give them.

6 The designer of the gaps?

The design arguments of natural theology are arguments for the existence of God. However, while most proponents of ID also believe that the designer is God, they argue that the design argument itself does not establish the designer's identity. Here ID's position has been subjected to diametrically opposed criticisms. On the one hand, methodological naturalists have argued that ID's design argument is not religiously neutral enough, and that its designer therefore cannot qualify as part of the natural sciences. On the other hand, theological critics have argued that ID's talk of an intelligent designer is too non-religious and too far removed from the classical theological tradition to be of any religious value. The designer has even been argued to be like an idol, a false image of God, making ID close to a theological heresy.

Another philosophical and theological critique of ID has been based on understanding ID as a fallacious 'God of the gaps' argument. This critique is commonly presented by both theistic and naturalistic critics of ID; article collections on ID usually feature several articles making the critique.[1] However, here too there is a large amount of variety. Some thinkers make the charge of the God of the gaps against all theistic arguments, while others would allow for other theistic arguments to work. There is some disagreement about what exactly makes an argument a God of the gaps, and how theistic arguments might avoid the fallacy.

The purpose of this chapter is to clarify these theological and philosophical discussions. I begin by examining ID's understanding of the nature of the 'intelligent designer', and how this compares to traditional design arguments. In the second section, I consider the critique of intelligent design as idolatry, and how this compares to critiques of natural theology. In the next two sections, I consider differences between ID and mainstream theistic natural theology relating to how we conceive of the problem of the God of the gaps.

1 See, for example, Dembski and Ruse, eds (2004, 67, 142, 238), Pennock, ed. (2001, 158–159, 184–185), Petto and Godfrey, eds (2007, 309–338, 416–417), Comfort, ed. (2007, 86) and Young and Edis, eds (2006, 3–5, 24–25 178–182).

ID's understanding of the designer

ID's separation between the designer and God

Design arguments have historically been among the most popular and most widely believed of natural theology's arguments in support of belief in the existence of God. Even Immanuel Kant wrote that the teleological argument

> always deserves to be mentioned with respect. It is the oldest, the clearest, and the most accordant with the common reason of mankind. It enlivens the study of nature, just as it itself derives its existence and gains ever new vigor from that source. . . . Reason, constantly upheld by this ever-increasing evidence which, though empirical, is yet so powerful, cannot be so depressed through doubts suggested by subtle and abstruse speculation, that it is not at once aroused from the indecision of all melancholy reflection, as from a dream, by one glance at the wonders of nature and the majesty of the universe – ascending from height to height up to the all-highest.[2]

Kant did also criticize the design argument. He argued that the argument can provide evidence only for the existence of some kind of designer, not the existence of God. The crucial problem is the finiteness of the universe, which means that it can (Kant argues) be explained by supposing the existence of a very wise and very powerful being, without the need for an infinite Creator.[3]

Since the biological design argument is also an argument of natural theology, and since proponents of ID wish to connect theology and science, it would not unreasonable to also classify ID as a minimalistic form of natural theology. Nevertheless, proponents of ID do not use this term of themselves, and mainstream natural theologians such as Swinburne have distanced themselves from ID. The mainstream of contemporary natural theology and proponents of ID diverge significantly in their responses to the Kantian critique. Natural theologians typically disagree with Kant on many levels. For example, Swinburne argues that an infinite Creator is a simpler hypothesis than a finite Creator and that natural theology does not need to provide absolute proofs, only evidence and cumulative arguments. Whereas Kant assumed that our conclusions cannot exceed that which is required by the evidence, Swinburne argues that even theories within natural science go beyond this requirement. For example, on the basis of observation of a small part of the cosmos, we make theories about physics which concern the whole universe.[4]

In contrast, proponents of ID frame their conclusions about the identity of the designer quite similarly to Kant, arguing that design arguments can at

2 Kant 1957 [1781], 520; quoted in Plantinga 1990 [1967], 95.

3 Kant also had other arguments for the same conclusion; see further Rossi (2014).

4 Swinburne 2011a and 2011b. See also Tapio Luoma's analysis of Thomas F. Torrance on this point (Luoma 2002, chapter 5).

most prove the existence of an unidentified designer. They do agree that the designer can be identified as God using additional theological and philosophical argument. However, the movement also emphasizes, with Kant, that design arguments alone can at most prove the existence of an unidentified designer.

For example, Behe admits that God is culturally the obvious candidate for the role of the designer, but nevertheless 'the leap [from a designer] to God with a capital G short-circuits scholarly arguments that have been going on for millennia across many cultures'.[5] Behe argues that there are many different accounts of the designer that could in principle fit with the evidence, and the design argument itself cannot settle the debate over which idea of the designer is correct. For example, he argues that nature could in principle be the product of some highly advanced technology, rather than the creation of God. Dembski similarly argues that while ID is compatible with theism and creationism, it is also compatible with deistic views and Platonism, for example. Thus ID is argued not to 'prejudge such questions as who is the designer'.[6] This emphasis is so strong in the ID literature that some critics have even been misled to interpret proponents of ID as agnostics.[7]

ID's identification of the designer as God

But texts identifying the designer with God are also not uncommon in ID literature. In Phillip Johnson's early works, one is even hard pressed to find such a sharp separation at all. For example, Johnson initially constructed ID's argument as a comparison of creation and Darwinian evolution as explanations. Johnson's critique of methodological naturalism is also based on the idea that supernatural explanations should be allowed within natural science.[8] However, later Johnson has also defined the limits of the ID movement's argument more minimalistically: 'My personal view is that I identify the designer of life with the God of the Bible, although intelligent design theory as such does not entail that'.[9] Similarly, in an early article Meyer argues that intelligent design is part of the 'return of the God hypothesis'. Citing the arguments of natural theology favourably, Meyer argued that many lines of evidence provide epistemic

5 Behe 2007a, 277–288. Similarly, for example, Behe (2001a, 699–700). Even in some defences of natural theology, the selection of theism over other designer-alternatives can also be based on subjective personal and cultural reasons; see, for example, Sennett (2005).

6 Dembski 1999a, 252.

7 For example Nieminen, Mustonen and Ryökäs (2014, 277): 'These ID proponents [Behe as the prime example] seem to have mostly agnostic worldviews'. This is a misunderstanding that a broader reading of the ID literature would have corrected.

8 Johnson 1993. It would be going too far to suggest that ID developed from an openly theistic argument into the kind of minimalistic argument seen today, however. There are also important early ID works making the same distinction. For example, Thaxton, Bradley and Olson (1992 [1984]) and Davis and Kenyon (1993, 126–127).

9 Johnson 2007.

support for belief in God, though they do not prove his existence; he then proceeded to identify the biological design argument as one additional such argument.[10] However, in his later writings Meyer has also emphasized the distinction between the intelligent designer and God: 'neither the evidence from biology nor the theory of intelligent design'[11] can prove the identity of the designer as God. Nevertheless, he continues to hold that 'theism makes more sense of the totality of human experience than does any other worldview'.[12]

All of the major proponents of ID have indeed identified the designer as the God of theism and regard making this connection a very reasonable thing to do. For example, Dembski argues that ID forms a 'bridge between science and theology'[13] and that the debate over ID is ultimately about 'whether reality at its base is purposive and intelligent or mindless and material'.[14] According to Johnson, materialists reasonably fear that 'even the most minimalist version of a deity will tend to become understood as something like the God of the Bible, who communicates with humans and cares about how we behave'.[15] He thus sees ID as a 'wedge' which will open a discussion about the nature of the ultimate reality and make it easier to trust in the God of the Bible.[16] According to Behe, evidence for design has the effect of strengthening a believer's faith in God,[17] and philosophical, historical and religious arguments exist which support seeing the designer as the God of Christianity. For example, Behe argues that an infinite series of designers is implausible, and so God is the most plausible designer.[18]

Given these views, it seems perplexing that the ID theorists so often emphasize the distinction between the designer and God, rather than the connection between the designer and God, which they also believe. Some critics of the ID movement have argued that the separation between the designer and God is merely a strategic ploy. By saying that ID does not reveal the identity of the designer, the design argument keeps the appearance of non-religiosity and can be taught in public schools in the United States.[19] Elliott Sober (representing naturalism) and Robert J. Russell (representing theistic evolutionism) have argued separately that not identifying ID's designer as God is very difficult. Identifying the designer as a space alien, for example, leads to the additional question where these space aliens came from. If evolution is not a viable answer, then our alien

10 Meyer 1999c.

11 Meyer 2010, 439.

12 Meyer 2010, 440.

13 Dembski 1999a.

14 Wiker 2002, 11.

15 Johnson 2007. Craig (2008) indeed uses the ID movement's design argument as part of an apologetic for Christian theism, arguing that the existence of an 'intelligent designer' fits better with theism than atheism.

16 Johnson 2000.

17 Behe 1998.

18 Behe 2001a.

19 Shanks 2004, Forrest 2001. For a critique of Shanks, see Ratzsch (2005).

creators must themselves have also been designed. If we do not want to end up with an infinite series of designers, then at some point the chain must stop with God. As I have noted, Behe has also argued similarly, and he did this before Sober and Russell.[20]

It seems to me that there is no reason to regard the ID proponent's distinction between the designer and God as deceitful. Their understanding of the logic of the design argument does allow for this distinction. Even ID proponents themselves think that taking this extra step is very reasonable, they can without contradiction believe that this additional step does indeed exist. However, it still needs to be explained why proponents of ID so often leave the theological interpretation of their argument to the reader, rather than getting into theological and philosophical discussion. Here the best explanation that I have found is that this is motivated by the movement's desire to gain acceptance for its design arguments as a legitimate part of the natural sciences. It is also a response to broader culture's valuing of scientific reasons over theological ones. Proponents of ID want to engage popular culture on the scientific level, since science is so highly respected. However, I worry that this results in a kind of strategic acceptance of scientism for the purposes of the argument. I will have much more to say about this in Chapter 10.

It is interesting to ponder whether the debate over the identity of the designer would not be quite different if the cultural scientism influencing the debate were to be challenged and overturned. In the debate on ID, defenders of the design argument emphasize the difference between the designer and God, while critics emphasize the supernatural nature of the designer. This is a complete reversion of the debate between Hume and Paley, where Hume emphasized the distinction between the designer and God, and Paley the identification. Suppose instead that there was no pressure to have ID qualify as part of natural science, and the central cultural issue was instead the credibility of theism. With this change, it seems likely that theistic defenders of ID would emphasize the connection they see between the designer and God, while the atheistic critics of the movement would once again argue that the design argument can establish only the existence of some designer, but not God.

In their critiques of ID, Russell and Sober aim to show that ID's vision of the designer is plausibly understood as theistic and supernatural. Their purpose is to argue that ID violates methodological naturalism and therefore should not be considered to be a scientific theory. On the other hand, some theological critics of ID have drawn the opposite conclusion from ID's separation between the designer and God: that ID's image of the Creator is too far removed from the Christian God to be credible theologically. I turn now to analysing this critique.

20 Russell 2005, Sober 2007.

Natural theology and ID as idolatry

The critique of idolatry and ontotheology

Most proponents of ID believe that their unidentified designer is actually the Christian God. But is this identification possible? Some theologians have argued that describing God as a designer presents a false image of God, which actually leads away from the knowledge of the true God. For example, theologian Conor Cunningham argues that ID's designer is actually closer to a devil than the true Creator, because the designer is just like a human being, only more powerful and more intelligent. Cunningham even argues that atheists like Dawkins could more effectively criticize traditional Christian belief in God by adopting ID, rather than by defending evolutionary biology.[21]

Relating this critique to the discussion on natural theology will be instructive, since in some critiques of natural theology it is also argued that there is an insurmountable difference between the 'God of the philosophers' and the God of Christianity. Some kind of difference does indeed seem to exist, as is poetically described by mathematician Blaise Pascal's description of his mystical experience in 1654: 'From about half past ten in the evening until half past midnight. FIRE. God of Abraham, God of Isaac, God of Jacob, not of philosophers and scholars. Certainty, certainty, heartfelt, joy, peace'. For Pascal this did not mean the rejection of philosophical apologetics, though he did think that the arguments of natural theology are insufficient for real religious belief.[22] However, others have used the difference between philosophical and religious understandings of God to argue that all images of God constructed on the basis of human reasoning are mere idols in violation of the commandment that 'thou shalt not have other gods'.

The critique of idolatry springs from two very different sources. The first is the Barthian argument that Christian theology and belief should be based on revelation, rather than fallen human reasoning, which will inevitably end up constructing an idol. Only the revelation of God can bring knowledge of God. Barth's famous 'Nein!' (1934) to natural theology was written in response to his friend Emil Brunner's (1889–1969) moderate defence of natural theology. Brunner had argued that some sort of human capacity for the reception of revelation and remnant of the image of God is required by Christian doctrine and tradition. Barth was concerned that we should not repeat the errors of Nazi-friendly German theology, which enslaved theology to serve the supposedly rational principles of the National Socialist party.[23]

The second source for this critique of natural theology as idolatry is quite different: philosopher Martin Heidegger's (1889–1976) philosophical

21 Cunningham 2010, 275–280.

22 Adamson 1995, chapter 7.

23 T.J. White 2010 and Holder 2012.

critique of 'ontotheology'. The critique of ontotheology is that using God as an explanation inevitably makes God into just another creature among creatures, part of the system of the world.[24] Though the concept of onto-theology was popularized by Heidegger, the idea that God is very different from any creature is nevertheless a staple of classical Christian theology. In the theology of Aquinas, for example, God is not just a normal 'being among beings', but 'being itself'. Any application of terms to God is analogical, not direct.[25]

Responding to the critique

In my view, though the danger of creating a false image of God is always present in theology, the critique of idolatry is not a good argument against all natural theology, and similar responses can also be developed on behalf of proponents of ID. For example, McGrath has argued that the Barthian critique of natural theology has an inner tension, because the Bible and traditional Christian theology themselves seem to contain grounds for natural theology. In this situation, the Barthian reliance on the Bible should lead to the acceptance of some sort of natural revelation, where the contents of Christian doctrine are found to resonate in some ways with what we observe in nature.[26]

Actually, the problem of fitting together different images of God is not just a problem for natural theology, but all of Christian theology. For example, the God of the Old Testament is not openly Trinitarian, though the Old Testament can be interpreted from the viewpoint of Trinitarian theology. Within Christian theology the prophets of the Old Testament are thought to speak of the same God as the New Testament.[27] Why could not the God described by philosophical natural theology also be interpreted as the same Trinitarian God? The images of God are not wholly different: proof texts for most of the attributes of the theistic God (such as omnipotence, omnipresence, omniscience, moral perfection and so on) can also be found in the Bible.[28]

Thomas Aquinas described the relationship of the God of the philosophers through an interesting metaphor. If we see someone from far away, we may be able to tell that it is a human person and only later recognize that it is Peter. When seeing the person far away, we were seeing Peter, even while we did not recognize him. Similarly, the God of the philosophers can be interpreted to be, on closer inspection, the God of Abraham, Isaac and Jacob who is known more

24 McCord Adams 2014.

25 Turner 2004.

26 McGrath 2008, chapter 7; 2001, chapter 6; Barr 1994.

27 On the historical importance of the Old Testament for Christianity, see Pelikan (1971, 13–27).

28 For example, see the articles in Flint and Rea (2009), which often quote biblical passages alongside philosophical reflection.

fully through faith.[29] It seems to me that ID's talk of a designer could similarly be interpreted as a vague and distant glimpse of God.[30]

The question of ontotheology requires thinking about the nature of theological language. In what sense can human concepts be applied to God at all? The question is not just about concepts like 'being' or 'design' but also applies to concepts like the love of God and the properties of God discussed in various biblical passages. Because we are human beings, we must necessarily use human concepts when talking about God. It is arguable that in formulating our account of theological language, we must simultaneously include both affirmation and negation. Claiming that God is wholly other and that human concepts cannot be applied to him would make God irrelevant to humans and dismiss the central Christian doctrines of God's revelation and incarnation. However, believing that we can wholly comprehend God would lead to creating a false image of God to fit into our philosophies.[31]

Theologian Denys Turner argues that natural theology can be formulated in a way that avoids the ontotheology error. The key is that in proving the existence of God (or at least providing evidence supporting this belief) natural theology is proving the existence of a mystery that reason cannot fully grasp. Paradoxically, just as natural theology leads us to understand that God exists and that God has certain attributes, it also leads us to understand God's transcendence and mysteriousness.[32] The same point is poetically expressed by Augustine, as quoted previously: 'though the voices of the prophets were silent, the world itself, by its well-ordered changes and movements, and by the fair appearance of all visible things, bears a testimony of its own, both that it has been created, and also that it could not have been created save by God, whose greatness and beauty are unutterable and invisible'.[33]

ID and the breadth of christian doctrine

How then could the breadth of the doctrine of God be combined with ID's design arguments? As Cunningham argues in response to ID, the doctrine of creation is about much more than the idea that God is the designer of the empirically studied order of nature. It is, according to Cunningham, primarily

29 Turner 2004, 18–19.

30 Similarly Feser 2008, 87–88.

31 Turner 2004.

32 Turner is a representative of the tradition of negative theology, and all proponents of natural theology do not accept as strong a sense of the mysteriousness of God. As Alston (2005) points out, modern Anglo-American philosophical theologians generally trust in the capacity of the human reason to understand quite a lot of the properties and intents of God, though no-one believes that they fully comprehend God. For two different perspectives of how we can talk of God's 'properties', see also Holmes (2007) and Wainwright (2009). It may be that a univocal understanding of theological language fits ID and much of contemporary natural theology better than an analogical understanding. See further Alston (1989) and Williams (2005) for defences of univocity.

33 *De civitate dei*, XI, 4.

a metaphysical doctrine explaining why there is something rather than nothing, explaining the fundamental dependency of all things of their Creator.[34] It seems to me that Cunningham is saying something important here: ID does not speak of this aspect of the doctrine of creation and thus provides at best an incomplete defence of belief in the doctrine.

However, proponents of ID do recognize that God is more than a designer. This is already implicit in ID's differentiation between the designer and identifying the designer as God. If God were not more than a designer in ID's understanding, than this kind of strong differentiation should not be possible. The implied understanding is that God is more than a designer, but also not less than a designer. This is in line with Turner's description of theological language: our language fails not because it says too much of God, but because it says too little. Analogy always includes both a denial and affirmation.[35]

Though ID fails to describe the full depth of the doctrine of creation, there is also commonality with the doctrine of God as Creator of the order of the nature. In studies of the historical development of the doctrine of creation, it is often even argued that the idea of God as the conqueror of the forces of chaos and the creator of order in the cosmos preceded the doctrine of *creatio ex nihilo* and metaphysical developments of the doctrine. McGrath thus argues that 'the theme of ordering is of major importance to Old Testament conceptions of creation'.[36] The fact of existence is not the only thing explained by the doctrine of creation; it also seeks to explain the rationality and beauty of the world God has created. It is with this part of the doctrine of creation that ID's 'designer' who purposefully creates order can find consonance.[37]

In the end, it seems to me that natural theologians and proponents of ID have a great deal of common ground in the debate on theological language. The descriptions of God used in mainstream natural theology are far more robust than in the ID literature. Nevertheless, the language of design and purpose are also used within mainstream natural theology, and natural theologians have developed responses against the critique of such language as an onto-theological error. It seems that at least many of the responses are also in principle available to the ID movement, if the movement would engage more with design as a theological and philosophical question, rather than attempting to restrict the discussion to the natural sciences.

34 Cunningham 2010, chapter 7.

35 Turner 2004, chapters 7 and 8.

36 McGrath 2001, 155; however, see Craig and Copan (2004).

37 This is not to say that all versions of the doctrine of creation will be compatible with ID. For example, from the standpoint of process theology, a creator ordering nature could be seen as coercion and contrary to love. Oord (2010) indeed criticizes ID on this basis. However, the creation of form could also be seen as a gift. Here the discussion depends on our overall understanding of ontology: what is meant by coercion, and is non-violent existence even possible? On this see the discussion in Hart (2003).

The God of the gaps critique

The basics of the God of the gaps critique

The God of the gaps critique against ID has been made by thinkers representing highly varied viewpoints.[38] Though the term 'God of the gaps' has Christian origins, it is used in many different ways and has recently also been used against all kinds of theistic argumentation, not merely creationism and ID. In such critiques, it is claimed that we should expect science to eventually replace talk of God altogether with scientific explanations of the same things.[39] Proponents of ID themselves vigorously deny the allegation that their arguments are examples of the God of the gaps fallacy. In this situation, it is important to clarify just what the term means and exactly what the problem is with God of the gaps arguments.[40]

Two main critiques of God of the gaps arguments have been made. First, such arguments are often called *arguments from ignorance*: the divine explanation is argued to be correct mostly on the basis that we have no scientific explanation of the phenomena. Now it should be recognized that science can study not only the powers of nature, but also the limits of nature. For example, the first law of thermodynamics tells us that we should not expect an overall increase in energy in closed systems. Because of this, it does seem in principle possible to argue that there are limits to natural explanations.[41]

But when God of the gaps arguments are criticized as arguments from ignorance, what is meant is that divine explanations are invoked at points where it would be more reasonable to wait for natural explanations, and where there is no good motivation to invoke theistic explanations. Dietrich Bonhoeffer famously argues this point in a letter written while imprisoned by the Nazis in Tengel in 1944 that 'It is wrong to use God as a stopgap for the incompleteness of our knowledge. If in fact the frontiers of knowledge are being pushed further and further back (and that is bound to be the case, then God is being pushed back with them, and is therefore continually in retreat. We are to find God in what we know, not in what we don't know; God wants us to realize his presence, not in unsolved problems but in those that are solved'.[42]

38 See for example Cunningham 2010, 275–280, Haught 2004, 238, Dawkins 2006a, 152–153, and Pennock 1999, 163–172. Even where this characterisation of ID is not present, the question of what we should think about mysteries currently unexplained by science is still often there.

39 For example Stenger 2004, 182.

40 Plantinga (1997) and Rusbult (2004) similarly argue that the term 'God of the gaps' is not useful without a precise definition of what is meant.

41 Walton (2009) even argues persuasively that the absence of evidence (or ignorance of evidence) can indeed often be evidence. When we are in a position where we should by good reasons be able to observe something if it exists, then not observing that thing is evidence against its existence. I analyse the issue of God of the gaps arguments as 'arguments from ignorance' somewhat more in Kojonen (forthcoming).

42 Bonhoeffer 1997, 311; see also Drummond (2008 [1883], 166).

The second main line of critique against God of the gaps arguments is that they present a wrong understanding of divine action. In gaps arguments, theistic explanations are thought to work on the same level as scientific theories, whereas the biblical accounts present God as the Creator of all things, including the regularities of nature. Furthermore, to be on a secure foundation, theological beliefs should be based on what we do know, rather than what we do not know. Charles A. Coulson put the point succinctly: 'when we come to the scientifically unknown, our correct position is not to rejoice because we have found God; it is to become better scientists'.[43]

Limit questions good, God of the gaps bad?

But the central problem now becomes: how do we know that ID's design arguments are God of the gaps arguments, and are problematic in the ways presented? To show how muddled the waters are, consider limit questions, which Barbour defines as 'ontological questions raised by the scientific enterprise as a whole but not answered by the methods of science'.[44] In contrast with gaps arguments, these are typically seen as quite legitimate by theologians. Examples of such questions include ethical questions related to the doing and use of scientific research, but also metaphysical questions, such as the question of the origin of the cosmos and the orderliness of the laws of nature. In such cases, it is argued that limit questions are clearly disanaloguous to the questions normally studied by the natural sciences. In his arguments for the existence of God, Swinburne similarly argues based on phenomena that are 'too odd' or 'too big' for natural science to explain.[45]

An idea of the hierarchy of the sciences often underlies the distinction between limit questions and the God of the gaps. For example, Arthur Peacocke presents a hierarchical model of the relationship of the different sciences, where each science proceeds by its own method to study those questions which its methods are best suited for analysing. There can be overlap and connections between the different fields, but by and large each science does its own thing. In the discussion on theology and science, the critique of the God of the gaps has been a reminder of the broad metaphysical nature of many theological doctrines and the compatibility of religious faith and science.[46]

But what are the criteria for differentiating between limit questions (which are legitimate) and God of the gaps arguments (which are thought to be illegitimate)? As in my discussion of methodological naturalism, I would argue that the most credible way of defending this distinction is based on experience. From our collective human experience, we know that the natural sciences are

43 Coulson 1958, 16.
44 Barbour 1997, 90.
45 Swinburne 2004a, 74–75.
46 Peacocke 1993, page 217, figure 3.

highly fruitful in studying certain kinds of questions, but that other methods are more fruitful in studying other questions. God of the gaps arguments argue for God based on mysteries where we have reason (based on experience of similar phenomena) that science will ultimately find good solutions for present mysteries. Limit questions are based on phenomena that our experience shows are vastly different from mysteries that science has been fruitful in solving. This kind of understanding of the issues seems to underlie Haught's critique of ID as a God of the gaps: 'ID is a "science stopper" since it appeals to a God-of-the-gaps explanation at a point in inquiry when there is still plenty of room for further scientific elucidation'.[47]

However, if classifying some particular point as the true limit of science and the beginning of theology is based on experience, then people may have different understandings of which claims are limit questions and which are God of the gaps arguments. The experiential grounding of the distinction between God of the gaps and limit questions does not provide grounds for an *a priori* argument against ID, since proponents of ID do not agree that our experience shows the folly of ID. Rather, they believe that our experience shows that biological information and irreducibly complex systems are best explained by reference to intelligence, and that there are grounds against expecting natural explanations to be found for such mysteries.

Possible worlds arguments are again relevant here. We can imagine a world where the origin of life happens through a natural chemical process, whether deterministic or indeterministic; indeed most of the scientific community believes that we live in this kind of a world. In this possible world, the origin of life is clearly not a limit question, but can be studied and explained exhaustively on the level of the natural sciences. However, it is also possible to conceive of a world where the origin of life cannot happen by any naturalistic process, but can only happen as a divine miracle, an event beyond what nature could produce on its own. In such a world the origin of life is indeed a limit question, since it can never be explained by naturalistic processes. In such a world, ID's arguments about the origin of life would be true, and the origin of life would be a limit question. Again, we must argue what kind of world we live in based on experience.

As noted, science does currently establish also some limits to natural processes. Following this precedent, we can at least imagine a situation where the empirical evidence would count strongly against any naturalistic explanation of the origin of life, for example. Ratzsch argues that if we had already done 10,000 years of research on naturalistic origin of life-hypotheses and the problems seemed similar to those afflicting the creation of perpetual motion machines, we would certainly be in a position to argue that these results tell us something about the inability of natural processes to produce life.[48] And if it

47 Haught 2004, 238.
48 Ratzsch 2001, 142.

is possible after 10,000 years, it may as well also be possible sooner. It seems in principle possible that something like the distinction between life and non-life could be a fundamental limit of the natural sciences, just as some natural theologians consider the explanation of consciousness in terms of non-conscious causes a limit of science.

There are differences between the arguments of the ID movement and some arguments of natural theology, such as the cosmological argument. Like the natural theologians, proponents of ID are also attempting to make claims about the fundamental nature of the world. However, we can at least imagine a world where evolutionary explanations for information and irreducible complexity work without needing to invoke the actions of a designer working beyond the laws of nature. But while something like the Leibnizian cosmological argument is also not totally removed from experience, it depends on much more general features of the world, which could be argued to be true in all possible worlds. So there seems to be some degree of difference here between ID's argument and the arguments of the natural theologians. Some questions seem be more clearly 'too big' or 'too odd' for the natural sciences, as Swinburne says.

However, mainstream natural theologians also do make use of arguments that depend even on highly precise empirical details of our world, which are not shared by all possible worlds. For example, the fine-tuning argument refers to the precise properties of the laws of constants of nature, and arguments from religious experience and miracles refer to particular religious experiences and particular historical accounts of miracles. These are not arguments that could be made in any possible world, yet they are not considered examples of God of the gaps arguments.[49]

So, though the difference between limit questions and gaps arguments is in principle clear, in practice the border is quite muddled and difficult to discern. I submit that from our subjective perspective, we should think of the difference between limit questions and God of the gaps arguments as a continuum, where different claims are classified based on how likely it seems to us that a particular point is a true limit of science. Just where each argument will fit on the continuum will depend on how strong we think the premises of each argument are and how analogous we think the issue is with questions that have been successfully explained by using methodologically naturalistic scientific methods.[50]

Where each argument should be placed on the continuum from limit questions to God of the gaps arguments will depend on our estimates of the evidence. For example, a proponent of ID might place ID's biological design arguments at about the same point as natural theologians place the fine-tuning argument. On the other hand, someone who believes that all of reality will ultimately be explainable through scientific methods would place all of the arguments on the God of the gaps side of the continuum; while perhaps even rejecting the

49 See, for example, the articles in Craig and Moreland, eds (2010).

50 Collins 2012, 224.

legitimacy of those questions which would still remain outside the province of the natural sciences, such as the question 'why is there something rather than nothing', which underlies Leibnizian cosmological arguments. Ironically, this kind of position might even be called an 'atheism or the gaps'[51] or a 'naturalism of the gaps', since it assumes that the solution of any and all mysteries will be naturalistic.

Often critics of ID make use of a very high view of scientific progress, where it is argued that all currently scientifically unexplained matters will ultimately be explicable in terms of naturalistic science.[52] For example, Stenger and Dawkins argue that the success of science in explaining past mysteries should also lead us to expect that science will find solutions to mysteries like fine-tuning.[53] In other words, the past history of theistic arguments and the success of science in overthrowing them should make us cautious about making arguments based on present scientific mysteries.

However, arguments by analogy depend on a relevant similarity between the compared objects. Our experience about scientific explanations being found for one type of phenomenon does provide us evidence that science will likely be able to explain similar mysteries in the future. However, if some mystery is of a completely different kind, then the past progress of science does not provide us equally good grounds for believing that these mysteries will be solved. So, it is worth noting that the phenomena which theists believe to be genuine limits of the natural sciences are believed by these theists to be very different from the phenomena that are normally explained.

It is also worth noting that the case for the inevitability of scientific progress is often stated too strongly, as Ratzsch argues: 'Gaps have certainly evaporated in some cases under pressure of scientific advance, but I don't know of anyone who has actually done the work of constructing a historical induction for the usually assumed constant drumbeat of collapsing empirical gaps. – And intriguingly enough, at least one gap – cosmic fine-tuning – seems to be gaping ever wider the more fully it is investigated. The platform for this induction is missing a couple legs'.[54]

In conclusion, it seems to me that applying the terms 'God of the gaps' or 'an argument from ignorance' to either ID's arguments or to natural theology does not allow us to bypass the evaluation of the premises of these arguments. Proponents of ID have attempted to argue in a way that I think is in principle possible; as I've argued, there is a possible world where something like ID is true for the origin of life, for example, and where ID's argument would be highly credible. Our question should be whether the data support the idea that we are

51 Alexander 2009.

52 Or at least that if some phenomenon is scientifically inexplicable and then no other way to explain that phenomenon could be valid either. This relates again to the discussion on scientism in Chapter 1.

53 Stenger 2004, 182; Dawkins 2006a, 152–153.

54 Ratzsch 2006.

living in such a world. When understood in this way, the condemnation of ID as a God of the gaps argument can only be made as the conclusion of a critique of ID, rather than as the starting point.

Theologies of the gaps

Models of divine action

Though the critique of the God of the gaps often takes a philosophical form, and has been used even by atheists, the term does have theological origins. I have already referenced two theological critiques of God of the gaps arguments: (1) such arguments are thought to needlessly restrict divine activity merely to mysteries, rather than understanding that God is also present in natural processes that we do understand, and (2) gaps arguments are argued to be apologetically dangerous: if faith in God is based on the existence of gaps, then the progress of science in closing these gaps will tend to undermine faith. I will now analyse these theological issues in more detail.

In criticizing God of the gaps arguments, Russell suggests that they problematically locate God's activity primarily in interventions into the natural order, rather than realizing God's presence in also in the 'web of natural processes'.[55] The problem of gaps arguments is, then, that they do not adequately recognize God as the creator of natural laws and processes and create an unnecessary conflict between natural explanation and belief in divine activity.[56] This kind of broad concern about gaps arguments is widespread in the theology and science community. Some who have this concern about the God of the gaps formulate an understanding of divine action and argue against all belief in miraculous divine action, also referring to problems like theodicy. Others are concerned merely with the overt emphasizing of miraculous divine action and bypassing general divine providence.[57]

Russell's warning is an important reminder of the breadth of divine activity. In practice some proponents of ID's biological design arguments do seem to make the rationality of belief in creation almost depend on the existence of gaps in nature, as I will argue in Chapter 10. In this kind of debate, the warning against the God of the gaps can serve to remind us of the breadth of the doctrine of creation – its credibility does not depend on finding gaps in the abilities of naturalistic evolutionary processes.

55 Russell 2006, 584.

56 McGrath 2009b, chapter 8. See McGrew (2013) for a discussion on different concepts of miracles and Carroll (2010) for a discussion of different understandings of 'natural laws'.

57 I am content to use the old, somewhat simplistic distinction between general and special divine providence here, since here the question is simply if God acts in the world in a way that goes beyond general providence. For a more nuanced categorisation of different types of divine action, see Tracy (2006). For a further critique of the distinction between general and special divine action, see, e.g. Gregersen (2009).

Nevertheless, it is also clearly possible to defend a biological design argument without limiting divine activity merely to gaps. Despite their sometimes harsh words against theistic evolutionism, proponents of ID do also typically recognize God as the creator of the entire natural order and do not restrict his activity merely to gaps. Here it is useful to distinguish between three broad models of divine action in nature.[58] The first (1) argues that God acts only through miracles, not at all through natural laws. This view comes close to occasionalism, which holds that all events happen by the will of God, and nature does not have any causal powers of its own. The second view (2) argues that God acts both through natural laws and through miracles (understood as acts of God which supersede what nature normally does). This view suggests that God acts both in the web of natural processes in its gaps. This is the traditional view, is the view of Russell and is also the typical view of ID proponents. The third view (3) is that God acts only through natural laws and processes. In this view, it is argued that general divine providence is sufficient for theology, and miracles would be in violation of God's nature or at least against the way God chooses to interact with the world.

There are many different models of divine action, and following the third option just outlined, it is possible to formulate an understanding that makes all appeals to divine interventions in history theologically dangerous. Much depends on what kind of metaphor of the God-world relationship we use. For example, on the metaphor of the world being like a machine created by a divine artificer, it seems odd to think that the artificer would have to repair the machine after its creation. A well-built universe should contain all that it needs without intervention. On this metaphor the existence of gaps in nature would actually be evidence against the existence of God, rather than evidence for God. But on the metaphor of the world as God's kingdom, temple or musical instrument, it becomes much more credible that God would also act in the universe beyond the laws of nature. One would expect a perfect king to have a personal interest in his domain and subjects, acting to influence the development of his kingdom in a positive direction.[59]

I submit that Christian theology allows for several different possible models of divine action and historically has also allowed for divine action beyond the laws of nature. This means that at least on the traditional understanding, we cannot rule out something like a miraculous origin of life out *a priori*. However, if we accept God's ability to also act through natural processes, as traditional Christian theology does, then we also cannot rule out *a priori* the possibility that God could have used natural processes to create life. Again, I submit that we

58 Larmer (2014, chapter 1), uses a similar distinction. Rusbult (2004) provides a more complete description of the possibilities with seven different types of gap theologies. Here I have used Sorri's (2013) simpler threefold division.

59 The possibility of different metaphors is discussed perceptively by M.J. Murray (2006), modifying his earlier critique of ID (M.J. Murray 2003).

should take the empirical evidence we have into account when arguing about what kind of theological model we should adopt. This means that our theological models also allow rejecting something like ID's design argument *a priori*, but only after an evaluation of the evidence.

Apologetic concerns

The second theological concern with God of the gaps arguments is apologetic: if belief in God is primarily based on gaps in nature, then the progress of science in filling these gaps will tend to undermine belief in God.[60] Based on the history of science, many argue that is better to present evidence of God as based on phenomena which are not expected to ever be open to scientific study. As Haught points out, theological accounts of nature are typically understood to concern the ultimate character of reality, rather than operating on the level of scientific theories.[61] The traditional question 'why is there something rather than nothing', for example, does not seem liable to be ever answered by natural science. Thus natural theology based on this question does not seem as liable to be falsified with the progress of science as gaps arguments.[62]

Even if divine interventions into history are a possibility allowed by our theology, it may still be a good idea to be careful about making such claims about divine action. Since the main focus of theology is outside God of the gaps arguments, at least faith should not be thought to depend on gaps arguments. As Allan Harvey has noted, there is a temptation 'to forget God's work in routine things and only acknowledge his hand in obvious miracles'.[63] The theological critique of the God of the gaps can guard against this temptation.

However, as Ross McCullough has argued, we should note that these apologetic concerns are pastoral and practical in nature.[64] This has the consequence that these arguments are more about the practical consequences and usefulness of gaps arguments, rather than their truthfulness. Such considerations are valuable; however, something like ID's design argument could well be true even if we do not like it.

Another consequence is that these concerns are related to the attitudes of those making the arguments, rather than the validity of the arguments themselves. It seems possible for someone to defend an argument for divine action beyond the laws of nature while at the same time admitting that the grounds of faith lie elsewhere. For example, a Catholic Christian might defend the veracity of the healings that are claimed to have happened through the intercession of Pope John Paul II, but the Catholic faith has much broader grounds, and the

60 Brooke 2010, 78–79.

61 Haught 2008, 35.

62 Turner 2004, chapters 11 and 12.

63 Harvey 2000.

64 McCullough 2013.

entirety of the faith would not be threatened even if some particular healings were proven to be forgeries. Similarly, natural theologians usually employ several different arguments to increase the credibility of the proposition that God exists; the loss of one argument would not be fatal to natural theology.

Similarly, let us assume that someone has no theological objection to the origin of life being an event that can be explained purely in terms of chemistry, with no need of divine intervention. Suppose further that this person knows all the usual stuff about the nature of religious faith and the broad basis of religious belief, so that his/her faith is not at all insecure. But suppose this person just finds the origin of life too improbable to have happened by any naturalistic process and is honestly convinced that the features of life are best explained by the actions of a designer. This person would then be an advocate of a biological design argument without making their faith depend on it. And this would seem to avoid the pastoral problem with gaps arguments. In practice this type of position may be rare, but this does not mean that it is impossible. In any case, it is the attitude that I would recommend to ID proponents.

Yet another point that follows from the pastoral and practical nature of this critique is that other practical considerations might also enter into play, and perhaps some of these could be in favour of taking the risk of making a gaps argument. Aquinas argued that 'by no other means can it better be made manifest that all nature is subject to the divine will, than by the fact that He sometimes works independently of the order of nature'.[65] Applying this type of thinking to contemporary gaps arguments, McCullough argues that if a gaps argument for a miracle in human history or natural history was successful, it would serve as powerful evidence against any naturalistic worldview and so may be worth the risk of being proven wrong.[66] One could also argue that the risks of making a biological design argument could be offset by using the previously mentioned strategy of not basing our entire faith on the success of a particular gaps argument. Natural theologians also use arguments with less than completely certain premises in their cumulative case arguments. Because of the possibility of this type of response, the pastoral critique is not decisive against God of the gaps arguments, though it does serve as a useful warning against a narrow dependence on such arguments.

I would argue that our proper response to the pastoral concern should also depend on what we think about the evidence. We will have to ask if we can honestly say that we are in a position to make an informed assessment that the proposed gap is a real gap in nature, rather than merely a gap in our knowledge. If it looks like the progress of science is likely to close a particular gap, then it will seem like an extremely risky strategy to advocate an argument based on this gap. On the other hand, if some phenomenon looks like a genuine limit of science, then there is much less need to be afraid of an argument on limits being

---

65 *Summa Contra Gentiles*, Book 3, chapter 99.

66 McCullough 2013.

proven wrong, particularly if our faith is robust and seeking to shore it up is not our primary reason for making such an argument.

So, theists can follow the evidence in deciding whether and what sort of 'gaps' there are in nature. This applies to theistic evolutionists as well. Thus theistic evolutionist Keith Ward can also argue that 'if there is a God, a Creator of the universe, it is plainly possible that God might perform miracles, might bring about events that no created cause has the power of itself to bring about'.[67] Acceptance of something like miracles or ID as an in principle possibility in some possible world that God could create does not logically require accepting that a particularly claimed instance of such divine action has actually happened in our world. However, it does mean that using the critique of the God of the gaps against ID is not a simple matter. As much as I have criticized scientism, the scientific and experiential arguments should nevertheless come first in critiques of ID's biological design arguments.

Summary

Proponents of ID make a strong distinction between the designer and God, but simultaneously also believe that it is reasonable to identify the designer as God. The temptation of scientism is visible here: the scientistic tendencies of the surrounding culture drive proponents of ID to keep theological and philosophical arguments in the background. If the philosophical problems of scientism were more widely known, the shape of the debate might well be different.

In critiques of God of the gaps arguments, the temptation of scientism can be seen in the easy assumption that all problems must have solutions that can be found by the methods of natural science. Theologians are right to warn against the error of the God of the gaps, but it could also be in principle possible for methodologically naturalistic science to come to the end of the road and to find real limit questions that require philosophical and theological discussion. Whether we think biological design arguments are a God of the gaps or a legitimate limit question should depend on what we think the evidence shows.

67 Ward 2002, 742.

7 The intuitive possibility of design

When discussing biological evolution, I noted that majority opinion of the scientific community is one factor that weighs against ID for many. It is, I think, generally reasonable to trust the majority opinion of experts in matters where one does not personally have any great expertise. However, there are also factors that offset the weight of this majority opinion for many people. Generally speaking, we are hesitant to accept the ideas of experts when these ideas run counter to what seems evident according to our own senses and sensibilities. In the case of biology, most people experience an intuitive feeling of designedness. Because of this, it comes as no surprise that people are hesitant when they are told by thinkers like Dawkins that this experience is actually an illusion. If evolution were taught more widely to be compatible with the general idea of design, as many theistic evolutionists believe it is, then perhaps ordinary people would be more inclined to accept the theory already on the basis of testimony.

Here it is important to differentiate between different senses of the word 'intuition' in order to be clearer. In philosophy, intuitive beliefs are understood as belief in truths that appear to be so obvious to our minds that they can be assumed to be true without further argument. Some have likened intuition to 'seeing' a truth, like 2 + 2 = 4, or the laws of logic. Philosophers often disagree about what actually is intuitively true in this way, and thought experiments are one way of arguing about the matter. So, intuitions are not necessarily thought to be infallible, and beliefs based on them be revised in virtue of further reasoning and evidence. It seems to me that these kinds of philosophical intuitions are used on all sides of the debate. For example, this unavoidably happens when discussing questions like 'what makes an explanation have explanatory force?'[1]

There is also a different sense for the term 'intuition', however. In the cognitive sciences of religion intuitive beliefs are understood as beliefs that are easy for the cognitive structure of our minds to adopt, in contrast to beliefs which require a great deal more cognitive effort for us to adopt, such as the theories of the natural sciences or the contents of systematic theology. In this sense, it has been argued that belief in the designedness of the cosmos may be natural

1 See van Woudenberg (2005) for a defense of philosophical intuitions and Pust (2012).

and easy to acquire for our sorts of intellects. Some postulate that we have an 'agency detection device', which tends to activate when perceiving the order of nature, thus producing design beliefs.[2]

In this chapter, I will analyse the significance of intuitions for the debate over ID. I will begin in the first few sections of the chapter by showing how different intuitions about design (in the philosophical sense) can be debated using thought experiments. In the latter few sections I then go on to discuss the connection between design intuitions and design arguments.

The importance of thought experiments

The laboratory of the mind

Testability has traditionally and rightly been considered an important criterion of scientific theories. In situations where two different scientific theories compete as explanations of the same data, scientists will attempt to find an additional empirical test that will enable us to finally see which theory is better. In the discussion on ID, the conflict is not just between different understandings of the empirical data – though that is certainly important – but also between different philosophies. For example, parties differ on what constitutes evidence of design and what would be the legitimate point where accepting design as the explanation is preferable over a search for further non-design-based explanations. But here we have a problem: how can these different philosophical understandings be brought under testing? It is often difficult to find an empirical test that will help us sort between different philosophies like these ones.

However, philosophy has another way to test these kinds of ideas: thought experiments, also called the 'laboratory of the mind'. They are hypothetical scenarios meant to tease out the implications and test the viability and coherence of the intuitions behind different philosophical ideas. In the debate on design arguments, thought experiments have often been used to defend the possibility of evidence for design against common critiques and examine how detection of nonhuman design could be possible. Proponents of ID, but also proponents of natural theology use thought experiments to argue that it is in principle possible to have strong evidence of purposeful design in nature.[3]

There are many types of thought experiments and precise classification is difficult.[4] Thought experiments are usually thought to be essential to philosophy, but they have also played a surprising role in natural science. For example,

2 See further De Cruz and De Smedt (2015).

3 For example, Leslie 1989 uses thought experiments in defense of the fine-tuning argument, and Swinburne (2004a) uses a thought experiment about a poltergeist to establish his category of personal explanation.

4 For different analyses of thought experiments, see Wilkes (1988), Sorensen (1992) and Häggvist (1996); for general reviews of the discussion, see Brown and Fehige (2011).

Galileo Galilei (1564–1642) used a thought experiment to argue that Aristotelian physics is contradictory,[5] and modern physicists also use thought experiments in discovering the implications of theories.[6] In philosophy, famous thought experiments include the 'brain in a vat', arguing the possibility that our perceptions are just illusions; 'monkeys and typerwriters', arguing that chance can generate order given infinite resources; and Searle's 'Chinese room', designed to show that computers do not think or understand. The examples listed are all controversial, and this goes to show that a thought experiment seldom ends the debate. A philosopher who wants to dispute the conclusion of the thought experiment can argue that the experiment is built on false or improbable assumptions and thus leads to an erroneous result, or that it is not really analogous to the case being debated. However, thought experiments are nevertheless useful tests of our thinking.[7]

The necessity of intuitions for the debate

The significance of thought experiments is disputed. This is particularly in thought experiments which are used to argue for strong metaphysical conclusions, as is sometimes done in the philosophy of mind. For example, it can be argued that since we are able to conceive of the existence of our minds without our bodies, this is at least some kind of evidence that our bodiless existence is actually possible. This assumes a connection between conceivability and possibility: if we can conceive of something like bodiless existence, then this makes it at least somewhat more likely that bodiless existence is possible. Our own self-awareness is the only way we even know that consciousness exists, so it seems reasonable that our own intuitions about what our minds are like should also count as some kind of evidence. But this has been disputed. For example, using this kind of intuition as evidence may be problematic because the intuition itself may be influenced by our prior worldview, rather than merely reflecting our self-knowledge about the kind of beings we are.[8]

In any case, the thought experiments in the discussion on ID are not meant to argue for metaphysical conclusions in this way. These thought experiments are not aimed at providing evidence for the existence of a designer, but at testing our intuitions about different models of design-based explanations. In response to this use for thought experiments, a critic could argue that intuitions are generally unreliable, and thus thought experiments testing our intuitions do not yet tell us much. In practical research intuitions have often been found to be misleading in some way from the point of view of physics. Furthermore,

5 Palmerino 2011.
6 See, for example, Hossenfelder (2013, 11–22).
7 Brown and Fehige 2011.
8 See Gender and Hawthorne (2002) and Taliaferro (1994) for different perspectives on this.

philosophers themselves have conflicting rational intuitions about matters, and not all intuitions can be correct.[9]

Despite the fallibility of intuitions, it seems reasonable to think that at the very least our philosophical intuitions about explanations continue to be important and cannot be dismissed even in the natural sciences. As philosopher of science Petri Ylikoski argues, 'science has its origin in common sense cognition. There should be some kind of continuity. Of course, it now includes much that is apparently incompatible with common sense, but I seriously doubt that this incompatibility also extends to the general principles of explanatoriness'.[10] If our philosophical intuitions can tell us anything, then they should be able to tell us about principles of explanation. Actually, if our intuitions cannot tell us about principles of explanation, then all kinds of thinking become very difficult, if not impossible. How are we to evaluate evidence at all, if our minds are simply unsuited to the task? It seems that we must begin by assuming that our philosophical intuitions are at least somewhat reliable, and that we can discuss them reasonably.[11] Furthermore, if our intuitions are wrong in the cases of the thought experiments, it would at least be desirable to be able to explain why and how they are wrong.

Examples of thought experiments

Thought experiments are not just important in the contemporary debate on ID but also in the historical debate on natural theology. Since this discussion also helps clarify the debate over ID, I will consider two examples here: the 'voice from heaven' in Hume's *Dialogues Concerning Natural Religion* (1779) and William Paley's famous 'watch on a heath' in his *Natural Theology* (1802). These thought experiments have the same purpose as the modern ones I will consider: they aim to defend the in principle possibility of evidence for design and also a certain account of what constitutes such evidence.

The voice from heaven

The thought experiment in the *Dialogues* is made in discussion between the character Cleanthes, defending the design argument, and the character Philo, who makes sceptical objections against natural theology. In the preceding section, the sceptic Philo has argued that repeated observation is the only reliable way to demonstrate the connection of cause and effect. Because we have not observed the generation of several universes, we cannot make general claims about what is required to make one. Philo argues that there is a profound

9 See further De Cruz and De Smedt (2015, 33–39).

10 Ylikoski (2001, 51) is not commenting on thought experiments here, but on principles of explanation.

11 See Ratzsch (2009) for a similar argument.

dissimilarity between human works of art and the cosmos, rendering analogical design arguments unsound.[12] With his thought experiment, Cleanthes wants to demonstrate that Philo's critique is flawed. Here is how Cleanthes states the experiment:

> Suppose, therefore, that an articulate voice were heard in the clouds, much louder and more melodious than any which human art could ever reach; suppose that this voice were extended in the same instant over all nations and spoke to each nation in its own language and dialect; suppose that that the words delivered not only contain a just sense and meaning, but convey some instruction altogether worthy of a benevolent Being superior to mankind – could you possibly hesitate a moment concerning the cause of this voice, and must you not instantly ascribe it to some design or purpose? Yet I cannot see but all the same objections (if they merit that appellation) which lie against the system of theism may also be produced against this inference.[13]

The problem, according to Cleanthes, is that Philo's objections would also make it difficult to consider such a voice from heaven designed. For example, we could argue that we have no example of any previous event that is precisely like this, and so our previous experience should not enable us to affirm that the voice is indeed produced by a person, if we were to accept Philo's principles of explanation. Rather, we would need to observe several such voices caused by divine beings before being able to make the inference. Cleanthes argues that this and Philo's other objections are intuitively absurd, when applied to this case: of course everyone would be able to notice that the voice is generated by intelligence. This, according to Cleanthes, reveals the emptiness of Philo's scepticism: 'You see clearly your own objections in these cavils; and I hope too, you see clearly that they cannot possibly have more force in one case than in the other'.[14]

Cleanthes' thought experiment is an attempt to test the cogency of Philo's sceptical arguments by applying them to a new case. It is a *reductio ad absurdum* where Cleanthes is trying to show the falsity of Philo's premises by extending them to a logical (but intuitively absurd) conclusion. His argument is that either Philo's sceptical arguments also work against the evidence in the thought experiment, or they do not work at all. So Philo should either reject the intuitive conclusion of design in the case of the voice of heaven, or also accept it in the biological world. For Cleanthes, the design argument works both in the case of the voice and of the cosmos.

12 *Dialogues*, part II.
13 *Dialogues*, part III.
14 *Dialogues*, part III.

The watch on a heath

Paley's famous example of a watch prepares the ground for his design argument in many ways, but the example has some core similarities with Cleanthes' argument. Paley also uses the example to ridicule potential responses to his design argument.

> In crossing a heath, suppose I pitched my foot against a *stone* and were asked how the stone came to be there, I might possibly answer that for anything I knew to the contrary it had lain there forever; nor would it, perhaps, be very easy to show the absurdity of this answer. But suppose I had found a *watch* upon the ground, and it should be inquired how the watch happened to be in that place. I should hardly think of the answer which I had before given, that for anything I knew the watch might have always been there. Yet why should not this answer serve for the watch as well as for the stone? Why is it not as admissible in the second case as in the first? For this reason, and for no other, namely, that when we come to inspect the watch, we perceive (what we could not discover in the stone) that its several parts are framed and put together for a purpose . . . Every indication of contrivance, every manifestation of design, which existed in the watch, exists in the works of nature; with the difference, on the side of nature, of being greater and more, and that in a degree which exceeds all computation.[15]

This is the part of Paley's example that is usually quoted, and here it is not clear that it is actually a counterfactual thought experiment like the voice from heaven. It seems that finding a watch on a heath, while unusual, would not be as strange as a voice from heaven, for example. However, Paley's further analysis of the example moves it further from our actual situation in the direction of counterfactuality. Through nine modifications of his example, Paley attempts to respond to different possible critiques of his design argument.

For example, Paley argues that it wouldn't weaken the conclusion of design if the person observing the watch had never seen one made or known anyone capable of making one. Thus background knowledge of and previous experience of the designer's capabilities is not, according to Paley, absolutely necessary for the design inference. This is an indirect response to Hume's argument that only inductively gathered experience of the creation of life forms would make the design argument possible. Paley also argues that small errors in the operation of the watch would not invalidate the conclusion of design. This is in response to the problem of natural evil. He makes several further arguments as well: for example, he argues that the conclusion of design would be only strengthened if the watch possesses the capacity to reproduce itself, since this

15 Natural Theology, chapter 1.

would only require more functional complexity if the watch were to be capable of reproduction, so this would only strengthen the design argument.[16]

So, Cleanthes and Paley both reject criticisms of design arguments by constructing scenarios in which the objections would lead to denying even obvious evidence of design. Cleanthes' thought experiments are purposefully fanciful, while Paley's thought experiment starts out quite close to our practical reality. Its initial closeness to our actual situation gives Paley's thought experiment some rhetorical force – the critic finds it difficult to deny that we can see the designedness of watches, since in our actual experience we do find that they are designed. This may make it more difficult to evaluate how our intuitions are formed: would we indeed have the intuition that watches are designed, if we did not have previous experience of them?[17]

A critic of Paley could argue in this vein that it is difficult to get beyond our knowledge that watches are designed to get a good sense of our intuitions regarding what we would think if we did not already possess this background knowledge and merely discovered watches whose order was a natural consequence of the operation of natural laws. One response to this objection is provided by the more fanciful sort of thought experiments outlined by Cleanthes. In these cases, we are dealing with something that is merely highly analogous to the products of human design, yet the conclusion of design seems intuitively quite clear. If the intuitions seem to be very similar as in Paley's more realistic case, then it seems that the degree of fancifulness in the thought experiment is not greatly responsible for the way our intuitions operate in these cases. The general strategy of argument seems to be sound.

The incredible talking pulsar

Like their predecessors from the time of the English Enlightenment, proponents of ID present both fanciful and realistic thought experiments. They often use thought experiments to illustrate situations in which it would be reasonable to infer the existence of an intelligent designer, despite some objection that is usually deployed against ID. The first thought experiment in the ID literature that I know of occurs in Dembski's early essay 'On the Very Possibility of the Design Argument'.[18] The point of the essay is to defend the possibility of ID's project of seeking evidence for intelligent design in nature, and Dembski's thought experiment of 'The Incredible Talking Pulsar' is the central argument used. Dembski aims to show that the detection of supernatural design is in principle possible, and thus the exclusion of design from consideration of possible explanations is not rational.

16 Natural Theology, chapters I–II.

17 Similarly, McGrath (2011, 110).

18 Dembski 1994.

Briefly, Dembski asks us to suppose that a pulsar star some billions of light years away emits regular radiomagnetic signals, which are found to be a message in Morse code. As the worldwide scientific community studies the signal, it is found that the pulsar is communicating itself to be 'the mouthpiece of Yahweh, the God of both Old and New Testaments, the Creator of the universe, the final Judge of humankind'. To confirm this claim, the pulsar agrees to answer any questions we might put to it. Soon, through the messages, medical doctors learn how to cure AIDS, archaeologists find lost civilizations, physicists find their unifying theory of the forces of nature and mathematicians obtain proofs for problems which are impossible to solve without infinite computational resources. Dembski argues that this would be clear evidence of divine design.[19]

Dembski acknowledges the outlandishness of his example, arguing that no theologian would expect God to reveal himself in this way. Thus the example is for Dembski a mere logical possibility, not something that would realistically happen. The example merely demonstrates that 'design has at least the possibility of becoming perfectly evident'.[20] This then makes it possible to ask whether our universe has some more subtle evidence of design.

Science fiction and island adventures

In this early text, Dembski presents this thought experiment as his main argument for the possibility of detecting intelligent design. In his later texts, Dembski has used many different strategies for defending design arguments. For example, in his book *No Free Lunch* (2002) Dembski begins with the importance of design-based explanations for practical life, and only later uses more fanciful, science-fiction-based examples to show how we could in principle also detect the existence of nonhuman intelligence.[21] Similarly, Behe's discussion of design detection in his *Darwin's Black Box* (1996) begins with thought experiments describing ordinary events such as scrabble games and trap construction. Only after this does Behe reference more fanciful examples of design detection taken from science fiction in order to show that the detection of nonhuman design is also in principle possible.[22]

Examples from science fiction are quite popular in ID literature. Dembski, Behe and Meyer have all referenced the search for extraterrestrial intelligence project (SETI) as an example of how the methods of intelligent design are already used in science. Here their central illustration is SETI pioneer Carl Sagan's science fiction book *Contact* (1985, also as a movie in 1997). In *Contact*, a signal from space is found to contain a long series of prime numbers. When

19 Dembski 1994, 113–138.

20 Dembski 1994, 129.

21 Dembski 2002a, 1, 6–8. However, Dembski (2009, 91–92) again uses the 'Incredible Talking Pulsar'-example.

22 Behe 2006a, 192–196; 196–199.

scientists investigate the signal deeper, they discover the blueprints for a vast machine. The signal is understood to be a message from an alien civilization. Proponents of ID agree that this conclusion would indeed be the only reasonable one, and argue it would be foolish to insist that we search for a materialistic, non-personal explanation for the message. Again, this is thought to show how nonhuman design can in principle be detected, and insistence that reference to designers is always a vacuous God of the gaps explanation can be unreasonable. Proponents of ID then go on to argue that the same kind of information-rich order is also found in nature, warring the design argument.[23]

As noted, some of the thought experiments used by ID proponents are not as fanciful. For example, Behe uses a thought experiment about a shipwreck onto an apparently uninhabited island while discussing the effect of background beliefs on the assessment of evidence for design. Behe argues that even if we are initially quite convinced that nobody else is living on the island, finding stones arranged to form the words 'WELCOME, SURVIVOR' would change our minds. Behe argues that design can also at least in principle be evident in the order of nature, even for those who do not begin by assuming God's existence. This functions as a response to those claiming that the design argument can only be convincing to theists. But Behe acknowledges that atheism and theism do effect the evaluation of the strength of the design inference: an atheist, giving a low prior probability to the hypothesis of design will require more evidence for the conclusion of design than the theist, for whom even supernatural intervention into nature can be a possibility.[24]

The idea of ID's thought experiments is that design can be explanatory in the situations described, despite objections. Based on this, it is argued that there can be no general ban on design-based explanations, but the evidence could in principle also support them in the case of biological life, for example.

Critical responses to thought experiments

Some responses from the literature

There are two main critical lines of argument available for critics. First, it can be argued that the assumptions and logic of these thought experiments are somehow faulty. Second, critics can simply accept the conclusion, but argue that our situation is very different from the examples. In my reading of the literature responding to ID, I have encountered only few responses to these kinds of thought experiments, despite their presence in so many ID-friendly texts.

23 For example, Dembski (1998c, 17), Dembski (2002a, 6–8), Behe (2006a, 196), Behe (2000b, 7) and Meyer (2004a and 2004b). The ID link to SETI is also prominently expressed in the ID friendly Illustra Media films *Unlocking the Mystery of Life* (2003) and *The Privileged Planet* (2005). See also McGrew (2004, 13).

24 Behe 2001a, 105.

Sober, Pennock, Matt Young, Mark Perakh and SETI-researcher Seth Shostak nevertheless have presented some critiques. Their critiques focus on the difference between the thought experiments and our actual situation.

Pennock argues that Dembski's example is misleading because of the difference between the 'Incredible Talking Pulsar' and the biological evidence: 'in each case we infer an intelligent signaller not because these are cases of complex specified information in a generic sense, but because the pattern of information matches a previously known pattern that we associate with intelligence'.[25] Shostak similarly contests ID's use of SETI as an example, arguing that SETI does investigate the contents of the signal. Rather, it focuses on finding intensive narrow-wavelength signals, which are known to be produced by civilizations, but are not produced by nature.[26] Both of these criticisms come close to the ID position, however. Pennock and Shostak both argue that because some property is found to be a marker of intelligent life in our experience in the human context, it can also function as evidence of design in the cases of the thought experiments. But this is also largely the logic the ID proponents use, as I will show in Chapter 8. Pennock and Shostak do not here seem to differ on the logic of the argument, but only on what properties constitute evidence of design. This leaves the door open for proponents of ID to argue that features like teleology, specified complex information and irreducible complexity are also strongly associated with intelligence.

Perakh and Young make their critical comments analysing Ratzsch's example of an alien bulldozer – one of several thought experiments Ratzsch presents in his analysis of design arguments.[27] Ratzsch argues that should we find a bulldozer on another planet, we could recognize it as designed despite not having previous knowledge about the designer. But Perakh and Young argue that the example is different from ID, since we can infer so much about the designer. The designer might be of a certain height to sit inside the bulldozer, he or she needs bulldozers to create buildings and so on. In contrast, in the case of biological organisms, the purposes of the designer must be very different from human designers and cannot be known by studying biology. So, for Perakh and Young, the explanatory power of the design argument is dependent on being able to make such more detailed judgements about what the designer is like.

This criticism illustrates the way the assumptions and conclusion of a thought experiment might be questioned. However, it seems to me that the line of critique adopted by Perakh and Young will not apply to all thought experiments of this type. For instance, consider John Leslie's example, where Leslie asks us to imagine that 'particles regularly formed long chains which spelled out "GOD CREATED THE UNIVERSE", this then being shown to result inevitably

25 Pennock 1999, 254.

26 Shoshtak 2005.

27 Perakh and Young 2006, 194–195; Ratzsch 2001, 21.

from basic physics'.[28] Here the designer is clearly different from humans, yet design does seem to have explanatory force. Dembski's example of the talking pulsar also makes the same point. Moreover, even considering the example of the bulldozer, it could be argued that our conclusions about the designedness of the bulldozer are more certain than our conclusions about what the designer is like. For example, we might eventually conclude that the aliens are actually very different from humans, and created the bulldozer simply to mimic human technology, and to thus communicate with humans. Furthermore, at least in the human context it is often possible to recognize that some artefact is designed, without knowing what its purpose is.

Sober's critique is much more weighty. Sober recognizes that Cleanthes' thought experiment about the voice from heaven presents a challenge for his position that background knowledge of the designer's existence and motivations is necessary for making the conclusion of design: 'These arguments do not require us to say anything concerning how probable it is that an intelligent designer who lives in the dark or in the clouds will produce an English sentence. . . . And who knows how inclined a celestial intelligence would be to boom English sentences down to Earth?'[29] Sober recognizes that Cleanthes' design argument is based on an inductively observed connection between the type of order seen and intelligent design as a cause and grants that 'there is nothing wrong with inferring that the voice in the dark and the voice in the clouds were both probably produced by an intelligent being'.[30]

Yet Sober denies that this makes ID's biological design arguments plausible. His reasons for this are twofold. First, Sober argues that while there is good evidence to establish a high-frequency connection between intelligible voices and intelligent agents, there is insufficient evidence to establish any such high-frequency connection between purposeful complexity and intelligent designers. Second (and this is the more weighty criticism in Sober's own estimation), the biological design argument does properly take into account evolutionary biology: Sober is convinced that evolutionary mechanisms can indeed explain life, whereas they cannot explain the voice.[31] This critique is one that proponents of ID would agree with, if they did not contest the viability of evolutionary explanations.

Most examples of purposeful complexity occur outside the context of human activity, so it seems correct to say (following Sober) that proponents of ID cannot argue that there is a high-frequency observed connection between all examples of purposeful complexity and intelligent design. Nevertheless, as I will examine in more detail in Chapter 8, proponents of ID can still argue that there is a somewhat weaker connection that still gives design-based explanations some

28 Leslie 1989, 109.
29 Sober 2008, 171.
30 Sober 2008, 174.
31 Sober 2008, 175–176. Perakh and Young (2006, 194–195) also make the same criticism.

explanatory power. It would be strange to argue that the connection has to be as clear as in the case of the voice example before the design argument starts to have any explanatory power at all. It seems more credible that the evidence of design does not have to be either completely convincing or completely absent. Perhaps the amount of evidence and the quality of arguments we have is rather somewhere between these two extremes.

The possibility of scepticism

It seems to me that thought experiments do count against many too far-reaching objections to design arguments. In the previous chapters while analysing God of the gaps critiques and methodological naturalism, I have also assumed that we can imagine a situation where we would have evidence of design, and categorical denials of the possibility of design arguments do not make sense. Thought experiments like the ones analysed in this chapter can help support this conclusion. Under some of the critiques, even if we found the words 'GOD MADE THE UNIVERSE' regularly created by the normal operation of the laws of nature (to adopt Leslie's example), explaining this by reference to design would only be a vacuous God of the gaps. If the naturalist adopts this line of argument, then he can answer the design argument based on metaphysical philosophical arguments alone, rather than the empirical evidence usually valued by naturalists. But this is a line of thought that is vulnerable to ID's criticism of naturalistic science as merely applied philosophy, not empirical investigation based on the unending search for truth.

However, this still leaves room for more moderate critiques following the critics' line of argument. Because thought experiments are hypothetical, they do not themselves provide evidence of design, but only test our concepts. So, critics can essentially admit the point of the thought experiments: yes, evidence of design is possible. Critics also do not need to argue that the situations of the thought experiments are completely dissimilar from our own, such that we do not have any evidence fitting the design argument. Rather, a critic can simply argue that the situations of the thought experiments are sufficiently dissimilar to our situation that scepticism of design arguments is made possible. In nature, we do not find talking pulsars or 'MADE BY YHWH' labels on human DNA. We do find rational order, fine-tuning and astounding complexity, but the evidence for design isn't of quite the same, unavoidable nature as in the thought experiments.

Despite these criticisms, the major point of the thought experiments seems to stand. If seeking to explain the patterns described in the thought experiments in terms of design and purpose would be rational, then this seems to make it possible to consider that there may also be other situations in which the design argument is rational, and that we may ourselves live in such a situation. As in my chapters of methodological naturalism and the God of the gaps, I have once again found myself defending the in principle possibility of ID's design arguments. But is ID indeed primarily about such arguments, rather than intuitive belief?

Design as an intuitive belief

ID proponents on the commonsensical nature of ID

I have been considering the role of our philosophical intuitions in the debate over ID, and thought experiments as one way to discuss these intuitions. But the ID movement does also argue that belief in design is intuitive in the sense that it is a commonsensical explanation of the order of nature. Design is understood as a reasonable mode of explanation that all humans intuitively use in their everyday life. However, it is argued that design can also be refined into a rigorous scientific explanation.[32]

The intuitive credibility of design as an explanation is a commonly stated background assumption of the ID movement. For example, Behe argues that 'the overwhelming appearance of design strongly affects the burden of proof: in the presence of manifest design, the onus of proof is on the one who denies the plain evidence of his eyes'.[33] Behe is saying that the appearance of design can be very clearly perceived in nature, and this means that the burden of proof should be on those who dissent from this commonsense conclusion. According to Dembski, his mathematical design arguments give 'theoretical support to intuitions that most people have for a long time harbored'.[34] Dembski argues that humans tend to intuitively infer design when they perceive a complex pattern conforming to some 'specification' or rational pattern. For Dembski, this sort of intuitive design inference also triggers when humans perceive the order of natural objects such as animal organisms. Meyer also argues that his design argument on DNA leads to the same conclusion as 'commonsense reasoning' on the matter.[35]

Recognizing the perceived commonsensical nature of the design inference helps make sense of a perplexing attribute of some early ID works, such as Johnson's *Darwin on Trial*. The book contains little explanation of why design is a good explanation and instead focuses merely on critiquing Darwinism. But supposing that Johnson's critique of Darwinian evolutionary theory were to be accepted, how would this lead to the conclusion of design? Often, our current ignorance of natural explanations can simply lead us to search further. So, it is initially puzzling that Johnson does not appear to see the need to provide a positive argument for design. However, if the background assumption of the commonsensical nature of belief in design is taken into account, Johnson's argument becomes more intelligible. Johnson is assuming design as an obviously logical and intuitively apparent explanation of biological life. Design is the default explanation for the ordered complexity of nature, as in Behe's writings. Refuting the credibility of all alternatives means that design will continue

32 According to Edis (2006, 9) this is the primary purpose of the ID movement.

33 Behe 2006a, 265.

34 Dembski 2005a.

35 Meyer 2009, 17.

to reign as the best explanation by default, without requiring any further positive argument in its favour.

Recall also ID's frequent use of quotations like Dawkins' definition of biology: 'biology is the study of complicated things that give the appearance of having been designed for a purpose'.[36] Proponents of ID argue that if even a strong critic of religious belief like Dawkins can acknowledge the appearance of design as a central feature of biology, then that appearance must be very strong indeed. The intuitiveness of design is then used as part of the argument for at least considering the possibility of design as an explanation, rather than just dismissing it *a priori*: 'there is something curious about the scientific denial of our ordinary intuition about living things'.[37]

The intuitiveness of design-based explanations helps make plausible the ID proponent's contention that design beliefs are different from the identification of the designer as God. If the conclusion that nature's order is designed is initially reached through the same cognitive apparatus that is also responsible for detecting human design, then the initial basis of the conclusion is not based in any religious tradition. In that case our subconscious cognitive processes will only supply us with the initial idea that there is design, but the identification of the designer will depend on some other process.[38] A conclusion that is initially arrived at in this manner could later be integrated into a religious tradition and supported by it. Actually, this is just what some cognitive scientists of religion are postulating indeed is happening with regard to belief in design: those outside religious traditions give up this intuitive belief, while those in religious traditions continue to interpret nature through the teleological intuition.[39]

The intuitiveness of design in the cognitive science of religion

In recent decades, the idea that humans intuitively see nature as designed has received support from research in the cognitive science of religion. Teleological explanations are argued to be natural to us humans in the sense that they accord with our natural cognitive tendencies, and so are easy for us to accept. Some even argue that children are 'intuitive theists'.[40] Even adults appear to have the same intuitive tendency to explain things by reference to purposes. As Ratzsch puts the point, 'design thinking may be natural to our sorts of intellects'.[41] There is some controversy over interpreting these results. While most agree that this natural tendency can help explain the persistence of belief in the designedness

36 Dawkins 1991, 1.

37 Meyer 2009, 20. See also, for example, Behe (2006a, 264–265) and Dembski (1999a, 125).

38 Mullen 2004, 4.

39 See further De Cruz and De Smedt (2015).

40 For example Kelemen 2004.

41 Ratzsch and Koperski 2015.

of nature, there is disagreement over whether this undercuts our rationale for believing in design.[42]

Some sceptics of design arguments have claimed that our detection of purpose in nature is an evolutionary accident; a mechanism which has evolved to serve in the recognition of natural agents erroneously also activates when observing the order of nature.[43] Justin Barrett has argued that the postulated human cognitive mechanisms responsible for detecting agency are hyperactive: in our distant evolutionary past, it may have been useful to have a bias to regard noises produced in the forest as the product of agents, since this would have allowed our ancestors to avoid predators.[44] Barrett himself avoids making strong conclusions based on this thesis, but others have used it to argue for sceptical conclusions. For example, Stuart Guthrie argues that such evolutionary explanation for the functioning of our design-detecting faculties should lead us to be sceptical about our intuition that nature is designed.[45]

Is the design intuition reliable?

What should we think about these results? One possible conclusion is that we should reject all of our intuitive judgements about design as unreliable, and only believe in design when a rigorous argument in favour of design can be made independently of the intuition of design.[46] However, I think this is taking the results too far. First (1), it would be strange indeed to discard some explanation as unreliable merely because it fits with our cognitive architecture. This would be saying that un-intuitiveness is a merit of theories: we believe them because they are absurd. Yet it seems that many of the beliefs that are in accord with our cognitive structure are also true. Second (2), our propensity toward teleological explanations does not make all our intuitive teleological explanations unreliable. Those of us who believe in the existence of human minds believe that we can indeed reliably identify human artefacts as designed and identify that other humans also have minds, so it appears that our design detection is still reliable most of the time. Furthermore, sometimes our intuition of design is far stronger than at other times. For example, in the case of the noise in the forest it is far weaker than when reading a book, or when observing the structure of organisms or the rationality of the laws of nature.[47]

---

42 See De Cruz and Smedt (2010) for an excellent review of different positions within the cognitive sciences of religion, and analysis of the arguments.

43 Guthrie 2006.

44 Barrett 2004.

45 Different explanations for why we intuitively perceive design in the universe lead to different conclusions regarding the reliability of this perception. The existence of the HADD could help atheists explain the persistence of religious beliefs, but from a different standpoint theists can argue that the Creator has designed us to be able to see the order of nature as evidence of his existence. (See Leech and Visala 2011; Visala 2011, DeCruz and De Smedt 2015.)

46 Nagasawa 20010, 56–57.

47 See Leech and Visala (2011), Visala (2011) and de Ridde (2014b, 42–51) for further discussion.

In our everyday lives we can differentiate between the weak evidence of design presented by conspiracy theorists and the reliable knowledge that a computer is designed. It seems that we are not at the mercy of our 'agency detection device', but can evaluate how convincing it is at least in some way. If the same process causes us to perceive design in both human artefacts and in nature, we need to be able to specify why we reject the intuition in one case but not the other. Otherwise it seems more coherent to accept the *prima facie* reliability of the intuition either in both cases or in neither.[48]

It is clear that human intuitions and beliefs are often mistaken. This conclusion is supported both by scientific research and our common human experience.[49] However, the idea that we should adopt a *prima facie* trust in the beliefs formed by our cognitive faculties does not imply that we should believe our cognitive faculties to be infallible. Defenders of commonsense rationality allow that our commonsense beliefs can be altered and defeated by the evidence. They simply argue that we must have at least some trust in our intuitions and common sense for the process of rational inquiry to get even started.[50]

If this kind of trust in our common sense is adopted, it seems plausible to claim that the triggering of our design detection faculties in the case of nature does provide at least some reason to believe in design. However, as with other commonsense beliefs, this initial reason could be overthrown by some further arguments. This is just what many critics of design arguments in fact claim. For example, Dawkins sees biology as the study of things that appear to be designed, but he goes on to argue that Darwinian evolutionary theory shows that this design does not have its origin in a designing mind, but in the operation of natural selection.[51] Discussion of the validity of these defeaters can also make discussion on the reliability of our intuitions on design possible. Thus Alvin Plantinga, for example, argues that Darwinian evolutionary theory actually doesn't provide a defeater for belief in design even if it is correct, so the design intuition retains its force.[52] In contrast, the ID movement argues that Darwinian evolutionary theory does not actually explain the appearance of design in biology.

---

48 This strategy is taken up by Mullen (2004). To determine the triggering conditions of our design detection, Mullen analyses several examples of design detection, as well as potential defeaters for the reliability of the design perception. This is one possible way of bringing the discussion forward, even if design detection is seen as an intrinsic human capability not amenable to description as an argument.

49 Trout 2002.

50 See, for example, Dougherty (2014a, 57–61).

51 Dawkins 1991, 1.

52 Plantinga 2011, chapters 1–2. See also de Ridder (2014) and Kroeker (2014) for discussion and expansions of Plantinga's position.

Perception of design or design argument?

Design arguments as unnecessary

To recap, the results of the cognitive sciences of religion seem to lend credence to the idea that forming design beliefs about nature is in some way natural or easy for us humans. Those who trust in our intuitive perception of design in nature see our design detection as just another human cognitive faculty that we simply have to trust in *prima facie*, just as we have to have some trust in our other perceptual capabilities. So, could belief in design be based on this kind of faculty, rather than design arguments?

Already Thomas Reid (1710–96) argued that belief in design is based on a non-inferential capacity to detect design that all humans have and that is required to detect even the intelligence of other humans. According to Reid, design arguments can act to reinforce the reliability of this initial perception, but such arguments are not necessary for belief.[53] Some defenders of this idea of design detection go further and argue that all design arguments in fact presuppose the reliability of the design intuition. The argument is that design arguments do not really add anything to our certainty of design, but only succeed in restating the intuition. William Whewell (1794–1866) stated this view eloquently:

> When we collect design and purpose from the arrangements of the universe, we do not arrive at our conclusion by a train of deductive reasoning, but by the conviction which such combinations as we perceive, immediately and directly impress upon the mind. 'Design must have a designer'. But such a principle can be of no avail to one whom the contemplation or the description of the world does not impress with the perception of design. It is not therefore at the end but at the beginning of our syllogism, not among remote conclusions, but among original principles, that we must place the truth, that such arrangements, manifestations, and proceedings as we behold about us imply a Being endowed with consciousness, design, and will, from whom they proceed.[54]

In this quotation, belief in design is understood to emerge as the result of how the order of nature influences the mind. The mind is not portrayed as a wholly passive recipient of this natural revelation. Rather, the mind interprets nature through the principle that certain types of order imply a designer. Design arguments can be formulated only if we already believe in design before the argument.

---

53 *Essays on the Intellectual Powers of Man* (1785), essay V.

54 Whewell 1834, 344, quoted in Ratzsch and Koperski 2015; see also Ratzsch 2003.

As noted, Plantinga has also defended the idea that design beliefs are based on the normal functioning of our cognitive faculties, rather than arguments. Just as we immediately form the belief that other minds exist, so also certain types of order elicit in us the belief in design. According to Plantinga, belief in the designedness of the cosmos arises not primarily through arguments, but through design discourse. This means that the description of certain features of the cosmos causes in us a powerful impression that there must be an intelligent cause, and this is sufficient justification for believing in design. Plantinga is not opposed to design arguments as such, but argues that beliefs based on this non-inferential design discourse may be more resistant to critiques than beliefs based on arguments.[55]

Design arguments as developments of intuitions

The debate about whether our own subjective experience of design already provides us with sufficient grounds for belief in design resembles the contemporary epistemological debate about the necessity of natural theology. The idea that we should trust in all of the beliefs formed by our belief-forming faculties until we have reason to doubt them is defended by a broad variety of thinkers based on very different epistemological views. For example, it is accepted in both the reformed epistemology defended by Plantinga[56] and the evidentialism of Swinburne.[57] The difference between the viewpoints here is whether it is necessary to also provide arguments for religious belief in addition to these subjective reasons. Evidentialists like Swinburne believe that in the presence of disagreement about the reliability of religious belief, presenting publicly available evidence and detailed arguments in favour of the existence of God is important.[58]

The extent to which design arguments depend on prior intuitions about the world is a question that can only be settled by a detailed examination of the logic of design arguments. It seems to me that the argument does indeed depend on the ability of our mind to recognize a conceptual link between certain types of order and the purposeful actions of an intelligent agent as a good explanation for this type of order. Furthermore, as I will argue in more detail in Chapter 8, the credibility of the argument will indeed depend on our prior beliefs about theism. However, design arguments do not necessarily assume the conclusion of the argument. As I argued in Chapters 3 and 4, they usually do not assume the reality of teleology before the argument, but merely the appearance of teleology.

55 Plantinga 2011, chapter 2.

56 Plantinga 2000. See also Alston (1991), Koistinen (2000).

57 Swinburne 2004b.

58 Swinburne 2004b.

Both proponents of ID, their critics and research in the cognitive sciences of religion agree that design beliefs are intuitive for humans. There may also be ways to defend the reliability of our design intuitions, even accepting Darwinian evolutionary biology, as Plantinga claims; this is contentious. But does this mean that there is no use for further arguments? In the discourse on natural theology, it is often also argued that the many of the arguments of natural theology develop certain human intuitions about the world into arguments, and thus help expand and evaluate the basis of our intuitive beliefs.[59] The credibility of our commonsense beliefs can often be tested by reflective thinking. It can be asked: how does my subconscious cognition come to the conclusion that nature is designed? Furthermore, how sound is the basis of the intuition? Discussion on the credibility of the design intuition would similarly be helped if it could be developed into a rigorous argument. If the design argument's premises can be shared by both the theist and the atheist, and the argument is good, then this will help the case for the reliability of the design intuition. If the credibility of the argument depends to a great extent on our prior religious and ideological commitments, then this will also be good to note.

Furthermore, even if belief in design gains some *prima facie* credibility from the commonsensical design intuition, it does not follow that the strength of our beliefs in design could not be influenced by arguments. Our beliefs could be motivated by a mixture of inferential and non-inferential support, rather than having to choose either one as the exclusive method of forming justified beliefs. Intuitively accepted beliefs can gain or lose support based on what further research and analytic arguments show about the same issue.[60] This means that both supporters and critics of design arguments can find value in studying and discussing design arguments, even if they accept the idea that the design intuition grants *prima facie* plausibility to design. Supporters can argue that the reliability of this intuition can be further supported by arguments, while critics can argue that arguments show the unreliability of the initial intuition by providing a sufficient amount of counterevidence. This also helps develop dialogue between the different positions.

In the next chapter, I will turn to analyse how its design argument should be understood and whether it can avoid some further philosophical critiques that are commonly directed against it.

Summary

The capacity to recognize intelligence in others and in patterns is important in everyday life, and similar pattern recognition also acts as a trigger for many in the case of nature. Proponents of ID also appeal to the intuitiveness of belief in design when attempting to argue that the possibility of design should be

59 Evans (2010) makes the case for this understanding of natural theology well.

60 Similarly, Von Wachter (2014, 60).

investigated further. Indeed, though there continues to be debate over the matter, there does not seem to be any reason to reject the rationality of such beliefs simply because of their commonsensical nature. However, the intuitiveness of beliefs does not preclude us from attempting to formulate further arguments to corroborate or disconfirm such intuitive beliefs.

In addition to intuitions about design, philosophical intuitions about what kind of explanations are good and in what situations design arguments could be justified are also at work in the debate over ID. Thought experiments are one way to test different intuitions about situations in which something like ID's 'intelligent designer' could in principle be explanatory. These thought experiments work by imagining some situation in which (it is assumed) all parties of the debate could agree that design is indeed detected, even though the situation does not appear to avoid some broad *a priori* critique of design arguments (such as the idea such arguments are always unexplanatory 'God of the gaps' arguments). Both natural theologians and proponents of ID can use thought experiments to defend the in principle possibility of cosmological and biological design arguments. But only a more detailed evaluation of the evidence and the premises of the argument can tell us whether such design arguments are valid also in our world and not just in the imagined situations of the thought experiments.

8 The logic of design arguments

Design arguments are at the centre of the ID movement's thought. Like the traditional design argument, ID's argument gains much of its appeal from the intuitive link between teleological order and the operation of a mind as a teleological cause. This is stated succinctly by Dembski: 'Intelligent Design is one intelligence determining what another intelligence has done'.[1] Again, this underscores the idea of a link between the sort of order seen in nature and intelligence. Proponents of ID agree on this general principle, but have presented several different ideas of how, exactly, the logic of the argument works. For example, design arguments can be divided into analogical, inductive and abductive forms. Dembski has also attempted to formulate a new kind of 'eliminative' design argument.

In this chapter, I will analyse some formulations of the argument and compare them with critiques, as well as formulations used in natural theology. In the first section of the chapter I analyse some traditional formulations of the design argument and move on to the inference to the best explanation in the second section. Having identified some critiques of the argument, I then turn in the third part of the chapter to analyse different strategies for defending design arguments. In the fourth section I consider Dembski's distinctive design argument. Throughout, I will contrast the argument with critiques and point out ways in which the argument could be developed further.

Traditional formulations of the design argument

Analogical arguments

Traditionally, discussion on design argument in textbooks of the philosophy of religion centres on William Paley and David Hume. I will also begin at this point, though the contemporary discussion in both natural theology and ID

1 Dembski 1998c, 19.

seeks to go beyond this discussion. In Chapter 7 I already quoted Paley's example of the watch:

> Every indication of contrivance, every manifestation of design, which existed in the watch, exists in the works of nature; with the difference, on the side of nature, of being greater and more, and that in a degree which exceeds all computation.[2]

Paley argues that nature has the same indications of design as the watch, only that the evidence of design in nature is even stronger. Because of the prominence of the analogy at the beginning of Paley's *Natural Theology*, Paley's argument has often been understood to be an analogy also by its logical structure. So understood, the conclusion of design is formed on the basis of nature's likeness to human artefacts.[3] Here the logic of the arguments runs roughly as follows:

1 Biological organisms resemble machines in their goal-directed order. For example, the eye resembles a camera.
2 Machines possess goal-directed order because they are products of intelligent design.
3 Similar effects typically have similar causes.

Therefore:

4 It is probable that nature exhibits goal-directed order because it is also designed, like machines.

David Hume criticized this type of argumentation on several points in his *Dialogues Concerning Natural Religion* (1779), though I should note that Hume was not writing in response to Paley – rather, Paley was writing partly in response to Hume.[4] Hume argued, against premise 1, that the analogies between nature and man-made machines are too distant to lend the inference much strength. As I've noted in Chapter 4, here contemporary proponents of ID differ with Hume: they believe that the progress of science makes the analogy between natural order and man-made machines close indeed. For example, Behe argues that 'the analogy between a watch and a living organism could be made very strong. Modern biochemists probably could make a watch, or a time-keeping

2 Paley 2006 [1803], chapter 1.
3 For a critique of this reading of Paley, see Oppy (2006, chapter 4). Oppy argues that Paley actually meant his argument as a deduction; however, I concur with Schupbach (2005) that Paley's argument was an inference to the best explanation, not a deduction.
4 Hume's *Dialogues* was published posthumously in 1779, well before Paley's work. Paley explicitly mentions Hume's arguments on the problem of natural evil in chapter XXVI of his *Natural Theology* (1809). Hume's argument may well have been directed against Newtonian cosmic design arguments more than biological design arguments (Hurlbutt 1985).

device, out of biological materials – if not now, then certainly in the near future'.[5] Here the debate on evolutionary biology is again significant: as I've noted, evolutionary biologists consider the ability to reproduce to form a crucial difference between machines and biological organisms.

However, setting this debate aside, Hume also has much to say against premise 3. In the *Dialogues*, the sceptic Philo argues that comparing humans and dogs, and observing that humans have circulation of blood, we might infer by analogy that dogs also likely have circulation of blood. Comparing humans and vegetables, the analogical argument would be far less reliable, because of the many differences of properties. The differences between the cosmos and machines, and between biological organisms and machines are vast, and Hume argues that this renders the analogy unreliable.[6] As Ratzsch notes, the criticism here is based on the fact that 'any two (groups of) things have infinitely many properties in common and also differ in infinitely many respects'.[7] So, how can an observed similarity in some properties lead reliably to the conclusion that the two objects are also share some other property (such as being designed)? After all, the other property could also be one of the differences. It must be shown that the similarity is somehow relevant with respect to the conclusion, or the argument fails.[8] And indeed it seems that proponents of analogical design arguments have typically had such a link in mind: the appearance of teleology is thought to be somehow aptly explained by teleological causes. The perceived connection between machine-like features and teleology as a cause is why the analogy is thought to be relevant. In the ID movement, Behe and Dembski have both defended analogical design arguments in this vein, though they state that analogy is not their preferred formulation.[9]

The *Dialogues* is a wonderful book because of its good presentations of different viewpoints. In this case also, the *Dialogues* actually contain material allowing for an even deeper consideration of analogical design arguments. The character Cleanthes actually makes a similar reply as Behe and Dembski do: he argues that it is enough for the purposes of his argument that the cosmos resembles machines in the crucial respect of 'adjustment of means to ends'. So the argument is not about comparing all of the properties of the compared objects, but only a relevant subset. Recall that Cleanthes also responds to Philo's criticisms by way of thought experiments. But most of the Philo's criticisms of the analogical design argument come only after this adjustment. In addition to the points about the distantness of the analogy, Philo refers to possible other

5 Behe 2006a, 218.

6 *Dialogues*, chapter II.

7 Ratzsch and Koperski 2015.

8 On this, see Juthe 2005 and McGrew 2004. However, no general theory of analogical arguments yet enjoys general acceptance.

9 Behe 2006a, 218; Dembski 2002, 211n84; Dembksi 1999a, appendix. Meyer (2009, 383–386) also discusses Hume's criticism of analogical arguments and responds that his design argument is not analogical, but an inference to the best explanation.

explanations of biological complexity and to the problem of evil as counter-evidence. Here it seems that proper evaluation of the design argument requires comparing design as an explanation to other explanations, and this is better done by understanding the argument as an inference to the best explanation.

Inductive arguments

Design arguments can also be described as inductive arguments, meaning generalizations based on our past experience. Inductive reasoning is about observing the connection in a sample of test cases and then extending the generalization to objects that belong to the same class.[10] So, the logic of an inductive design argument is based on our experience of how certain types of objects are created, and then applying this inductively also to similar living objects. On this understanding, the design argument is a kind of inductive analogy.

Behe, Dembski and Meyer have all referred to induction in justifying their argument. For example, Dembski writes that connecting 'specified complexity' with intelligence happens through 'a straightforward inductive argument: in every instance where the complexity-specification criterion attributes design and where the underlying causal story is known (i.e., where we are not just dealing with circumstantial evidence, but where, as it were, the video camera is running and any putative designer would be caught red-handed), it turns out design is actually present'.[11] Dawes formalizes Dembski's logic as follows:

1 Every observed instance of specified complexity that we can trace back to its origin is explained by the acts of some intelligent agent who brought it about.

Therefore:

2 Every instance of specified complexity is explained by the acts of some intelligent agent who brought it about.[12]

This is very similar to commonly used inductive arguments, as Dawes points out. So, if we accept inductive reasoning in general and we accept the truth of the premises, the inductive design argument does succeed in establishing some plausibility for design as an explanation. According to Dawes, the actual problem with the argument is again not logical, but empirical: we have other explanations for specified complexity because of Darwinian evolutionary biology.[13]

10 See further Chalmers (1982).
11 Dembski 2002a, 25.
12 Dawes 2007, 76–77.
13 Dawes 2007, 76–78.

Behe similarly argues that 'cellular machines and machines in our everyday world share a relevant property – their functional complexity, born of a purposeful arrangement of parts – so inductive conclusions to design can be drawn on the basis of that shared property'.[14] Here Behe is making an analogical induction: because the property of 'irreducible complexity' is known to be explained by design in the case of human machines, we should also explain it by reference to design in the case of biology.[15] Meyer states that 'undirected materialistic causes have not demonstrated the capacity to generate significant amounts of specified information. At the same time, conscious intelligence has repeatedly shown itself capable of producing such information'.[16] Even the Discovery Institute's official definition concurs: research on design 'is conducted by observing the types of information produced when intelligent agents act. Scientists then seek to find objects which have those same types of informational properties which we commonly know come from intelligence'.[17] So, in ID's argumentation, a link between a certain type of order and intelligent design as its cause is often based on our inductive experience.

Rather than relying on the ID proponent's own terminology alone, it should be asked what type of logical structure best captures the ideas of Behe's inference. And one idea that is not present in the inductive formulation is the comparative nature of the inference. Earlier in the same article, Behe writes that 'a theory succeeds by explaining the data better than competing ideas'.[18] This is the sort of language that fits better with understanding the design argument as an inference to the best explanation, as I will argue shortly. But this inference to the best explanation is supported by inductive knowledge which is argued to link certain kinds of effects with certain kinds of causes, and rule other kinds of causes out. Dembski, too, favours his eliminative form of the design argument, where the elimination of other possible explanations occurs before the inductive design inference.

More than induction

Intriguingly, the ID movement's own literature also contains grounds for critiquing an inductive linking of the categories of (apparent) teleological order and teleological causes. First, it seems that induction cannot be the only possible way of gaining knowledge about intelligence. Dembski argues that we must have been able to see evidence of intelligence at some point without

14 Behe 2006c, 89–90. Similarly, Behe (2006a, 218): 'the irreducibly complex Rube Goldberg machines required an intelligent designer to produce it; therefore the irreducibly complex blood-clotting system required a designer also'.

15 Based on this quote, Sober (2008, 168n37) argues that Behe's design argument is indeed inductive.

16 Meyer 2010, 341.

17 Discovery Institute 2015.

18 Behe 2006c, 82.

having prior experience of it.[19] If we can only find evidence of design based on our prior experience of design, then how was this prior experience gained? At some point, we must have gained evidence of design through some other way than induction. There must be some feature of the world which is evidence of design in itself. For the ID movement, features like specified complexity and teleology are such features. Design is an 'inherently teleological' process, thus it is able to explain teleological patterns.[20] Here using design as an explanation is not based on induction, but on a conceptual understanding of cause and effect.

Second, it is argued that we need a way to differentiate between different things human beings produce. Not all we produce is equally a product of intelligent design. For example, we might accidentally break vines in a forest, or we might designedly form a trap from these vines. Finding merely a statistical correlation between human activity and some product is not enough, since it does not allow us to distinguish only those things we produce through design. According to Behe, 'we know that all these things were designed because of the ordering of independent components to achieve some end'.[21] So, understanding the properties of objects created by humans and the powers of designing intelligence is crucial for understanding some properties as evidence of design.

In these arguments, the rationality of explaining teleology by teleology is not based on just an inductive generalization, but a connection between the essential features of designing agents and these types of order. This is a link based on the understood nature of the cause and the effect, rather than just on an empirical correlation between them. It could be that the conceptual link is believed because of rational intuitions that our cognitive capacities tend to produce. However, it could also be that we learn to understand the existence of such a conceptual link between design and some property only based on our subjective experience of the human capacities that are needed create new artefacts. The inductive argument for design would be strengthened by appealing more clearly to our own subjective experience of what it is like to be an intelligent designer. This is seen sometimes in the ID literature, such as when Dembski writes that 'Intelligent Design is one intelligence determining what another intelligence has done'.[22]

Another problem in the induction is based on the relatively small sample size of the induction. As Ratzsch notes, an inductive case for the connection between design-likeness and design as a cause must be based on human artefacts, while the majority of design-likeness resides in natural objects, whose

19 Dembski even argues that we detect our own intelligence through observing the kind of specified complexity he describes. Of course, we don't intuitively use the term 'specified complexity', but Dembski claims that we nevertheless use the methodology Dembski describes (Dembski 2004a, chapter 32).

20 Dembski and Wells 2007, glossary.

21 Behe 2006a, 196; Behe 2000b, 7.

22 Dembski 1998c, 19.

origins ID cannot directly investigate. Thus the generalization is being made based on a small sample and extended into a different category. According to Ratzsch, this should at least lower the probability of the conclusion of design, though it does not entirely remove the value of induction.[23]

Ratzsch's point is important and shows that the possibility for other explanations of design-likeness cannot be dismissed. I submit that the goal of the analogies and inductions should not be to demonstrate the conclusion of design beyond a doubt. Rather, the goal should be merely to show that design is in some way a relevant contender for explaining certain types of order. In order to possess explanatory power, design must be at least better than an appeal to chance, the null hypothesis. If such inductive arguments can give design as an explanation, even the modest probability described by Ratzsch, they will already be valuable. In this case thinking about design as an explanation for such features of nature is not an *ad hoc* type explanation, but one arising naturally from our experience. This does not yet demonstrate that it is the best explanation, but it is still valuable in constructing the argument as an inference to the best explanation.

But this conclusion also allows for criticisms of the design argument. It seems to me that the best line of response from a critic of design arguments should not deny the connection between design-likeness and design, or teleological order and teleological causes altogether. Rather, even the argument that the conclusion is not necessary already potentially opens the way for other interpretations of nature. We can construct arguments that design-likeness can be created without design, and that in some case (such as biological evolution) the non-purposeful explanation can be superior to the design-based explanation. Here the detailed consideration of the evidence and the background probabilities that go into the inference will be necessary for determining the conclusion.

The inference to the best explanation

Principles of abductive reasoning

Because of the comparative nature of the design inference, the inference to the best explanation (IBE) seems to be the best way of formulating the argument. This is a well-known argument form that has in recent decades also emerged as one of the most promising ways to formulate the logic of scientific and also many non-scientific arguments. Something like the inference to the best explanation is often used in arguments of natural theology, and I will argue that it is the best way to understand ID's arguments as well.

The basic logic behind these is generally thought to be 'abductive' as described by C. S. Peirce. The idea is that if our empirical evidence would be

23 Ratzsch and Koperski 2015.

a reasonably expectable occurrence given the truth of some hypothesis, then this gives us evidence in favour of this hypothesis. Peirce formulates this logic as follows:

1 The surprising fact C is observed.
2 But if A were true, C would follow as a matter of course.
3 Hence, there is reason to suspect that A is true.[24]

Many believe that this is the basic form of inference which underlies many forms of science, Darwinian evolutionary theory being one standard example.[25] For example, if all animals have a common ancestor, then we would expect them to have biological similarities. Biological similarities exist, so we have grounds for believing the hypothesis of common descent. This kind of abductive reasoning can fail, because the same evidence can fit several different hypotheses. In practice, abductive explanations (hypotheses) are evaluated based on several different criteria such as explanatory power and scope, and fit with already accepted theories, fruitfulness, precision, unifying power and such like.[26]

Related to this, philosopher Peter Lipton makes the distinction between potential and actual explanations. A potential explanation is one that entails the data in some way; an actual explanation is simply a true potential explanation. Different criteria can then be used to try to identify the most likely actual explanation from the pool of potential explanations we have available.[27] In the case of 'design-like' objects in nature, potential explanations could include evolutionary explanations, design-based explanations, explaining the apparent rationality as an illusion created by our minds and so on. However, if design is at least a potential explanation – if it has explanatory force – then this comparison could in principle lead to the result that design is the best explanation. In my view, the value of the analogical and inductive arguments for ID's argument is precisely in getting design into this pool of potential explanations for features of life.

The history of science knows many examples where the same data could be explained by several models. In Galileo Galilei's time, the Earth-centric cosmology of Tycho Brahe was able to explain the same data as the heliocentric cosmology of Copernicus and Galileo. However, over time the situation has changed in favour of the heliocentric model of the solar system. This feature of inferences to the best explanation is known as explanatory underdetermination.[28] The ID proponent's claim that the design argument does not reveal the

24 Peirce 1955, 151. See also Dawes (2009, 20–23), Ratzsch and Koperski (2015).

25 See Banner (1990, 125–130). For more on the general logic of inferences to the best explanation, see Lipton (2004).

26 Ratzsch and Koperski 2015.

27 Lipton 2004, 56–66. For Lipton, the inference to the best explanation is indeed concerned with finding reasons to believe in some hypothesis. However, it is also possible to interpret the inference to the best explanation as merely a heuristic method for comparing hypotheses that will then have to be confirmed using some other methodology (Iranzo 2007, 340–341.)

28 Lindberg 2003.

identity of the designer makes sense in terms of underdetermination: the same data can be explained based on a wide variety of different design hypotheses. For example, perhaps the designer could be a Platonistic demiurge, a space alien or Zeus instead of the God of the Bible. In this way of framing the argument, it makes sense to claim that additional background assumptions or further arguments are needed to identify the designer as God. On the other hand, such background assumptions may also be needed to make the design argument as an inference to the best explanation credible, as I will discuss shortly.

Within the ID movement, Meyer explicitly refers to his argument primarily as an inference to the best explanation, whereas Behe makes several different formulations of the argument. However, the probabilistic nature of Behe's argument makes seeing it as an inference to the best explanation credible. As I've noted in Chapter 4, Behe argues that the probability of the design conclusion varies based on the properties of the natural systems under analysis. The more complex and purposeful the order appears, the more certain our conclusion of design becomes for him.[29] He compares the likelihood of design and natural explanations and argues that our background religious and non-religious beliefs effect our assessment of the probability of the conclusion.[30] He further argues that the presence of consilience (several independent lines of argument leading to the same conclusion) lends more probability to the design argument.[31] These are features of inferences to the best explanation.

Ratzsch formulates the design argument as an inference to the best explanation (IBE) as follows. Here the first premise is related to Pierce's premise that 'the surprising fact C is observed' and the second premise is the hypothesis which explains this datum. After comparison with alternative explanations, it is concluded that the design hypothesis is the best explanation and probably true:

1 Some things in nature (or nature itself, the cosmos) exhibit exquisite complexity, delicate adjustment of means to ends (and other relevant *R* characteristics).
2 The hypothesis that those characteristics are products of deliberate, intentional design (Design Hypothesis) would adequately explain them.
3 In fact, the hypothesis that those characteristics are products of deliberate, intentional design (Design Hypothesis) is the best available overall explanation of them.

Therefore (probably)

4 Some things in nature (or nature itself, the cosmos) are products of deliberate, intentional design (that is, the Design Hypothesis is likely true).[32]

29 Behe 2006a, 256.
30 Behe 2001a.
31 Behe 2007, chapter 10.
32 Ratzsch and Koperski 2015.

The conclusion (4) is not always included in formulations of the inference to the best explanation. It simply states the common belief that if some explanation is the best, then we have grounds for believing that it is also probably true, not just the best currently available explanation. This may not always be true. If none of the available explanations are very convincing, or the best explanation is only slightly better than the rest, then we may still not have grounds for believing that it is true. However, assuming that the criteria for selecting the best explanation are conducive to truth – that is, assuming the reliability of our rational intuitions concerning explanations and the philosophy of explanations – it seems that often we are at least rationally justified in accepting the best explanation as probably true.[33]

Critiques of the design argument as an IBE

In the preceding formulation of the argument, premises 2 and 3 are the crucial controversial premises of the argument. As Dawes argues, there are two alternative lines of critique which can be made against abductive theistic explanations. These can also be applied against ID. First (1), it can be argued (against premise 2) that theistic explanations actually don't explain at all, meaning that they are not part of the pool of potential explanations. Divine action or (in the case of the ID movement) the actions of an unidentified intelligent designer do not show why we should expect to observe the data. This is an 'in principle' objection to design arguments. Taken to the extreme, this would mean that no matter what the universe looks like empirically, design cannot explain it. This would mean that there is no conceivable evidence that could speak in favour of design – a very strong conclusion that runs into trouble with the thought experiments analysed in Chapter 7. However, the critique of premise 2 can also be formulated in a more moderate way: perhaps design can fit in the pool of potential explanations, but just barely. Such a poor explanation will then be easily superseded by any explanation that does a better job. Furthermore, if design is a very poor explanation of the data, we may not be warranted in believing it to be true, even if it is currently the best explanation. So discussion of premise 2 is certainly relevant.

According to Dawes, the more promising critique of the argument is a 'de facto' critique based on the competition between different potential explanations of the same data. This critique is targeted at premise 3 – the comparison of explanations. Though theistic explanations and design could in principle explain natural order, in practice naturalistic explanations like Darwinian evolutionary theory can be argued to work better and thus make design an

33 Dawes 2009, chapter 6.

unnecessary explanation. Or on a theistic perspective, theistic evolutionism can be argued to make more sense of the overall evidence better than ID.[34]

Common critiques of the explanatory power of ID concern its lack of independent support and the claimed frivolous, *ad hoc* nature of design hypotheses. Elliott Sober has illustrated the difficulties facing design arguments with an interesting parable. Suppose that we hear a strange sort of rumbling from the basement. We could argue that the hypothesis 'the noise is caused by a bunch of trolls bowling' explains the noise quite well, as it predicts the observed empirical evidence. This is causally sufficient explanation involving designers, but it does not feel quite satisfactory.[35]

Two related difficulties help understand the unsatisfactory nature of the troll hypothesis. First (1), we do not have any independent reasons for believing in trolls, which means that the prior probability of the troll hypothesis is very low. We will rather hold out for a more reasonable explanation than accept something this strange. Even though the evidence increases the probability of the troll hypothesis, it is not sufficient to raise the probability into the realm of credibility, since the beginning probability is so low. Second (2), any data can be explained by a modified troll hypothesis, supposing that the trolls are postulated to have the motivation and adequate powers for producing the evidence we see. The technical term for this frivolousness is that the troll hypothesis is *ad hoc* – a hypothesis artificially constructed just to explain this one piece of data, but which has no other grounds.[36]

According to Sober, to avoid these difficulties, the design argument needs to be supported by independent evidence of the existence of the designer, and there needs to be a plausible reason for supposing that the designer has the motivation for producing the order we see in nature. This is the only way to avoid frivolous design hypotheses which can be invoked to 'explain' anything at all, but which we nevertheless have no grounds for accepting. Sober's conclusion is very Humean: we can reliably infer the presence of human design, since we already know much about humans, but our inferences about supernatural design are far less certain.[37]

For a design argument to be credible as an inference to the best explanation, the reasoning behind premises 2 and 3 must be made as clear as possible. It must be specified what is required before a design hypothesis can possess explanatory power, and to assess how much evidential support this really gives to the design hypothesis in relation to other hypotheses. Here the strategies of theistic natural theologians and the ID theorists differ.

34 Dawes 2009, chapter 2.

35 Sober 1993, chapter 2.

36 This is related to what Kitcher (1981, 528) has called the problem of spurious unification. See also Dawes (2009, 43–46) and Pennock (1999, 275).

37 Sober 2004. Similarly, for example, Pennock (2001) and Hurd (2004).

Different strategies for defending the argument

Defences within natural theology

The arguments of theistic natural theology are different from the troll hypothesis because they are not just artificially constructed to explain one facet of reality. Rather, there is a cumulative case of many theistic arguments which support each other. If – as many argue – the explanatory dimensions of theistic belief are not the reason for its origination, then this seems to show that theism is not an *ad hoc* hypothesis invented to explain some small amount of data. If we already had other evidence for the existence of trolls, and if the observed result was highly consistent with what we already believe about the nature of trolls, then the troll hypothesis would also be better supported.[38]

As Dawes notes, it is also not the case that just any data could be explained by reference to the theistic God. This is why many theistic believers would find the existence of gratuitous evil in the world very puzzling. God is thought to have certain attributes which make some ideas about what God would do more reasonable than others. For example, because God is good, he is expected to create a good world. The arguments of theistic natural theology thus often depend on clear ideas about God's nature and motivations.[39]

It is clear that such theistic explanations are quite different from scientific explanations based on lawful regularities, and natural theologians make no secret of the fact. Rather, natural theologians believe that their argument works on a different level from the natural sciences. In classical theology, God is thought to be free and thus it is difficult to argue that any empirical result could be derived from the existence of God as a 'matter of course'. This difficulty doesn't seem fatal, if we believe that personal explanation can have explanatory power at all. Even explanations referring to human intentionality can rarely predict something absolutely. We can never be sure that another human being has the exact intention which will result in exactly this sort of behaviour, though we may have very good reasons to believe so. Theistic philosophers of religion can argue that the same is true of personal explanations referencing the intentions of God. Though God is free in his actions, he does not act without reason. Thus some actions seem to be more in line with what we believe about the divine nature than other actions, and the theistic hypothesis gains explanatory power.[40]

Defences within ID

ID could be defended in this way as a theistic project, beginning from the presupposition that God exists. This would then supply the basic knowledge that

38 Similarly Himma 2005, 1.

39 Dawes 2009, 43–46.

40 Dawes (2009, appendix) argues that intentional explanations are deductive, whereas Swinburne (2004a) sees them as probabilistic.

a designer capable of creating life exists and help offset the *ad hoc* nature of the hypothesis. The aim of ID's project would then be to determine whether signs of the divine intelligence can be seen in the order of nature and whether God created life through evolution or through miracles surpassing the laws of nature. ID could function (for those who accept the premises of its argument) as part of a broad array of theistic arguments. However, ID's approach is different, and typically its design arguments are stated without the support of a cumulative case of other theistic arguments and without appealing to such theistic presuppositions. Proponents of ID do recognize that theistic background beliefs can make their design argument more credible (or less credible, for theistic evolutionists). However, proponents of ID also believe that the design argument can be convincing on its own, as long as the possibility of design is not dogmatically denied *a priori*. As a consequence, they generally leave the question of the precise nature and motives of the designer open.

Theistic natural theologians, such as Swinburne, usually refer to the goodness of God as a way of limiting the range of results that one can expect from the theistic hypothesis. In this way they believe that their hypothesis can acquire explanatory power. The ID movement, in contrast, uses the connection between the appearance of teleology and intelligence as a way of getting explanatory power. Sober's thought experiment about trolls in the basement can be modified to show how I believe proponents of ID conceive of this connection. Suppose that the noise from the basement was not just some random rumbling, but was analogous to beautiful orchestra music, or why not also punk rock? Then the hypothesis of design would seem to be the best explanation, even if we did not have prior evidence of a designer in the basement. The pattern itself would be evidence enough. However, the structure of the design argument would not allow us to make the additional conclusion that the designer is a troll. Rather, because of our background knowledge, the most reasonable possibility would be a human designer. Even the outlandish possibility that we are being visited by a highly musical group of burglars would be more credible than the troll hypothesis.

The Bayesian probability calculus can be used to further elucidate the differences between ID and natural theology. Bayesian logic allows for the calculation of the probability of the hypothesis given the evidence. The probability of the hypothesis depends on both the background probability of the hypothesis without the evidence, the background probability of the evidence and the degree to which the hypothesis predicts the evidence.[41] Natural theologians assess all of these factors, but the ID literature only directly addresses the background probability of the hypothesis without the evidence and argues that this surprising evidence is well explained on the hypothesis of design, but poorly explained without it. ID assumes that the background probability of the design hypothesis can even be very low, but it will still be confirmed by the data, since

41 See Joyce (2003) and Howson and Urbach (2006) for more on Bayesianism.

the data is so poorly explained without it. As long as the prior probability of the design hypothesis is not set to zero (in which case no conceivable evidence could confirm it), we can indeed imagine a body of evidence that would be sufficient to confirm the hypothesis. A suitable thought experiment to that effect can be constructed following the examples in Chapter 7.[42]

It seems reasonable to suppose that independent evidence of the designer would indeed help the design argument. Any conclusion is strengthened when it is supported by multiple independent lines of evidence. However, we should note that according to proponents of ID, the design argument already works based on multiple lines of evidence. The cosmic and biological arguments for design are collections of a vast variety of facts which are all thought to be explained by the same hypothesis of design. So, in a way the design argument is itself also a cumulative case argument. Our estimates of the strength of the evidence of design will determine how much other supportive argumentation we would need to accept the conclusion of the argument.

As in Chapter 7, here I have also been arguing against *a priori* criteria for excluding the possibility of design inferences, and in favour of adopting criteria which allow for arguments like ID in principle. But again it is important to notice that this does not mean the end of the discussion. Even if something like ID could in principle be convincing apart from very robust religious convictions working in the background, this does not mean that it works in this way in our actual situation. I accept the idea that nature bears the appearance of design, but I would still argue that this appearance of design is a good deal more ambiguous than in thought experiments where 'YHWH made the universe' was visibly written on living cells. In our situation, the balancing of many arguments to evaluate the conclusion of design seems legitimate, and limitation of the discussion to just design arguments seems undesirable. Rather, the issues should be considered in their full philosophical and theological breadth.

The inference to the only explanation

Inferences to the only explanation

I have argued that the inference to the best explanation is a promising way to formulate the design argument's logic. However, often ID proponents go further than merely propose ID as the best explanation. Rather, they want to argue that ID is the only explanation for some things and that all remotely plausible competing hypotheses can be decisively eliminated. I believe it is fruitful to

42 The case has an interesting analogy in the discussion of the probability of Jesus' resurrection. Swinburne (2003) argues that the credibility of Jesus' resurrection is highly dependent on having at least a moderate background probability for the existence of the kind of God who might reveal himself in history. In contrast to Swinburne, T. McGrew (2009) argues that the historical evidence favouring Jesus' resurrection is so strong that even a much smaller probability for the existence of this kind of God will suffice for the argument.

relate this argument to what philosopher of science Alexander Bird has called the 'inference to the only explanation' (IOE).[43] Bird's purpose is to develop the logic of the inference to the best explanation further so that it can give a stronger guarantee of the reliability of the hypothesis. Bird's development of the idea follows the logic of Sherlock Holmes: 'when you have eliminated the impossible, whatever remains, no matter how improbable, must be the truth'.[44]

It is important to note that, according to Bird, not all rational inferences even in natural science can be legitimately called inferences to the only explanation. The problem of underdetermination prevents this – often there will be several different explanations for the same data, and not all of them can be decisively eliminated. Showing other alternatives to be improbable is sufficient for rational belief and the use of the inference to the best explanation, but the inference to the only explanation requires more than improbability – it requires elimination.[45] In an inference to the only explanation, the initial background probability of the hypothesis can be very low, as long as the hypothesis is strongly confirmed by the evidence, and all other explanations can be eliminated. In this way it is clearly in line with what proponents of ID want from the design argument.

The eliminative argument

Though all major proponents of ID believe that design is the only remotely adequate explanation for features of life like irreducible complexity, Dembski's methodology perhaps embodies the idea of elimination of alternative explanations most clearly. Dembski calls his methodology an 'eliminative design inference' or the design filter, where design is inferred only after all other explanations have been eliminated. Dembski himself rejects the characterization of the design argument as an inference to the best explanation.[46] However, I will argue that Dembski's eliminative design argument cannot stand alone and needs the kind of support that inferences to the best explanation can provide. Indeed, usually when other proponents of ID cite Dembski's argument, they cite them as auxiliary support for something like an inference to the best explanation.

Dembski's argument is complex and multi-staged, construed as an eliminative argument where a pattern exhibiting 'specified complexity' is seen as designed after finding reasonable grounds for eliminating chance and necessity (coincidences and law-like regularities) as plausible explanations.[47] A short sequence of letters like 'CAT' is specified but not complex – finding such a pattern written in Scrabble letters might still be explained as the coincidental

43 For example, Bird (2005, 2007, 2010).

44 Doyle 1892, 'The Adventure of the Beryl Coronet'.

45 Bird 2005, 26–28.

46 For example, Dembski (2005b, 35–37), Dembski (2004a, chapter 32).

47 For example, Dembski (1998a), Dembski (2002), Dembski (2004) and Dembski (1998c, 98).

result of pieces dropped randomly. A long sequence like 'QNEDFJEFOIJK-FEES . . . ' is complex but not specified – it does not match a previously known pattern. A Shakespearean sonnet, on the other hand, is both complex and specified. Specified complexity like this is, for Dembski, a reliable sign of intelligent design and far too difficult to explain by referring to chance processes or the regularities of nature.

Dembski's description of designed patterns as 'specified complexity' and his arguments for the elimination of chance and necessity are the most original parts of Dembski's project. Briefly, Dembski's method for eliminating chance as an explanation is based on the statistical methods developed by mathematician Ronald A. Fisher (1890–1962). Fisher uses a statistical approach for testing hypotheses. If the observed measurements are far from what would be expected based on a random distribution (that is, they lie in the 'rejection region'), then the chance hypothesis can be discarded. Dembski argues that if some improbable event also has a clear pattern (a specification), then the chance hypothesis can be eliminated, as in Fisher's statistical analysis.[48]

How improbable does the specified pattern have to be before chance-based explanations can be rejected? In Dembski's understanding, this depends on what we think the 'probabilistic resources' available to generate the pattern without design are, and how certain we want to be before eliminating chance. Not all examples of specified complexity we observe must be due to design, because the probabilistic resources must also be considered. In poker, a straight flush is a specification, but a player can get a straight flush without cheating. However, a player who always gets a straight flush will be considered a cheater, because this is so extremely improbable (complex) and the outcome is specified. Dembski formulates a 'universal probability bound', meaning the amount of specified complexity that he argues is impossible to produce by chance, given the limited temporal history and finiteness of the universe. This is calculated by multiplying the amount of atoms in the observable universe, the amount of maximum physical interactions that can occur in a second, and a billion times the age of the universe in seconds. The resulting number (10^{150}) is fantastically large, and according to Dembski, we usually will not need to set the universal probability bound this high before we can eliminate chance-based explanations. In practice he argues even smaller amounts of specified complexity (such as multiple straight flushes) can be justifiably seen as designed.[49]

48 For example Dembski (2005b, 12–13): 'specifications are patterns delineating events of small probability whose occurrence cannot reasonably be attributed to chance'. Specified complexity, for Dembski, can also be characterized as having low descriptive complexity while having high probabilistic complexity. Dembski also links the concept to mathematical 'Kolmogorov complexity'.

49 Dembski 1998a, 167–174. Elsberry (2007, 285) criticizes Dembski's unwillingness to define the precise point where we can use the criterion of specified complexity as a reliable marker of intelligent agency. Dembski simply states that we can set the limit arbitrarily based on how confident we want to be of the conclusion of the argument.

Problems in Dembski's approach

There has been quite a lot of discussion over Dembski's proposal, and most critics have thought that other forms of the design argument are more promising. Only a minority of the criticisms have been directed against Dembski's method of eliminating chance as an explanation. One such critique is the claim that Dembski errs in arguing that patterns can be recognized even if the 'rejection region' is not specified temporally before seeing the event being discussed (for example biological complexity or some other putative example of specified complexity). In Fisher's statistical reasoning, the pattern must be really predicted. However, for Dembski it is sufficient that there is independent reason to think that such a pattern is special.[50]

But this does not seem to be a weak point of Dembski's analysis. The natural sciences abound in examples of how a real pattern can be found in some data after its initial discovery. For example, biological order has become better and better understood over time. Support for similar reasoning can even be found in critics of creationism like Dawkins, who uses similar arguments against random chance instead of selection as an explanation for biological order.[51] Dembski himself provides the compelling example of cryptanalysis, where an apparently random signal is later deciphered by counter-intelligence officers and revealed to contain an encrypted message. In these examples, a real pattern is indeed found temporally after the event.[52]

A much more serious problem in Dembski's design argument comes from his initial definition of design simply as the exclusion of chance and necessity. As noted, Dembski's methodology is reminiscent of the previously quoted Holmesian method: 'when you have eliminated the impossible, whatever remains, no matter how improbable, must be the truth'.[53] However, to even qualify as 'improbable', design must have some positive arguments in its favour, not just arguments against alternatives. It is not enough to say that a chance-based explanation is impossibly improbable if design is equally improbable; rather, design must be a better explanation than chance.[54] Dembski himself recognized this problem already in his book *The Design Inference* (1998). In this work, Dembski wrote that 'the design that emerges from the design inference must not be conflated with intelligent agency. Though they are frequently linked, they are separate'.[55] As Ratzsch argues, Dembski seems to be presupposing that there is some further step, in addition to his explanatory filter, which is required for having evidence of intelligent agency.[56]

50 For example, Elsberry (2007, 253).
51 Dawkins 1991, 8.
52 Dembski 1998a.
53 Dembski himself recognizes the similarity to Holmes (2005, 28).
54 Himma 2005, 1; Dawes 2007, 74–75.
55 Dembski 1998a, 5.
56 Ratzsch 2001, 155.

In *The Design Inference* Dembski does indeed also argue that 'there is an intimate connection between design [as identified by the explanatory filter] and intelligent agency'.[57] Later Dembski has often written of specified complexity as positive evidence of the action of intelligent agency. Specified complexity, for him, eliminates chance and necessity as explanations and also acts as evidence for intelligent design as the true explanation of some event: 'Often, when an intelligent agent acts, it leaves behind an identifying mark that clearly signals its intelligence. This mark of intelligence is known as specified complexity'.[58] Here Dembski is clearly making an inductive connection between specified complexity and design as a cause, rather than relying just on the eliminative argument.

Unfortunately, Dembski does not focus much time in linking his eliminative argument and the inductive argument. Dembski emphasizes that specified complexity is linked in our inductive experience to intelligent design as a cause. However, as I have shown in Chapter 8, the ID literature also contains critiques of such a purely inductive linking. It should also be argued that intelligent design is somehow a particularly good explanation of specified complexity, rather than merely a statistically correlated explanation. But this conceptual connection is much clearer in the case of traditional categories like teleological causes and teleological order. And Dembski has not yet made it very clear what the relationship of specified complexity is to the traditional categories of teleology and rational order, which other ID proponents, and Dembski himself, use in their popular arguments for ID. Dembski does argue that information in the mathematical sense is conceptually linked to intelligence, because both information and intelligence are about making choices. But these definitions of intelligence and design are quite vague, and it is not clear how specified complexity can help us avoid referring to traditional evidences of design like the rationality, teleology and beauty of nature.[59]

Dembski has argued his case for specified complexity in at times highly technical and mathematical form, beginning with his book *The Design Inference* (1998). Both Behe and Meyer have agreed with specified complexity as a way of describing the designedness of nature. Behe's definition of design as the 'purposeful arrangement of parts' and his idea that the strength of the design inference increases as the complexity and specificity of order increases come rather close to Dembski. Behe also explicitly refers to Dembski as providing a possibly more rigorous definition of design.[60] Meyer, too, uses specified complexity in his work to argue against chance and natural law as explanations for the origin of life. For Meyer, Dembski's 'specified complex information' well describes the sort of information found in DNA.[61] However, neither Behe

57 Dembski 1998a, 62.

58 Dembski and Wells 2008, 165.

59 Similarly, Murray (2003, 7–8).

60 Behe 2006a, chapter 9, note 5.

61 Meyer 2009.

nor Meyer use Dembski's mathematical formulations, or Dembski's explanatory filter as a premise of their arguments. Rather, they rely more on the common understanding of inferences to the best explanation, with Dembski's arguments serving in an auxiliary role to help eliminate chance and regular natural processes as explanations. It seems to me that the argument is indeed more suited to this kind of auxiliary role.

The power of Dembski's argument to eliminate explanations based merely on chance is often acknowledged in the discussion. However, typically critics of Dembski have argued that nature itself might nevertheless possess self-organizing powers that do not rely merely on random chance or natural regularities, but on a dynamic evolutionary process combining both. It has been argued that evolutionary theory provides a counter-example to Dembski, because it shows that specified complexity can be generated by the regularities and probabilistic processes of nature. Evolutionary theory does not postulate any random events exceeding Dembski's universal probability boundary. Rather, biological order is thought to emerge through small, successive steps.[62]

In response, Dembski has attempted to provide a mathematical formula for showing that there is 'law of conservation of information' which makes the generation of new, specified complexity impossible even through combinations of lawful regularity and random chance. However, when responding to the above crucial evolutionary critique of his argument, Dembski depends also on other arguments against the plausibility of the Darwinian mechanism, such as Behe's irreducible complexity. Dembski argues that the problem of irreducible complexity shows that biological specified complexity cannot be broken up to sufficiently small steps; even the emergence of one new irreducibly complex biochemical machine is so improbable through Darwinian mechanisms that it would violate the universal probability bound.[63] Here it seems that the validity of Dembski's eliminative arguments is linked to the validity of ID's critiques of evolutionary biology and are not easily amenable to use by theistic evolutionists.[64]

Inference to the best explanation or to the only explanation?

The critique of alternative explanations is also important for inferences to the best explanation. The differences between the two arguments are mainly of emphasis and degree of certainty. However, it seems that it should already be interesting to argue that design is the most plausible explanation for some

62 Sober, Fitelson and Stephens 1999.

63 Dembski 2002a, chapters 4 and 5.

64 Dembski has recently expanded his argument to accommodate Darwinian evolution. According to Dembski, if evolution does work, then his information-theoretical arguments show then it must have been designed to do so. If this argument succeeds, then even the production of specified complexity through evolution would not necessarily provide a counter-example to Dembski. (See for example Dembski and Marks 2009.)

pattern in nature, without having to argue that design is the only possible explanation of this pattern. This is a highly ambitious conclusion that is much more than natural theologians like Swinburne want to claim for any theistic argument. Rather, contemporary natural theologians more typically claim merely that each of the arguments of natural theology increase the credibility or Bayesian probability of the existence of God. Different natural theologians have different estimates about the strength of each argument.

Proponents of ID emphasize the certainty of their conclusion and the elimination of error. These are good goals, of course, but yet there is also value in less certain conclusions. It seems that in principle it would already be interesting to argue that design is simply the most plausible explanation for some pattern in nature, rather than being the only remotely plausible explanation. This could still add to the overall probability of the existence of God for someone wanting to combine Swinburnean natural theology and ID. In a comparison of the relative credibility of theism and naturalism, arguments lowering the probability of naturalism can also be interesting. For example, if one believes that it is unlikely that the biological organisms can evolve by wholly unguided processes, then this would lower the probability of naturalism.

When formulated like this, it seems that proponents of ID could in principle find some value in their biological arguments, even if the arguments fall short of eliminating all other options, and short of certainty. Without other supporting reasons, such an argument may itself be insufficient to give up naturalism, and to adopt theism. The value of the argument will then depend on our background beliefs and on what we think about the justification of the particular premises, as with the other arguments of natural theology. Such arguments would not determine our worldview alone, but only as part of a broader evaluation of the matter. And of course many critics of ID would already disagree about the basic premises of the argument, such as the implausibility of a naturalistic explanation of evolution.

I have been arguing that the ID movement's design argument is best understood as an inference to best explanation, with inductive and conceptual arguments supporting the credibility of design as an explanation.[65] But the interesting conclusion is that these arguments are in principle quite possible. As Dawes has argued, 'While a great deal of abuse has been directed at intelligent design theory (ID), its starting point is a fact about biological organisms that cries out for explanation, namely "specified complexity" (SC). Advocates of ID deploy three kind of argument from specified complexity to the existence of a designer: an eliminative argument, an inductive argument, and an inference to the best explanation. Only the first of these merits the abuse directed at it; the other two arguments are worthy of respect. If they fail, it is only because we have a better explanation of SC, namely Darwin's theory of evolution by

---

65 Dawes (2009, 107–108) similarly argues that Stephen Meyer's design argument is an inference to the best explanation supported by inductive arguments.

natural selection'.[66] My analysis supports Dawes' contention that ID's analogical, inductive arguments and the inference to the best explanation could all in principle be convincing. Whether they actually are convincing depends on the state of the evidence. I also agree with Dawes that eliminative arguments without positive reasons to believe in design are not worth much for theists. Eliminative arguments must be used as part of an inference to the best explanation or an inference to the only explanation to be of use.

Proponents of ID and many commentators agree with Dawes that the critique based on naturalistic explanations for 'design-like' properties is the central critique of design arguments. This is the central reason why proponents of ID spend so much time arguing against naturalistic explanations. In my analysis of the logic of the design argument in this chapter, I have also presented reasons for seeing this comparison with natural explanations as crucial. However, in Chapter 10 I will be arguing further for the conclusion that biological design arguments and natural explanations do not have to be opposed, but could also be conceived as explanations that work on different levels. But before that I still need to say something about the counterevidence to design arguments: the problems of natural evil and bad design.

Summary

ID indeed does not rely on just our intuitive reasoning, but attempts to develop rigorous philosophical, even scientific design arguments. Proponents of ID have defended several different formulations of the design argument. I analysed formulations of the design argument as an analogy, an induction, an inference to the best explanation and an inference to the only explanation. Though design arguments have often been understood as analogies, I argued that ID's version of the argument is better understood as an inference to the best explanation or to the only explanation. These inferences work by positing that design best explains certain features of the cosmos and the biological world, such as fine-tuning and irreducible complexity. The critique of alternative explanations is crucial for these argument types, but a positive connection between intelligent design as a cause and the properties explained is needed.

I argued that the ID movement's design argument gains its explanatory power from the perceived connection between teleological properties and design as a teleological process. This connection is argued based on inductive observation, subjective experience of the nature of intelligence and rational intuitions. Many thinkers in the ID movement prefer using technical terms like 'specified complexity' instead of teleology when describing the complexity of nature. However, they typically move back to the language of teleology when it comes time to explain the explanatory power of the argument. It is argued that

66 Dawes 2007, 69.

the appearance of teleology in nature is best explained by a teleological cause: intelligent design.

My analysis of the logic of the design argument and thought experiments supports the possibility that this type of inference could indeed in principle work. Whether the actual world contains evidence that can be identified in this way is another matter. Many critics of design arguments also acknowledge that there are features of nature which are congenial to the design-based explanation. When design-based explanations are rejected, it should be done after first considering the details of the arguments, and the evidence presented.

To reject ID's design arguments, one should also argue that it is more reasonable to accept some other explanation than design, or at least that it is more reasonable to wait for such an alternative explanation, than to accept the conclusion of design. ID's design arguments require that such alternative explanations can be shown much less improbable than design. Just how improbable the natural explanations have to be shown depends on conceptions about the prior credibility of the design hypothesis. ID assumes an interpretation of the philosophy of mind in which intentionality can really be the true explanation of human behaviour, and even an unembodied designer could have sufficiently analogous properties for the argument to work. Furthermore, in order for the argument to work, the existence of this kind of nonhuman designer must be accepted as a possibility that could in principle be supported by the evidence.

9 Design, natural evil and bad design

The problem of natural evil is based on the existence of apparently non-beneficial, or even harmful order in nature. The problem of bad design is a subset of this problem, based on non-optimal order in nature. The question for proponents of ID is: if a good designer is indeed responsible for the order of nature, why does nature contain this kind of non-optimality? Theologians have discussed these kinds of questions for centuries, and the problem of natural evil is also the basis for some theological critiques of ID. It is argued that ID would lead us to believe in the kind of God who intervenes constantly in nature, and this makes it more difficult to understand why God has not also intervened to prevent the evolution of harmful order like droughts and diseases.

One might think that different opinions about design are influenced by temperament: theists could be understood as optimists who focus more on goodness and beauty in nature things and naturalists as pessimists who focus on natural evil and ugliness. But this interpretation is not credible. Naturalists, too, more typically emphasize the beauty of the natural order. For example, Dawkins' writings on evolution are full of wonder at the order of nature, even while arguing that nature contains bad design. The same contrast is already present in Darwin's, though. On the one hand, Darwin felt that there was 'grandeur' in his view of life and obviously felt love, rather than disgust, for the natural world.[1] On the other hand, he thought that natural evil was a problem for theism, writing that 'I cannot persuade myself that a beneficent and omnipotent God would have designedly created the Ichneumonidae with the express intention of their feeding within the living bodies of caterpillars or that a cat should play with mice'.[2]

Theists are also not strangers to suffering. The idea that suffering and evil in the world would somehow count as evidence against the existence of God can even seem strange from the Christian perspective, since the biblical narratives do not understand suffering in this way, and are full of depictions of sorrow and

1 Darwin 2009 [1859], 360.

2 Darwin 2012 [1860]. Desmond and Moore (1991, 622–637) argue Darwin evolved in his religious views from a theist into an agnostic. Even as an agnostic he wavered between belief and unbelief.

evil. Ultimately Christians do believe that good is and will be victorious over evil, so in this they may indeed be more optimistic than naturalists. But the main difference between religious believers and atheists is not in whether they observe natural good and natural evil, but in the theological and philosophical interpretations of evil.

Many good books have already been written on the problem of natural evil and how the existence of evil fits or does not fit into various worldviews and theological systems of thought. The task of this chapter is not to advance this general discussion about the problem of evil. Rather, I want to advance discussion of the problem in the particular context of the debate over Intelligent Design and relate it to the broader discussion. I will begin this chapter by describing how ID has been critiqued based on the problem of natural evil. In the following two sections I go on to analyse ID's different responses. The discussion over the problem of evil again reveals that the acceptance and rejection of design arguments is often based on theological and philosophical considerations, not just science.

Understanding the problem

The philosophical problem of natural evil

In Hume's *Dialogues Concerning Natural Religion*, the problem of natural evil is one of the core objections against all forms of natural theology, including design arguments:

> Look round this universe. What an immense profusion of beings, animated and organized, sensible and active! You admire this prodigious variety and fecundity. But inspect a little more narrowly these living existences, the only beings worth regarding. How hostile and destructive to each other! How insufficient all of them for their own happiness! How contemptible or odious to the spectator! The whole presents nothing but the idea of a blind nature, impregnated by a great vivifying principle, and pouring forth from her lap, without discernment or parental care, her maimed and abortive children.[3]

Dialogues presents four types of natural evil: (1) the capacity of organisms for pain, not just pleasure; (2) the governance of the world through regularities and natural laws, rather than through divine action that could prevent any evil; (3) the insufficient natural capabilities granted to living beings for taking care of themselves and finding happiness; and (4) the insufficient fine-tuning of the natural laws, which do allow for life, but also for natural disasters. The universe is compared to a poorly built house where the tenants live in suffering. The

3 *Dialogues*, part XI. (Hume 1999, 113.)

Dialogues then goes on to argue that this presents a problem for belief in God, because we would not expect to find this type of evil in a world created by an omnipotent, morally perfect Creator.[4]

In the philosophy of religion, there have been many different formulations of the problem of evil. I believe that the inference to the best explanation is also a good way to formulate this problem. In this formulation, one can admit that the existence of evil is logically compatible with the existence of a morally perfect, omnipotent God. A theist can always argue that God has good reasons for allowing evil, even if we do not know all of these reasons. So there is no logical incompatibility between evil and theism. But the problem of evil as an inference to the best explanation argues that the existence of this kind of natural evil is nevertheless not what we would expect given the existence of God, so it is at least some kind of evidence against theism.[5] Hume's own argument against natural theology works just in this fashion and goes even further:

> I will allow, that pain or misery in man is compatible with infinite power and goodness in the Deity, even in your sense of these attributes: What are you advanced by all these concessions? A mere possible compatibility is not sufficient. You must prove these pure, unmixed and uncontrollable attributes from the present mixed and confused phenomena, and from these alone.[6]

In the *Dialogues*, the problem of natural evil is not used so much to disprove the existence of the Creator as to argue against the possibility of proving the Creator's goodness. On this understanding, the imperfection of creation is in contradiction with the perfection of God, and so it is not what we would expect based on the theistic hypothesis. The strength of natural evil as evidence against theism will then depend on how contrary to theistic expectations these phenomena are. Hume's evidential argument from evil is based on a comparison of hypotheses: does an indifferent and impersonal Mother Nature 'impregnated with a great vivifying principle' that works 'without discernment or parental care' provide a better explanation of the facts than the hypothesis of a morally perfect, omnipotent Creator? Proponents of the evidential problem argue that the evidence of natural evil is better explained by the hypothesis that we are produced without divine design than the hypothesis of design.[7]

4 *Dialogues*, part XI (Hume 1999).

5 Howard-Snyder (ed.) 1996; see also Draper and Dougherty (2014) for further discussion.

6 *Dialogues*, part XI (Hume 1999).

7 For examples of the argument in the contemporary discussion, see Narveson (2003) and Dawes (2009).

The problem of bad design

Against ID, the problem of natural evil is typically formulated as the problem of bad design. Here the argument is a comparison of the explanatory value of the design and evolutionary biology, understood as competing and alternative explanations of the same data. Other writers promoting similar arguments are not difficult to find. A classic statement is provided by Stephen Jay Gould, who argues in his book *The Panda's Thumb* (1980) that 'if God had designed a beautiful machine to reflect his wisdom and power, surely he would not have used a collection of parts generally fashioned for other purposes.... Odd arrangements and funny solutions are the proof of evolution-paths that a sensible God would never tread but that a natural process, constrained by history, follows perforce'.[8]

This argument for evolution clearly is partly theological and philosophical, as some in the ID movement have argued.[9] The evolutionists here some expectations about what we could reasonably expect God (or an unidentified designer) to do. But the argument is not just that these features are evidence against design. Rather, they are also presented as positive evidence in favour of evolutionary theory. If evolution gives us good reason to expect such features, but we have no reason to expect them or their absence on the hypothesis of intelligent design, then the evidence of bad design favours naturalistic evolution over intelligent design.

Evolutionary biologists have identified four reasons for expecting that Darwinian evolution would not create perfect creatures. First, selection can act only on existing variations. If a mutation making some trait possible does not occur, then it won't evolve. Second, evolution is limited by historical constraints. Adaptation to new situations must begin from the body plan that already exists, rather than designing a new one from scratch. Third, adaptations are often compromises. For example, it may be difficult to simultaneously create a high amount of offspring and care for them all. Fourth, chance, natural selection and the environment interact. An adaptation that is good for one environment may not be as optimal when the environment changes.[10]

As I will show below, one of the ID movement's primary strategies for answering these kinds of critiques is simply to refuse to engage in theological speculation about what kind of cosmos God would create. Proponents of ID argue that even suboptimal or bad design can still be designed in the case of human artefacts, so why could we not also recognize suboptimal designs as products of an intelligent creator in the case of natural order? In this way, the existence of bad design would be logically compatible with the existence of a designer, just as the existence of evil is logically compatible with theism. However, this does not answer the evidential version of the problem – it may still be that the existence of bad design fits better with an evolutionary understanding

8 Gould 1980, 20–21. Similarly, for example, Coyne (2005, part VI).

9 For example, see Hunter (2001) and Nelson (1996).

10 Campbell and Reece 2007, 484.

of our origins, than with ID's understanding. So, proponents of ID also need other strategies for responding to the problem of bad design.

Natural evil as a theological problem for ID

The problem of natural evil has also been a cornerstone of several prominent theological responses to ID. Because of the problem, ID has even been argued to be theologically heretical or at least close to it. For example, biologist Francisco A. Ayala argues that ID attributes catastrophes, disasters, imperfections of the natural world to the Creator's design, and that this 'amounts to blasphemy'.[11] According to Ayala, 'Darwin's gift' to religion is the possibility to absolve God of the responsibility for any such natural evils. Others making a similar argument include *BioLogos* writers Karl Giberson[12] and Darrel Falk[13] as well as philosopher of biology Michael Ruse.[14]

These thinkers are saying that theists actually have a good response to the problem of natural evil, but that this response requires acceptance of evolutionary biology. The underlying presupposition is that is valuable for nature to be orderly and evolutionary, and pursuing this good gives God good reason for also allowing the existence of natural evil. Ruse explains the argument clearly:

> But supposing that God did (and had to) create through law, then Richard Dawkins of all people offers a piece of candy to the Christian. Dawkins argues that the only physical way to get organic adaptation ... the design-like nature of living beings ... is through natural selection, that very painful mechanism that worried Darwin! Other mechanisms are either false (such as Lamarckism, the inheritance of acquired characteristics) or inadequate (such as saltationism, change by sudden jumps). In other words, although Darwinism does not speak to all cases of physical evil ... the earthquakes ... it does speak to the physical evil that it itself is supposed to bring on. It is Darwinism with suffering, or nothing.[15]

The argument is that if God wanted to create through an evolutionary process, then he had to create through the Darwinian process and the existence of suffering was inevitable. In contrast, within ID's vision, it seems that the Creator likes to micromanage his creation, being involved even in minute details like the origins of irreducibly complex biochemical systems. This then leads critics

11 Ayala 2007, 160. See also Ayala (2006) and the discussion in Ayala (2008) and Doran (2009).

12 Giberson 2009.

13 Falk 2009.

14 Ruse 2011. For more detailed versions of the argument, see Ruse (2003, chapter 15 and 2001, chapter 6). Southgate (2011, 387–388) also argues that evolution as we know it 'was indeed the only way, or the best way, God could give rise to creaturely selves'.

15 Ruse 2011.

to ask why God has not micromanaged his creation a little bit more. This is a legitimate question that can be asked of proponents of ID.

However, the evolutionary theodicy itself also raises many questions, regardless of whether one is a supporter of ID or not. For example, the theodicy seems to assume that Darwinian evolutionary processes were the only possible method of creation available to God. But in the classical understanding, God is the creator of the laws of nature as well, and so is himself the one who determines what kind of evolutionary processes are possible. So, for example, if a Lamarckian evolutionary process were more beneficial, then God could have chosen to create life through such a process. These kinds of considerations lead Robert J. Russell – no friend of ID – to argue that Ayala's theodicy is actually a 'theodicy lite' that merely pushes back the problem of natural evil to the laws of nature. An omnipotent God could plausibly have created different laws of nature and optimized the process in a way that did not result in as much suffering.[16]

In order to build a more robust evolutionary theodicy, we need to present some kind of reason why God would choose to create life through just the kind of evolutionary processes described in contemporary evolutionary biology. In the discussion, three basic reasons for this divine choice have been presented.[17] First (1), it is arguably an intrinsic good for the universe to exhibit progress; such a method of creation is thought to be more beautiful than creating through miracles. But here we can still argue that the universe could also exhibit progress even with a shorter history, and there may also be value in creating a universe without suffering, and value even in miraculous testimony of the Creator.[18]

Second (2), some have argued that a universe possessing autonomy must be evolutionary. For example, Haught argues that in order for the universe to be truly distinct from God, it must be capable of evolving in any direction freely.[19] Though there is much more depth to this approach than I can do justice here, hard questions remain. The conception of autonomy in particular needs more work. In what sense would it destroy nature's autonomy if God were to create directly, rather than through an evolutionary process? As Michael J. Murray argues, it is hard to see why autonomy would be destroyed. In creating a painting, for example, a human artist does not merely create an appendage of himself; why should God be unable to create something distinct from himself? Furthermore, if creating directly merely creates an appendage of the deity, then it is difficult to see how evolution solves the problem. If we believe in the creation of the world out of nothing, then God has created the initial state that

16 Russell 2013. See also Russell (2008, chapters 7 and 8). Similarly, Alston (1994, 55–56).

17 For an alternate, more detailed classification of reasons, see M.J. Murray (2011, chapter 6).

18 On this see for example Murray and Wilkinson (2010).

19 Haught 2003.

evolution begins from. If this initial state is merely a 'part' of God (because it was directly created by God), why should we assume that further evolution will make the part distinct from God?[20]

Third (3), it has been argued that God chose to use the evolutionary process in order to keep himself hidden. For example, Miller argues that if God were to create life other than through an evolutionary process, then his existence would be so evident in the biological marvels of life that it would make human free choice impossible.[21] The presence of a policeman will make it very difficult for people to choose without pressure whether to obey the law or to disobey it. Similarly such pressing knowledge of God's existence might, it is argued, make it difficult for people to make a free moral choice between loving God and rejecting him. So, in order to make human morality possible, God must maintain a certain epistemic distance between himself and humanity. There is much to be said for the general idea of the necessity of at least some divine hiddenness, but the conclusion that God therefore had to use a Darwinian process is questionable. As Murray notes, a large amount of people in history have believed that the teleological nature of organisms provides excellent grounds for an argument for God's existence. It is hard to believe that none of these people had free choice, or that the free choice of ID proponents is compromised because of their belief in their own arguments.[22]

So, there are many open questions to evolutionary theodicies. Because of these problems, the argument that God must have used an evolutionary process remain inconclusive.[23] As Robin Collins argues, I believe that these kinds of arguments might at most lead us to prefer an evolutionist account, rather than ruling something like ID's argument out on theological grounds. Committing to building a proper theology of evolution can be motivated strongly enough by the empirical evidence for evolution and the rich resources of the Christian tradition. Theistic evolutionists do not need to think that there would be necessary theological reasons to believe in a theory like Darwinian evolution, if we did not have good empirical evidence.[24]

Having now presented the problem of natural evil for ID, I will go on to discuss the movement's responses.

---

20 M.J. Murray 2011, 170–175; 2009b, 365–367. It seems to me Hart (2003, 18–19) formulates a better model of autonomy.

21 Miller 2002, 290.

22 Murray 2011, 180. For a balanced natural theology combining divine hiddenness and divine revelation, see Evans 2010.

23 It may be that a more convincing case for the necessity of evolution could be made from the perspective of process theism, which already includes the process-like nature of creation in its basic philosophical background. But here the problem is that the particular metaphysics of process theism is itself controversial, and only accepted by a minority of theologians.

24 R. Collins 2009.

Explaining evil within ID?

Bypassing the problem?

Because ID's design arguments do not identify the designer as God, proponents of ID often argue that their design argument is not dependent on the philosophical and theological discussion of the problem of natural evil. For example, Dembski argues as follows:

> Critics who invoke the problem of evil against design have left science behind and entered the waters of philosophy and theology. A torture chamber replete with implements of torture is designed, and the evil of its designer does nothing to undercut the torture chamber's design. The existence of design is distinct from the morality, aesthetics, goodness, optimality, or perfection of design. Moreover, there are reliable indicators of design that work irrespective of whether design includes these additional features.[25]

Generally proponents of ID argue that their design hypothesis does not say anything about the moral characteristics of the designer. Behe similarly claims that 'we can determine that a system was designed by examining the system itself, and we can hold the conviction of design much more strongly than a conviction about the identity of the designer'.[26] So, the design argument cannot say 'whether the designer of life was a dope, a demon or a deity', and we need not deny the conclusion of design simply because the design appears evil to us.[27] Behe himself is quite consistent on this point, even arguing that the malarial parasite was intentionally designed to infect humans. Because the parasite's molecular machinery is an 'exquisitely purposeful arrangement of parts', it is not, according to Behe, credible to believe that it evolved without the direction of some intelligent designer.[28]

In Chapter 8, I have argued that the ID movement's design arguments indeed do not derive their explanatory power from any assumption about the designer's morality and motives. Rather, they depend on the perceived link between some types of order and intelligent design as a cause. Based on this, the ID movement's response to the problem of natural evil does have some initial plausibility: the argument does not depend on the goodness of the designer, at least in its most minimalistic form. But this does not mean that there are not also reasons why proponents of ID should take the problem of natural evil seriously. I will now present four such reasons.

25 Dembski 2000a.

26 Behe 2006a, 196.

27 Behe 2007a, 238–239.

28 Behe 2007a, 237.

First (1), in previous chapters, I have shown that proponents of ID sometimes move between a minimalistic and a more robust version of the design hypothesis. For example, in cosmology, they refer to the beauty, goodness and rationality of the cosmos as evidence that fits better with the hypothesis of intelligent design than with any naturalistic explanation. In biology, they feel awe in the face of the designed elegance of biological systems, which they feel fits better with intelligent design, than with belief in a haphazard evolutionary process as the engine of creation. But if proponents of ID indeed sometimes refer to considerations like the goodness, beauty and the degree of perfection natural order exhibits, then it would be inconsistent not to also face the problem of bad design.

Second (2), proponents of ID must face the problem of natural evil because it is presented not merely as evidence against design but also as evidence that is predicted by evolutionary biology. One interesting strategy that proponents of ID sometimes use at this point is to combine belief in design with acceptance of parts of evolutionary theory. The designer could have chosen to work through a historically constrained evolutionary process, leading to the same limitations in designs as mainstream evolutionary biology. The combination of ID and evolution can also lead proponents of ID to expect life to be imperfect in the way described by evolutionists. On this understanding, bad designs will simply be evidence for an evolutionary understanding of design, rather than against all design arguments. However, this strategy for bypassing part of the problem will only work for that minority of ID theorists who accept common descent. Others need to find further responses.

My third argument (3) for the relevance of the problem of natural evil to ID is based on the importance of worldviews and background probabilities for the design argument. Even if our Western culture is in some ways 'post-Christian',[29] the monotheistic God of Judaism, Christianity and Islam remains the most credible candidate for a designer for most people, including proponents of ID.[30] This cultural situation seems to make it reasonable to evaluate the design argument as part of this broader context of reasons to believe or disbelieve in the existence of God. Culturally the most credible alternatives are currently naturalism and some form of theism. So – to most people – either a designer is perfect, or there is no designer at all. In this cultural context, the hypothesis that there is a designer but that he is unable to create good design may be less credible than a wholly naturalistic scenario. Because proponents of ID wish to impact our broader culture, engaging in such broader discussion should also be desirable for them.

It may indeed be true that the culturally reasonable opposition between naturalism and theism does not capture all the options adequately. One way of showing that the problem of natural evil does not lead to atheism would be

29 Hart 2010.

30 Sennett 2005.

to argue that the problem should lead us to modify our conception of God, rather than to abandon belief altogether. For example, it is conceivable that belief in the God described by modern process theology could for many people be more credible than believing in a fully naturalistic account of evolution, even with the problem of natural evil. But most of the ID theorists themselves are very traditional theists, so this does not seem like a strategy they would endorse.

My fourth argument (4) for the relevance of the problem of natural evil to ID is based on the way proponents of ID themselves understand ID as a link between theology and science. They believe themselves to be constructing a science that is more consonant with theism than Darwinian evolutionary biology has been. Furthermore, ID has broad cultural aims beyond just promoting the design argument, as I've noted. It desires to provide a better ground for understanding the meaningfulness and value of life than atheistic evolutionism. But in order for ID's design argument to be useful for this kind of broader purpose, ID must be related somehow to this broader theistic vision. This requires more knowledge of the nature of the designer, and thus also requires dealing with the problem of natural evil.

Questioning examples of bad design

While it may in principle be possible to construct a design argument without interacting in great detail with the problem of natural evil, the broader context of the argument does not allow bypassing the problem this quickly. Thinkers within the ID movement have attempted to tackle the problem more directly, though these responses are rarely constructed in a thorough and systematic manner. First (1), proponents of ID have argued that some proposed examples of natural evil are not actually evil, or that at least we are not in the position to evaluate how optimal they are. Second (2), proponents of ID have attempted to support their design hypothesis with explanations for the existence of bad design. For example, as already noted, ID can be combined with parts of evolutionary theory, or it can be argued that the designer has some other reason for allowing bad designs and natural evil. This latter strategy already comes quite close to the theological discussions of theodicy.

While proponents of ID do concede that some natural evils are real, they also claim that some other examples of natural evil or bad design are unconvincing. There are two primary ways of doing this. First, it can be argued that examples of bad design are actually examples of good design, when they are evaluated more precisely. In one of his critiques of ID, Coyne argues that the wayward route taken by the human recurrent laryngeal nerve is evidence that it was not constructed by an engineer working to create the most efficient solution, but a historical process. It is 'one of nature's worst designs'.[31] In

31 Coyne 2009, 87.

response, ID proponents have argued that research actually shows this to be a functionally better solution than the straight route. Similar examples could be multiplied.[32]

Proponents of design arguments can also argue that some evaluations of bad design are based on incomplete criteria. Thus Witt argues that Gould's evaluation of the panda's thumb is flawed because it overemphasizes engineering efficiency:

> Must the cosmic designer's primary concern for pandas be that they are the most dexterous bears divinely imaginable? From a purely practical standpoint, might opposable-thumbed über-pandas wreak havoc on their ecosystem? From a purely aesthetic standpoint, might not those charming pandas up in their bamboo trees with their unopposing but quite workable thumbs be just the sort of humorous supporting character this great cosmic drama needs to lighten things up a bit? If Shakespeare could introduce a comical gravedigger into the tragedy of Hamlet, why cannot God introduce whimsy into His work?[33]

Witt does make a sound point here: judgements of optimality will inevitably be value judgements, and tidiness and engineering evidence should not be the only values considered. Rather, we should also consider the organism's role in the broader ecosystem, the beauty of the plurality of forms created and the possibility that the Creator might wish to commune with his creation before evaluating the goodness of the designs of nature. This seems reasonable from a theological perspective, but again requires a broader approach than just focusing on the minimalistic design argument.

Though proponents of ID can well argue that we are unable to evaluate whether organisms are fully perfect, or whether engineering efficiency should indeed be the primary goal of the designer, these arguments still cannot consistently bar all negative evaluations of nature. After all, the ID proponent's own argument also hinges on our ability to identify what kind of functions biological order has. As I showed in Chapter 4, Behe argues that we can reliably understand what a system's immanent functions are, even though the designer's ultimate purposes are unknown to us. But if we can understand the system's immanent functions, we might also in principle be able to understand if the system is somehow flawed. Certainly medical science depends on being able to diagnose when a system is not working properly – for example, when a heart is not able to pump as much blood as the organism needs. So, it seems that we can and do evaluate design.

---

32 For example, Luskin (2014).

33 Witt 2009. See also Behe (2006a, 223).

A balanced scepticism?

Here it is interesting to relate scepticism about our capability to evaluate the goodness of nature to another theistic strategy for responding to the problem of evil: sceptical theism. It is possible to argue that we cannot reliably predict that God would not create a world like ours, since we cannot be confident in our ability to judge such lofty things as the character and motives of God. Because of this, we cannot assert with any confidence that the existence of evil is incompatible with the existence of God. The basic intuition behind this strategy finds support in the tradition of negative theology, as well as the biblical book of Job. However, the problem is that if God is asserted to be fully unknowable, this includes very high costs for the rest of Christian theology. It also becomes difficult to speak of God's love for humanity, since we will have no basis of saying what such love means. Furthermore, in order to be meaningful, assertions of the unknowability of God must paradoxically always be based on some knowledge of what God is like. Otherwise, how could we know that God is unknowable?[34]

But perhaps there is a way to make a weaker sceptical response work: God could be unknowable in some weaker sense of the term. Perhaps there is some way of appealing to the complexity of reality and the limits of human knowledge that strike just the right balance between allowing for knowledge of God on the one hand, but nevertheless being sceptical of our ability to criticize God. This kind of response would argue that it is precisely in knowing God that we simultaneously come to know that we cannot criticize God. To make this kind of sceptical response work, one must balance a fine line where the Creator is both knowable and unknowable at the same time.[35]

Similarly, the sceptical defence of design arguments must be humble in the face of reality's complexity without abandoning hope for knowledge about it. It seems that we can indeed often detect design before being able to evaluate whether that design is optimal or not. For example, most of us do not know the design principles of computer hard drives. The sceptical defence of design arguments needs to say that our situation is similar with nature's order.

In this vein, suppose that we can recognize that the cosmos and life are designed by looking at their intricate complexity and rationality which far exceeds anything that human beings have created. If some intelligence was able to create such order, then it seems reasonable to conclude that the intelligence was far more capable than we are, to such a degree that we should think it likely that we will not be able to outsmart this intelligence. So as we come to know the Creator of life and understand his intelligence by analogy with human intelligence, we simultaneously realize that he is much greater than we can comprehend and thus above our ability to criticize. Just as in Christian negative

34 For discussion of sceptical theism, see Dougherty and McBrayer, eds (2014).

35 For one attempt at this kind of balance, see DePoe (2014).

theology, in coming to know God we simultaneously also come to know that he is a mystery.[36]

This line of argument has actually been taken up in the ID movement. Referring to Kant's argument of this type and the biblical story of Job, Dembski has argued that intelligent design actually helps answer the problem of natural evil, because it helps us understand that the designer of life is greater than we are, and thus it is reasonable to be sceptical of our ability to criticize him.[37] This is an attempt to balance on the fine line between knowledge and scepticism. This view does not lead to a similar doubt regarding our capability to recognize that some design is very good. Rather, it is just because we recognize that the designs are generally very good that we become sceptical of our own negative evaluations. As in the evidential strategy, evil is treated as an anomaly in the broader evidence which points to the wisdom of the Creator.

The difficulty of explaining evil away

The previous responses to the problem of natural evil are also open to theistic evolutionists, and can in some cases help alleviate the problem. However, they do not solve the problem completely. Though we can understand some cases of natural evil to be misunderstandings and see that in some other cases we cannot be confident of our ability to judge that the design is truly of poor quality, in other cases the degree of imperfection or evil seems to be so great that such solutions are implausible. If we are to be at all confident in our ability to evaluate nature (even to recognize the wisdom of its Creator), it seems difficult to believe that we cannot at the same time recognize the imperfection and evil in these cases.

One example of clear natural evil that is difficult to explain away is provided by Behe, who argues that the molecular machinery of the malarial parasite is an 'exquisitely purposeful arrangement of parts' and cannot be plausibly explained by naturalistic mechanisms.[38] By Behe's own logic, the malarial parasite is clearly designed. But a problem arises, because the parasite's design is producing a great deal of suffering, and so the intelligent design we observe seems to be clearly morally evil. Behe admits that this is a hard question theologically, but not one that affects the minimal design argument. This is in line with his earlier conclusion that 'we can determine that a system was designed by examining the system itself, and we can hold the conviction of design much more strongly than a conviction about the identity of the designer'.[39] So, the design argument cannot say 'whether the designer of life was a dope, a demon or a deity'.[40] So Behe

36 Turner 2004.

37 Dembski 2003a.

38 Behe 2007a, 237.

39 Behe 2006a, 196.

40 Behe 2007a, 238–239.

admits that some designs in nature are evil, but argues further that we cannot deny the conclusion of design simply because of this fact.[41]

Previously in this chapter, I pointed to Witt's argument that we should evaluate the beauty of nature, not just its efficiency. The example of parasites is one where nature seems ugly, though efficient. Parasite wasps are highly useful for human farmers because they kill off many pests. Sometimes humans have thus even helped parasite wasps spread so that they would protect human farms.[42] Nevertheless, there is something deeply ugly and unsettling about the whole phenomenon of parasitism. I have already quoted Darwin's assessment: 'I cannot persuade myself that a beneficent and omnipotent God would have designedly created the Ichneumonidae with the express intention of their feeding within the living bodies of caterpillars or that a cat should play with mice'.[43] The problem of natural evil is somewhat diminished once we realize that caterpillars surely have vastly different emotional lives than humans (if they indeed have emotions). This does not remove the ugliness of the phenomenon, however. And there are also parasitical worms which live in the intestines of humans and higher primates, so the ugliness of parasitism is not just a problem concerning caterpillars.[44]

In cosmological design arguments about fine-tuning, some proposed answers to the problem of natural evil are also not convincing. Consider earthquakes. Defending the design argument, Denton argues that earthquakes are a consequence of the activity of the Earth's geology, which is necessary to circulate heavier elements from the Earth's depths to its surface, where life can make use of them.[45] This response seeks to show that earthquakes, too, have a purpose for life: that even in this instance, nature is fine-tuned to benefit life. However, here Hume's question about the insufficient fine-tuning of natural laws seems pertinent. On a theistic view, one can ask whether it is really plausible that geological activity could not be so optimized by an omnipotent deity creating the world *ex nihilo* as to recycle the elements without causing earthquakes.[46]

A patchwork quilt of responses

Common theological responses to the problem

Though the preceding strategies used by the ID movement may help alleviate the force of the problem of natural evil, it seems that the entire problem

41 Similarly, Richards (2007).

42 See Pennisi (2010) for more details.

43 Darwin 2012 [1860].

44 On whether animals have emotions and experience suffering, see Murray (2011, chapter 2) and Dougherty (2014a).

45 Denton 1998. Murray (2011, chapter 5) also explores similar strategies.

46 On Denton's own view this is not a problem, however, because Denton does not believe that God created *ex nihilo*. Rather, Denton believes that the Creator worked on pre-existing matter and created the best world that this matter allowed for. On explaining natural disasters, see also Hart (2005).

cannot be answered using these strategies. It can still be asked (1) how imperfections in the natural world fit into the broader theistic worldview that ID's design arguments are designed to support, and (2) it can still be argued that the data of natural evil fit better with another theistic or naturalistic understanding of the cosmos. However, the preceding discussion also does not exhaust all of the responses available for proponents of ID. Several other responses can be discerned in the ID literature, thought they have not yet been patched together into a complete whole (or at least, the complete patchwork has not been revealed to the world).

Regarding how imperfections fit into a theistic worldview, I believe proponents of ID need to avail themselves of strategies developed during centuries of discussion in theology and in the philosophy of religion. It is true that evolutionary theodicies based on the value of the orderliness of nature are more difficult for proponents of ID to defend, since proponents of ID already believe that the Creator acts in the world to create effects that surpass the capacities of natural processes and laws. However, most theistic evolutionists also believe that God acts at least in some way beyond the laws of nature, such as in the events of salvation history like Jesus' resurrection. So, the difference between proponents of ID and theistic evolutionists may be a matter of degree here. The theological problem facing ID here is a very general one for all theories in which God acts beyond the laws of nature: if God acts in the world at all, why does he not act even more?

Since theists already typically believe that God acts in the world, it is difficult to limit precisely how much God can act before this becomes problematic for the regularity of creation and the possibility of creaturely freedom. If the one act of raising Jesus from the dead does not yet create massive irregularity in the world, why should directing the evolution of the bacterial flagellum create massive irregularity? It is difficult to evaluate such things. However, it seems that if the defence based on the regularity is to be valuable at all from the viewpoint of traditional Christian belief, then upholding the value of nomic regularity in the world must not rule out all divine intervention in the world. The Creator must be able to interact with his creation without jeopardizing its autonomy and regularity. Even within ID, thinkers such as Behe continue to argue that the Creator has given the processes of nature much autonomy and only directs the course of evolution when necessary.[47]

Much further, work must be done before it is possible to argue confidently that the amount and type of divine action required by ID is enough to make nomic regularity defence wholly impossible.[48] I do not think it does. However, proponents of ID indeed cannot use this kind of defence as broadly as theistic

47 Behe 2007c.

48 Considering the length of history and the size of the world, it can be argued that even thousands of miracles in the history of life would still not create massive irregularity in nature. On this point, see also the insightful discussion in Corabi (2009, 23–31).

evolutionists can. This is because some of the examples of natural evil, such as the malarial parasite, require the kind of highly complex molecular machines that the ID movement argues cannot be generated by the regular processes of nature themselves, without intelligent guidance. So proponents of ID must find some other way of accounting for many examples of natural evil.

The evolutionary theodicy based on the value of nomic regularity is just one of several responses available in the Christian theological tradition. For example, the idea of the world as a theatre of soul-making is one possible reason why God could have allowed the existence of apparent imperfections in the world. The basic argument (following theologian Irenaeus, 130–202 AD) is that the existence of hardships allows the development of virtue, and all evils will ultimately be defeated in the coming eschatological salvation. This view can also be criticized, like all theodicies; for example it seems that suffering does not always seem to lead to the growth of character. But the theodicy does not assert that we should already be able to see how evil will eventually won, rather only that this will happen at some point. The theodicy continues to have able defenders.[49]

Another common response to the problem of natural evil is the free will defence, stating that natural evil is somehow a result of the freedom of created beings, rather than the freedom of processes, as stated by the evolutionary theodicy. It is claimed that the existence of true creaturely freedom and true love are such great goods that their existence justifies allowing the existence of evil resulting from free choices of the creatures.[50] Typically free will defences have been used to explain the existence of evil in human societies after the 'fall' of humanity. Since the discovery that suffering existed before humans, this has become more difficult, though some still argue that God created nature to be a fitting place for sinful humans, since he had foreknowledge that humans would sin. This defence based on the foreknowledge of God has also been used in the ID movement by Dembski. Dembski believes that the Garden narratives of Genesis are essentially historical, showing that God initially sheltered humanity in a paradise-like garden, and that God then expelled humanity into the outside theatre of soul-making after the fall.[51]

Another option that avoids reference to divine foreknowledge is to explain the corruption of creation by reference to the fall of angels and the subsequent actions of these fallen angels. This solution is indirectly hinted at by Behe's wording that 'a demon or a dope' may be responsible for the evil designs in nature. Indeed, if we can make estimates of the wisdom and intelligence of the designer based on analogies with humans, why not also estimates of the designer's morality? However, I am unaware of any ID writer defending this model, and Dembski has even directly criticized it. Dembski argues that though

49 For example, Dougherty (2014a).

50 Plantinga 1977.

51 Dembski 2009.

it could be that God allows free creatures such as humans and fallen angels to produce evil in the world, this would not entirely eliminate God's responsibility for this evil. Rather, Dembski argues that Christians must accept that God bears the ultimate responsibility for evil, even if he merely allows it, and that no view can absolve God of this responsibility, even if God is only responsible by allowing the creation to suffer the consequences of human sin.[52]

The literature on different theodicies is in any case quite robust, and it seems clear that many different approaches and their combinations to explaining the existence of natural evil are in principle open to proponents of ID.[53] It is true that all of these approaches can be criticized, but the same is true of any philosophical argument, including the evolutionary theodicy. Therefore, it does not seem that proponents of ID are substantially worse off with the problem of evil than other theists. What remains is the other side of the problem of natural evil as evidence for a naturalistic understanding of nature, rather than merely as evidence against theism. Here there are again several different approaches that are open to proponents of ID.

Evil as an anomaly or evidence for theism

Many natural theologians are content with granting that the existence of natural evil is at least somewhat surprising given the existence a good God, and therefore constitutes evidence against the existence of God and in favour of naturalism. However, it may be that this counterevidence is simply too weak to override the evidence in favour of the existence of God. The approach of Swinburne, for example, is to minimize the power of the argument from evil by using theodicies and then to argue that the overall evidence is sufficient to render theism more probable than not.[54] Paley's response to Hume's argument in his *Natural Theology* was similar: Paley argued that there is much more good than evil in the world, and that we can often identify a good reason for the existence of purported natural evils.[55] In this approach it may be admitted that at least some natural evils are evidence against theism, but these are seen as anomalies in the broader pattern of evidence which supports theism. However, as in the natural sciences, anomalies do not always lead automatically to the rejection of an otherwise good theory.[56] The credibility of this approach depends on how strong we think the grounds of theistic belief are in contrast with the problem of evil.[57]

52 Dembski 2009, 150. See Boyd (2001, chapters 8–10) for an extended defense of the demonic theodicy and Murray (2011, chapter 3) for some mild critiques of this approach.

53 On combining different theodicies, see Murray's helpful analysis (2011).

54 Swinburne 2004a, chapter 11.

55 *Natural Theology*, chapter XXVI (Paley 2006, 237–276).

56 For a defence of thinking of evil as an anomaly for theism akin to the anomalies of scientific theories, see Dougherty and Pruss (2014).

57 See also Murray (2011, chapter 4) for further criticisms.

As Pierre Duhem and Willard Van Orman Quine noted, it is rarely possible to falsify even a scientific theory with just one experiment. Rather than being isolated hypotheses that can be tested in this way, scientific theories often form a complex web of mutually reinforcing beliefs and hypotheses. Thus it is often possible to save a hypothesis from falsification by modifying the system at some point and introducing other explaining factors.[58] Sometimes this is the reasonable and correct thing to do. For example, in the beginning of the 19th century it became apparent that the orbit of Uranus did not conform with the predictions of Newtonian mechanics. In this case, it was more reasonable to posit the existence of a new planet (Neptune) than give up the whole model.[59] In Chapter 4, I pointed out that defending the theory of biological evolution similarly requires believing that current mysteries do indeed have explanations that do not change the current theory radically. Ironically, referring to those hard-to-explain instances of natural evil as anomalies in the theistic framework is also the best way for proponents of ID to defend their design argument. It must be argued that natural evil is a mystery that theists have reason to believe will be solved, rather than a mystery that we have reason to believe won't be solved.[60]

Actually something like this approach makes sense on ID's understanding of the state of the evidence. Recall that proponents of ID argue that the non-purposeful evolutionary processes actually cannot explain the origins of most of life's complexity. If this were true, then evolutionary biology would not provide a good explanation for life. Even if the data of bad design fit well in the hypothesis, this would not be enough to save evolutionary theory, if the evidence were otherwise in favour of ID. The problem of natural evil is not by itself a sufficient argument against ID since it could well be that the probability that a naturalistic process could produce life at all could still be much lower than the probability that a good God would create suboptimal designs.[61]

A further theistic strategy takes the case even further and argues that the existence of natural and moral evil is actually evidence in favour of the existence of God, rather than against it. The argument is that naturalism implies that good and evil are merely human inventions, whereas theism implies that there is an objective standard of moral good and evil. Evil is understood as parasitic on good. Thus God as the highest good must also exist if evil exists. This approach has also been endorsed by prominent thinkers within the ID movement, notably Dembski,[62] Wiker[63] and Hunter.[64] Dembski puts this point as follows: 'The line I find most convincing is that evil always parasitizes good. Indeed, all our words for evil presuppose a good that has been perverted.

58 Quine 1953. See also Paul Murray (2010, 97–98).

59 O'Connor and Robertson 1996.

60 On this, see Dougherty 2014b.

61 This is argued in more detail by Corabi (2009).

62 Dembski 2000a.

63 Wiker 2009.

64 Hunter 2010.

Impurity presupposes purity, unrighteousness presupposes righteousness, deviation presupposes a way (i.e., a via) from which we've departed, sin (the Greek hamartia) presupposes a target that was missed, etc. Boethius put it this way in his Consolation of Philosophy: "If God exists whence evil; but whence good if God does not exist?"'.[65] This moral argument for theism based on natural evil is related to the controversial moral argument for God's existence. The literature contains much discussion of it, and objections to will be similar also in the case of ID. In particular, naturalists can argue that the problem of evil is about the internal incoherence of theism and ID, and that they as naturalists do not actually believe in the existence of objective evil, even though it is in practice difficult to live without assuming such categories. But perhaps the moral argument can at least somewhat lessen the evidential value of evil against theism.[66]

Summary

The problem of natural evil points to the apparently useless and chaotic arrangements, bad design and the ugliness of the world as evidence against design. While proponents of cosmic design arguments claim that the cosmos is fine-tuned for life and rational understanding, the problem of natural evil can be used to argue that our cosmos appears to be largely indifferent to the suffering of living beings. Rather than being the good world that onc would expect based on a theistic design hypothesis, our world is argued to be mediocre at best. Against biological design arguments, it is argued that living things are in many places poorly designed and not the sort that one would expect from a wise and powerful designer but are rather better explained by a haphazard, tinkering process of evolution.

Proponents of ID often attempt to bypass discussion of the problem of natural evil on the grounds that it is not relevant to their argument. In this they are partly correct: the explanatory force of their design argument derives from the connection between teleological order and teleological causes, not from the goodness of the designer. However, I have argued that the broader context of ID's design arguments should lead the ID theorists to also engage with the problem of natural evil in a deeper way. The credibility of ID's minimalistic design argument also depends partly on broader philosophical and theological issues, so the movement should engage and discuss these issues in a more systematic manner. In this they could well benefit from the way theistic natural theologians have approached the issue and the several strategies for arguing that a good God could well be expected to allow some evil in the world.

65 Dembski 2000a, quoting Boethius 1973 [524], 153.

66 Another response to the moral argument would be to state that moral facts can exist in some way even without being grounded in the reality of God. See further the excellent discussion in Garcia and King, eds (2009), as well as Evans (2014).

On the other hand, theological challenges to ID based on the problem of natural evil are also not very strong. Theists have many different responses to the problem of natural evil, and ID's arguments only make some evolutionary theodicies more difficult, rather than making the entire problem impossible. Moreover, evolutionary theodicies also have their own unsolved questions. A more throughout understanding of the options available could help both critics and defenders of ID formulate their positions more clearly.

10 Intelligent Design and theistic evolutionism

Because a central aim of ID is to oppose a naturalistic understanding of the world, ID would initially seem to have much in common with theistic evolutionism, since a theistic understanding of evolution is also opposed to naturalism. But as I have noted repeatedly in this study, there is much tension between ID and theistic evolutionism. In previous chapters, I have analysed some critiques of ID from a theistic evolutionist viewpoint, and have generally argued that ID could in principle be formulated in a way that avoids these criticisms, if only the evidence supports ID. In this chapter, it is time to subject ID's critique of theistic evolutionism to the same kind of critical analysis.

The ID movement's critique of theistic evolutionism is sometimes almost as fierce as its critique of a purely naturalistic understanding of evolution. Proponents of ID argue that the scientific evidence doesn't support evolution, and also present this as a major reason for rejecting theistic evolutionism. However, beyond this critique it is clear that major theological and philosophical reasons also underlie their rejection of theistic evolutionism. Combining theism and mainstream evolutionary biology is believed by most major ID proponents to result in almost incoherent views that greatly weaken the rationality of belief in God.

I will begin in this chapter by analysing the surface level of this debate: ID's understanding of design and evolution as competitive explanations. I will argue that the ID literature actually also contains the seeds for an approach reconciling design and evolution. In the second section of the chapter I will move to analyse what the debate between ID and theistic evolutionism tells us about ID's overall approach to reconciling science and religion. It is my belief that this is the point where the adverse effects of scientism on the ID movement's argumentation are most clear. Avoiding the temptation would make the movement's argumentation more robust and would help build dialogue with theistic evolutionists.

Design and evolution in competition

ID's understanding of evolution

In the history of design arguments, natural causes and the effect of minds have not always been opposed. Plato's demiurge, for example, created by using matter's existing properties, not out of nothing or contrary to laws of nature. For the death of Socrates, Plato saw several causes. While the poison drunk by Socrates was the material cause of his death, it would have been an error to see only this side of the issue. Instead, the political situation of Athens and the plans and purposes of both Socrates and his opponents were also important to note. For Plato, material and teleological explanation were thus complementary levels of explanation. On this model, a design argument is not necessarily in conflict with material explanations.[1]

In my discussion of cosmological design arguments, I already noted the strategy of level-shifting, where natural explanations for fine-tuning like the multiverse hypothesis are argued not to explain away the features that make design as an explanation appealing. Could a similar strategy also work in the case of biology? Proponents of ID are not opposed to the general idea that the designer, or God, could have worked through natural laws and mechanisms. For them, design and natural causes are both real. As Behe writes, the alternatives are not that of 'a cartoon world, where genies and fairies swirl about endlessly dispensing magic, or a world of relentless materialism where, say, the charitable work of a Mother Teresa is explained only in terms of evolutionary selection coefficients'.[2]

Accordingly, proponents of ID distinguish between several different meanings of the word 'evolution', most of which they believe to be compatible with ID.[3] But they believe that Darwinian evolutionary mechanisms are formulated specifically in a way that competes with design as an explanation: 'it is not evolution in general, but Darwinism's exclusion of design, that ID proponents reject'.[4] The problem for proponents of ID is that (to phrase the point in Plato's terms) while other natural explanations work on the level of material causes, Darwinism also attempts to reduce teleology to material causes. It attempts to provide a wholly naturalistic explanation of teleology, and to thus render references to purpose and direction unnecessary.

I noted in my discussion of level-shifting that sometimes the strategy might indeed not work, and a natural explanation might make appeals to design unnecessary, at least in the case of human design. Plato himself did also criticize the Epicurean system, which argued that teleology is ultimately reducible to material causes.[5] ID proponents believe that the case is similar in the competition between Darwinian evolution and design as explanations of biological teleology. Design explains teleology by reference to a teleological cause, whereas evolution reduces teleology to material causes. If evolutionary explanations are

1 Sedley 2007, chapter 4.
2 Behe 1999a.
3 Dembski and Wells 2007.
4 Wells 2010, 119. Similarly, Meyer (2010) and Johnson (1993).
5 Sedley 2007, chapters 4 and 5.

successful, then design-based explanations for the same features are no longer required, according to ID.

Because of the many different definitions of evolution, proponents of ID believe that it is it possible to define 'theistic evolution' in a way that is compatible with the design argument of the ID movement; namely as a process directed by the designer in some way.[6] But this, according to proponents of ID, is not compatible with mainstream understandings of Darwinian evolution. Rather, undirectedness is understood to be part of the very definition of the Darwinian process. For example, according to Johnson, '"Evolution", honestly understood, is not just a gradual process of development that a purposeful Creator might have chosen to employ. It is, by Darwinist definition, a purposeless and undirected process that produced mankind accidentally'.[7]

Following this understanding, proponents of ID tend to see the harmonization of theism and this kind of evolutionary theory as harmful for the rationality of religious belief. For example, Dembski argues that 'Theistic evolution takes the Darwinian picture of the biological world and baptizes it, identifying this picture with the way God created life. When boiled down to its scientific content, however, theistic evolution is no different from atheistic evolution, treating only undirected natural processes in the origin and development of life'.[8] Dembski recognizes that God could in principle have directed evolution in a way that is invisible to the natural sciences, but argues that atheists can easily dismiss this kind of theistic evolutionism by appealing to the principle that we should eliminate superfluous factors from our explanations. If God is not necessary to explain evolution, as ID posits, then he can be argued to be unnecessary for biology, and so biology would be identical for theists and atheists. So, Dembski argues that consistent theistic evolutionists should just give up the label 'theism' and simply call their view 'evolutionism'.[9]

Two examples of theistic evolutionism

The ID movement's critique of theistic evolutionism will become easier to understand and criticize when brought into dialogue with defences of the compatibility of Darwinian evolutionary theory and belief in God. I will use two examples of such dialogue: Stephen C. Meyer's critique of Dennis Lamoureux's evolutionary creationism[10] and William Dembski's critique of Simon Conway Morris' view that the phenomenon of convergence allows us to see a direction in evolution.[11] Both of these are examples of what I have previously called the theistic law-governed view of evolution.

6 Meyer 2010, 147.
7 P. Johnson 1993b.
8 Dembski 1999a, 110.
9 Dembski 1999a, 111–112.
10 Meyer 2010b.
11 Dembski 2004c.

According to Lamoureux, 'the Creator established and maintains the laws of nature, including the mechanisms of a purpose-driven teleological evolution'.[12] Lamoureux argues that we can see design in nature at a level deeper than biology. Like a brilliant billiard player, who can sink all the balls of the billiard table with one shot, God has made the evolution of humans possible already with his initial act of creation. In our universe, while no references to design are necessary on the level of proximate biological explanations, ultimately all of the workings of nature reveal the existence of its Creator and cannot be properly understood without reference to him. Lamoureux affirms the value of the design argument, and even calls his own view a form of intelligent design.[13]

Meyer is not satisfied with Lamoureux's harmonization of theism and evolutionary biology, however: 'it is difficult to see how Lamoureux's theory . . . differs in substance from conventional materialistic theories of evolution that rely on undirected contingency and deny any intelligent guidance or direction in the history of life'.[14] Meyer uses the origin of life's biological information as an example of this similarity. If the information of the first cell does not come directly from the mind of the designer, it must be mediated by natural laws. However, no such laws have been discovered, so in practice Lamoureux must, like atheistic evolutionists, also explain the origin of life by reference to accidental chemical events and the effects of selection.

Meyer concludes that in this case the contingent processes of chemical accidents do most of the work of creation instead of a personal Creator, and so Lamoureux does not really have grounds for referring to the Creator's activity as an explanation. Meyer acknowledges that Lamoureux believes the Creator designed natural laws which allow for the interplay of natural laws and natural events to create living organisms. However, for Meyer such a role is too small for the Creator. He wants the evidence to reveal the Creator's active involvement in the creation of life beyond the laws of nature, and no less will do.[15]

Dembski makes many of the same points in his critique of Simon Conway Morris' defence of theistic evolution. Palaeontologist Conway Morris' argument is based on the phenomenon of convergence. Evolutionary convergence means that similar features have evolved several times apparently independently during the course of evolution. It seems as if there are laws governing the shape the tree of life takes, and so it is not completely random after all. This supports the possibility of a theistic interpretation of evolution, where the direction of evolution is built in by the Creator into the natural laws, though Conway Morris does not write of proving theistic guidance of evolution.[16]

12 Meyer 2010, 149.
13 See, for example, Johnson and Lamoureux (1999) and Lamoureux (2008).
14 Meyer 2010, 162.
15 Meyer 2010, 163.
16 Conway Morris 2005.

In response, Dembski argues that this evidence can at most demonstrate merely that evolution is 'limited to fixed paths, not that it has goals'. Dembski acknowledges that Conway Morris has given some evidence for the teleological nature of evolutionary processes. However, he argues that this evidence is not strong enough. Design remains merely a metaphysical possibility, rather than a necessary component of explanation. So, it can still remain a reasonable possibility to argue that there is no real direction to evolution.[17]

So, both Dembski and Meyer emphasize the need for evidence to determine the question of evolution's purposiveness. To discover whether evolution was directed, they argue that we should look at the details of the process itself, ask where the limits of the natural processes are, and whether design is required to explain that which lies beyond those limits. The assumption in both critiques is that the defence of the faith requires very strong evidence of design, and that this evidence should be scientific in nature. Meyer and Dembski want to discover evidence of intelligent design on the level of biology, teleology which cannot be explained other than by reference to the purposes of a designing mind. Because of this, they do not appreciate Lamoureux's and Conway Morris' arguments which aim to discover evidence of design not on the level of biological theory but on the underlying explanatory level in the fine-tuning of natural laws.

However, it should be asked whether Meyer and Dembski do justice to theistic evolutionism in their critiques. While Meyer is correct in pointing out that theistic evolutionism does not differ from atheistic evolutionism on the level of biological details, this does not mean that there are no *other* 'substantial' differences from atheistic views. For example, these theistic evolutionists agree with proponents of ID that (1) the ultimate basis of reality is personal or analogous to personal, (2) there is evidence of purpose in nature and (3) atheistic interpretations of nature can be opposed with rational arguments. These are very large differences from atheism, and bypassing these differences causes one to wonder if these ID proponents think that only scientific differences are really meaningful – a move towards scientism. Here ID's strategy of concentrating on the differences of the views seems quite far from their broader 'big tent' strategy.

Why should ID proponents even be interested in theistic evolutionism?

As I have argued throughout this study, the ID movement emphasizes the importance of empirical research in deciding what sort of natural history our world has. Because ID proponents do not believe there is good evidence for the veracity of mainstream evolutionary biology, they also do not think we should accept a theistic evolutionist view. Rather, they believe that the open investigation of the scientific evidence should naturally lead us towards the ID

---

17 Dembski 2004c.

position. So theistic evolution is also an unnecessary harmonization of theism and science. According to Dembski, 'the design theorists' critique of Darwinism begins with Darwinism's failure as an empirically adequate scientific theory, not with its supposed incompatibility with some system of religious belief'.[18] Dembski has also written that he doesn't know of 'any ID advocate who claims that Darwinian evolution entails atheism'.[19] However, in the same book Dembski himself does also critique the theological credibility of theistic evolutionism.

It seems that proponents of ID assume that it is interesting to attempt to harmonize scientific theories and religious beliefs only when the scientific theories are likely to be correct. Thus Jay Richards argues that prior to examining 'such arcane possibilities' as the compatibility of Darwinism and theism, we should first ask the prior question of whether Darwinian evolutionary theory is even true.[20] If the theory is not true, then there is no need to harmonize it with Christian belief. I think this argument is partially correct, but partially incorrect. It is true that if someone believes a scientific theory is likely to be false, then he or she will not experience a psychological need to harmonize his or her religious beliefs with that theory. This is the psychological state the ID theorists find themselves in. However, I want to claim that even proponents of ID should find such harmonizations interesting in the case of evolution for other reasons.

First (1), the question of the in principle compatibility of natural processes and belief in creation is an interesting one. If theism and Darwinism are compatible, then understanding this possibility might provide us with a better understanding of the basis of Christian belief, the nature of the doctrine of creation, and its relationship to scientific theories. Second (2), a broader use of good theological and philosophical arguments, such as those theistic evolutionists rely on, would strengthen ID's overall argument against naturalism and scientism. Third (3), the theory of evolution is currently widely believed to be true in academia, even by many who are acquainted with the ID theorists' critique of Darwinism. Theological and philosophical arguments could help these people avoid embracing atheistic metaphysical interpretations of Darwinian evolutionary biology. Even if a scientific theory is likely to be incorrect, showing its compatibility with belief in creation might still be interesting for those who are not convinced by the case against the scientific theory. Fourth (4), the acceptance of theistic evolutionism as a philosophically and theologically defensible position would help avoid the impression that theological reasons are important motivations for ID's own opposition of evolutionary biology.

As I have noted in Chapter 5, one of ID's critiques against methodological naturalism as a principle of science is based on many ID proponents' understanding of the freedom of God as Creator. Because God was free to choose natural or supernatural means of creation, we cannot tell *a priori* what God has

18 Dembski 1999a, 112.

19 Dembski 2011.

20 Richards (ed.) 2010, 302.

done. Rather, we must study nature, and cannot rule out even supernatural acts of God *a priori*. This standpoint would seem to lead to the possibility that God could also have used Darwinian evolution as a way of creation. The critiques of theistic evolutionism proponents of ID make reveal a strong theological dislike of God choosing to create through Darwinian mechanisms. Thus their ideal of openness to many different accounts of natural history does not mean that they have no theological or moral preferences for what sort of method God should have used.

The ID movement's idea that empirical evidence should define what we believe about God's interventions in natural history seems appealing. As I have discussed in the previous chapters, it seems difficult to form a convincing theological or philosophical argument ruling out the possibility of ID's position *a priori*. However, the ID theorists' defence of this principle would perhaps be more consistent if they did not at the same time also argue so strongly against the possibility of a theistic evolutionist view.

The compatibility of evolution and design?

In their critiques of theistic evolutionism that I have just analysed, proponents of ID acknowledge that it is possible for a theistic evolutionist to believe in the designedness of life from a theistic standpoint. What they are criticizing is the lack of scientific arguments that theistic evolutionists present for belief in the designedness of life. To proponents of ID, it seems that the theistic evolutionists' combination of evolution and design relies on fideistic faith, rather than evidence and reason.

Level-shifting again

There are many different approaches to the dialogue of science and religion, and one way in which theistic evolutionists could indeed affirm the designedness of life would be to just openly begin from theistic premises, and then interpret nature accordingly from that perspective. Theists can have other reasons for their beliefs than the biological design argument, even if the strategy of level-shifting does not work in the case of the biological design argument. Nevertheless, there are interesting seeds in the ID literature for a level-shifting argument in the case of biological life, as well. Such an argument would admit that insofar as organisms are designed, they are designed through an evolutionary process that often appears highly contingent and haphazard. Nevertheless, a theistic evolutionist (or ID proponent) taking the line I will suggest could still argue that something of the Creator's wisdom is visible in the amazing organized complexity of biological organisms.

Recall again the central factor separating plausible and implausible level-shifting in these examples seems to be whether the natural explanation eliminates the reason why the design hypothesis was made in the first place. Del

Ratzsch has applied the same idea to biological design with an interesting thought experiment.

Consider the possibility of an automated VCR (video cassette recorder) factory. In this case one could give a 'complete causal account of the production and physical properties of VCRs from the initial factory state. But we'd still feel that something was missing – that there was something about the factory itself, perhaps implicit in the "givens" that demanded special explanation'.[21] According to Ratzsch, this would be true even if the explanation for some order like this could be traced back to the Big Bang. Explaining the VCR's production in terms of the properties of the factory would leave something unexplained that we would still have to explain through design. If the properties of the factory itself are designed, then this designedness 'is not a simple causal irrelevance, given that without that factory's designedness the VCRs would fail both to exist and to have key physical properties they in fact have'.[22]

In this type of view the possibility of cosmic design arguments makes it possible to also argue that the biological organisms created by evolution are designed, since their order also depends on the natural laws. Nobel laureate Christian de Duve pointed out already in 1984 that in evolution, 'chance did not operate in a vacuum. It operated in a universe governed by orderly laws and made of matter endowed with specific properties. These laws and properties are the constraints that shape the evolutionary roulette and restrict the numbers that it can turn up'.[23] Several lines of argument support the general idea that the way the mechanisms of selection and mutation act is dependent on the precise background conditions of the process.[24]

Beyond usually discussed examples of fine-tuning, there appears to be a high degree of constraint on protein evolution and organismal structure. As Conway Morris argues, this is exemplified by the phenomenon of convergence: over time, similar structures have evolved multiple times. Conway Morris argues that this evidence points to 'the existence of something analogous to "attractors", by which evolutionary trajectories are channeled towards stable nodes of functionality'.[25] According to Conway Morris, it is likely that the possible biological forms, and so also the form of the tree of life, are to a large degree determined in the laws of nature.[26] It is controversial exactly how much of the course of evolution is determined. In any case, it is clear that functional biological forms must be connected in the 'fitness landscape' or 'morphological hyperspace' in a way that makes tree-like evolution possible.

21 Ratzsch 2001, 130–131.
22 Ratzsch 2001, 130–131.
23 De Duve 1984, quoted in Giberson and Artigas (2009, 32–33).
24 Alexander 2009, 11–17.
25 Conway Morris 2005, 309.
26 Conway Morris 2009, 1331.

ID's arguments turned to the service of theistic evolutionism

I come now to arguments from the ID literature. The arguments that proponents of ID make against the possibility of naturalistic evolution can also be (if they fail) understood instead as arguments about what kind of preconditions the process of evolution needs in order to work. In this way, ID's arguments can contribute to the idea that evolution is dependent on the wider teleology of the laws of nature. For example, consider Behe's argument from irreducible complexity. Recall that Behe argues is that it is implausible to think that the development of such systems is possible, since in this case the same parts would need to have functions in a vast variety of different systems, forming a chain of functional systems leading up the present ones.

Commenting on protein evolution, ID proponent Ann Gauger admits that it is possible to conceive of this kind of evolutionary landscape. She argues that because of the high functional requirements of proteins, it is implausible. But were such a landscape to exist, it would, for Gauger, be evidence of design: 'unless someone paved a highway to Mt. Whitney that went uphill every step of the way, Darwin's engine would never get out of Death Valley. But a paved highway isn't evolution, it's design'.[27] Here Gauger comes quite close to admitting the possibility of theistic evolutionism. To answer ID's critiques of evolutionary biology, critics must argue that there serendipitously exists a series of functional forms in morphological space. This series must allow for the move from functional system to functional system, so that the requirements of evolution are met. The fitness landscape must be fine-tuned in a way that allows for parts of one system to be transformed into parts of a new system. The facts of homology arguably provide evidence in favour of such pathways, since evolution from a common ancestor would explain these similarities. Granting this, we can argue that the possibility of evolution is written into the laws of nature, and evolution could not proceed otherwise.[28]

Dembski and Robert Marks argue similarly that evolutionary computer programs, which are often used to demonstrate the power of evolutionary mechanisms, actually show that evolution can only create information when the efficiency of the evolutionary search is ensured by the engineer. This is also shown by the possibility of generating algorithms which rely on mutations and selection and which do not generate any interesting results. To generate blueprints for machines or instructions for a chess computer, quite a sophisticated evolutionary program is required. So: 'In these models, careful tailoring of fitness functions that assist in locating targets is always present and clearly teleological. If these models adequately represent biological evolution, then this teleological feature of fitness ought to be preserved in nature, implying that Darwinian evolution is itself teleological'.[29] The discussion of evolutionary

27 Gauger 2013.
28 A similar argument has also been made by Masel 2014.
29 Dembski and Marks 2009, 31.

computer programs and the discussion is beyond this study,[30] but it is interesting to note that with their teleological Darwinism, Dembski and Marks come rather close to theistic evolutionism.

In their article, Dembski and Marks themselves do not mean to say that their model of teleological Darwinism is close to theistic evolutionism. Rather, they argue that theistic evolutionism means by definition belief in the teleology of evolution without any evidence.[31] I am hard pressed to find any definitions by theistic evolutionists who would equate theistic evolutionism with fideism; rather, it seems to me that many theistic evolutionists also value evidence. But in any case Dembski and Marks seem here to be agreeing with theistic evolutionists that the Darwinian process can be designed by God, and that there can even be evidence in favour of such a wider teleology. There is a tension between their arguments for the possibility of teleological evolution and the claim that belief in Darwinian evolution is in tension with believing in design.

In this kind of theistic evolutionism, the evolution of biological design is dependent on very precise properties of the laws of nature. Though no references to design are required on the level of biology as a discipline, biology nevertheless depends on the 'wider teleology' of nature, to use McGrath's term.[32] Just as the properties of Ratzsch's VCR factory are not irrelevant for explaining the properties of the VCRs, so also it seems that the properties of the laws of nature are not irrelevant to explaining the properties of biological organisms. The rationality of the factory and so the design behind this rationality is also visible in the VCRs it produces, even though no interventions into the processes of the factory were made. In the same way, the rationality of the Creator could be visible in biological organisms, even if the Creator works through natural processes.

We can express this basic point with transitive logic. Suppose that A implies B, and B implies C. By basic transitive logic, it follows that A implies C. Now let us apply this to biology. If the order of biological organisms (A) requires the rationality of the cosmos (B), and the rationality of the cosmos is evidence for the Creator (C), then the order of biological organisms is evidence for the Creator (A->C). In this way, biological organisms could still provide indirect evidence of the wisdom of their creator even in an evolutionary cosmos. Furthermore, Darwinian evolutionary biology does not undercut design discourse, but merely makes the testimony of the Creator more indirect.

ID proponents Wiker and Witt argue that we can appreciate the beauty of biological organisms better when we realize how much fine-tuning is required for this beauty to be possible.[33] It seems to me that this statement can be turned around: we can appreciate the fine-tuning required for life better when we

30 See Simon (2013) for an extensive discussion.

31 Dembski and Marks 2009, 6.

32 McGrath 2009.

33 Wiker and Witt 2006, 242–243.

look at the remarkable complexity and 'designedness' visible in organism. So, it is possible to argue that on the evolutionary view, the fine-tuning and rationality of the whole cosmos becomes clearly visible in the order of biological organisms.

Now to be clear, the universe as such is quite different from an automatic factory. The process of evolution seems to be more haphazard and less constrained by its preconditions than a factory producing just toasters, for example. In this way the discussion on Conway Morris/Gould reflects this analogy. If we take a view more in line with Conway Morris, our view of evolution is closer to a factory. However, if we view evolution as a random walk through the space of possible forms like Gould did, we will tend to view the products of this evolution as far more separate from the background conditions.[34] However, this biological design argument doesn't require any very close analogy between a factory and the universe. The basic principle is what matters: the products of some larger whole can reflect the rationality and designedness of the whole.

Furthermore, the argument here does not require that the course of evolution needs to be predetermined. Rather, it is sufficient for the argument to be able to claim that evolution requires fine-tuning, even if its actual course is highly contingent. Of course, if evolution is highly free and unconstrained, it becomes difficult to argue that the actual products of evolution are intended by God. However, in this case we can still argue that we see the wisdom of the Creator in the products of evolution. The argument will simply be that the universe has to be a pretty wonderful place in order to allow for the evolution of such creatures, and these features of the cosmos are best explained from a theistic perspective.

Under this kind of vision, theistic evolutionists can also maintain some of the good parts of Paley's vision of the cosmos, where the 'the world from thenceforth becomes a temple, and life itself one continued act of adoration. The change is no less than this, that whereas formerly God was seldom in our thoughts, we can now scarcely look upon anything without perceiving its relation to him. Every organized natural body, in the provisions which it contains for its sustentation and propagation, testified a care on the part of the Creator expressly directed to these purposes'.[35] In Paley's vision of the world, the wisdom of the Creator can be seen in everything around us.

I have now very briefly outlined one way in which it seems to me that theistic evolutionists could believe that organisms are designed, and reflect God's wisdom and glory. In that case, theistic evolutionists could still speak of organisms as icons in the temple of nature, to extend Paley's metaphor of the cosmos as a temple. However, within theistic evolutionism, this would be understood as a philosophical and theological, rather than a scientific argument in competition with the theory of biological evolution. So this is an alternative vision that

34 Gould 1989; Conway Morris 2005.

35 Paley 2008 [1802], chapter XXVII.

proponents of ID could also develop, if they find it desirable to have a fallback position that would protect belief in design, while also allowing for the success of evolutionary biology.

Evolutionism as a way of thought?

Proponents of ID do also have further reasons for believing in the incompatibility of Darwinian evolutionary biology and atheism. For example, they understand it to be a whole worldview and system of thought, rather than merely a scientific theory. As Johnson puts it, Darwinism is an 'episteme, a way of thinking about things in general'.[36] Johnson agrees that the new atheists Dawkins and Dennett have presented the philosophical implications of evolutionary biology correctly – it is a universal acid that dissolves everything else 'into shifting sand by the acid of reductionism'.[37] Thus evolution, when correctly understood, is not just a biological theory, but the starting point for understanding all of reality. Because of this, while a theistic evolutionist might have completely 'orthodox biology', he or she will still be 'missing the point of the theory' if he ignores the episteme. This type of separation between evolution as a worldview and evolution as a scientific theory is 'barely possible', but it is a continual struggle and a source of cognitive dissonance for the theistic evolutionist.[38] According to Johnson, combining the Darwinian way of thought and the naturalistic way of thought 'has a fatal logical weakness that stems from the fact that it attempts to reconcile two fundamentally inconsistent ways of thinking. Theism asserts that God rules everything; naturalism asserts that nature proceeds on its own, without supernatural influence'.[39]

Johnson is correct that many defenders of evolutionary biology also believe that the theory has far-reaching implications for our worldviews. But these arguments can be challenged, and a separation between Darwinian evolutionary theory and materialistic thought. Johnson assumes that there is no reason to accept Darwinian evolutionary theory without the philosophy, since the philosophy, not the evidence, is the main reason for believing in evolution. But for those who believe in evolution on the basis of the evidence, the philosophy does become unnecessary. For them, the dross of materialistic philosophy can be separated from the gold of scientific theory, as Peters and Hewlett put the point.[40] Theistic evolutionists can reasonable ask: why should select a particular scientific theory (such as evolution) as our starting point for interpreting all other areas of life? Could we not rather interpret evolutionary biology's meaning for our life based on what we know through other means, such as through

36 Johnson and Reynolds 2010, 49.
37 Johnson and Reynolds 2010, 55.
38 Johnson and Reynolds 2010, 53.
39 Johnson 2001, 447.
40 Peters and Hewlett 2003, 22.

our everyday experience, our philosophy, and our theology? It seems difficult to base any whole way of thought on just scientific discoveries. This would require scientism, which is itself a highly questionable philosophical idea that theistic evolutionists can criticize with full justification.

If it is possible to begin from theological premises (adopted for non-scientific reasons), this makes it possible to formulate theistic evolutionism as part of a theology of nature. For example, theistic evolutionist Robert J. Russell argues that the indeterminism of the Copenhagen interpretation of quantum physics makes it possible to interpret an apparently random process of evolution as guided by God. By directing quantum events, God could have directed evolutionary mutations without this direction being in any way visible within the natural sciences. From this theological perspective, then, indeterminism and chance in nature does not imply God's absence from the world.[41] In my view, the ID movement's rejection of scientism should lead to also taking this kind of view of theistic evolution seriously, rather than disparaging it as no different from atheistic evolutionism.

Related to the question of whether evolution is more compatible with atheism than theism, I believe the previous strategy of combining belief in design and evolution may be interesting. Even if the argument is not successful in convincing sceptics who have very different background beliefs, at least it may undercut some of the reasons for thinking that evolution logically leads to religious scepticism.

Consider Dawkins' argument that Darwinian evolution functions as a 'consciousness-raiser' which shows that teleology can be reduced to material processes, and that we should not trust our intuitions about design in nature. He argues that 'a deep understanding of Darwinism teaches us to be wary of the easy assumption that design is the only alternative to chance, and teaches us to seek out graded ramps of slowly increasing complexity. – After Darwin, we should feel, deep in our bones, suspicious of the very idea of design'.[42] Dawkins argues that since Darwinism shows that reductionistic explanations for teleology are possible, it provides grounds for the reduction of all teleology to non-intentional material causes. This is one point where Johnson agrees with Dawkins: the success of 'Darwinism' would be evidence that materialistic explanations work. Johnson even quotes the preceding Dawkinsian argument favourably.[43]

The question that I want to ask is quite fundamental: why should Darwinian evolutionary biology show that design beliefs are wrong in the case of biology? Let us accept that no references to design are required in the discipline of biology in order to explain teleological order. But what if Darwinian evolution itself depends on design, in that it depends on the wider teleology built into the

41 Russell 2008, 169.
42 Dawkins 2006, 139.
43 Johnson and Marks 2010, chapter 4.

universe? In this case it would not be accurate to say that evolution produces teleology completely without design. Rather, evolutionary mechanisms bring forth the potential that is built into the creation. Following the analogy of the VCR factory, just as the designedness of a factory is not irrelevant to explaining the products, the designedness of the universe is not irrelevant to the production of organisms. So Darwinian evolution itself cannot prove that biology does not require design, and so Dawkins' argument cannot get started. To prove his premises, Dawkins would first have to tackle cosmological arguments, and to show that the laws of nature do not require a designer. Putting biology first is a philosophical decision. Without further arguments, one might just as well put cosmology, philosophy, theology or everyday experience first.

Theistic evolutionism and the evidence

ID's emphasis on evidence

Proponents of ID generally emphasize the importance of scientific evidence for defending theistic belief in creation against naturalism. This is also important for their critique of theistic evolutionism. They do recognize the possibility that God could have directed the process of Darwinian evolution in a way that remains invisible to the natural sciences. So they recognize that there is no logically necessary connection between evolutionary biology and atheism – it is possible to be a theist and accept mainstream evolutionary biology. However, proponents of ID believe that this greatly weakens the cultural credibility of theism, since in this situation theists will lack the necessary evidence to properly defend belief in creation.[44]

For example, Johnson argues that the Darwinian way of thought rules out an evidence-based belief in creation, but still leaves room for religion which is chosen for subjective reasons.[45] Evolution does leave room for a faraway first cause, a deistic God. However, it doesn't leave room for a God who makes a difference in the natural world and whose existence can be seen from his works: 'If God stayed in that realm beyond the reach of scientific investigation, and allowed an apparently blind materialistic evolutionary process to do all the work of creation, then it would have to be said that God furnished us with a world of excuses for unbelief and idolatry'.[46] According to Johnson, the biblical passages on natural revelation (such as Romans 1:20) show that in the Christian view, nature must point 'directly and unmistakably' toward the necessity of a Creator. Accepting Darwinian evolutionary theory would mean that natural revelation in biology can no longer be said to be 'direct and unmistakable'. Biologically created things can no longer be said to reveal a Creator, and a crucial

44 Wiker 2002; West 2007, chapter 10.
45 Johnson 1993a, 155–157.
46 Johnson 2001, 443.

piece of evidence for ID has been lost. For Johnson, this makes Darwinian evolution theologically problematic.[47]

Similarly, Dembski writes that 'within theistic evolution, God is a master of stealth who constantly eludes our best efforts to detect him empirically. Yes, the theistic evolutionist believes that the universe is designed. Yet insofar as there is design in the universe, it is design we recognize strictly through the eyes of faith. Accordingly the physical world in itself provides no evidence that life is designed. For all we can tell, our appearance on planet Earth is an accident'.[48] In this quote, Dembski places a great emphasis on the importance of scientific evidence for design instead of philosophical and religious evidence. The unfortunate, unintended implication of this seems to be that philosophical and religious reasons are not valuable at all in deciding whether the cosmos is purposefully created. It may be that Dembski has not chosen his words carefully, since surely he is aware of natural theology that does not depend on ID. But the quote is nevertheless indicative of a common emphasis in the ID literature.

Dembski also argues that ID is theologically valuable, because it provides evidence against a theory which is indispensable for atheists. For him, claiming that evolution implies atheism is 'logically unsound', but it is not unsound to claim that 'atheism implies evolution'. According to Dembski, atheists require some sort of natural explanation for the design-like complexity of the biological world in order to be intellectually fulfilled atheists. Without evolution, atheists would have to deal with a problematic amount of evidence for the existence of an intelligent designer, giving support to belief in God. Without evolution, atheists would also lack the possibility of justifying their Darwinian metaphysics in a scientific-sounding way. By accepting Darwinian evolutionary theory, theistic evolutionists are thus not using a potent weapon against Darwinism. For Dembski, evolution is a weapon which atheists are using to attack believers. He argues that ID breaks the weapon, while theistic evolutionism provides an ineffectual defence, because it leaves the weapon intact.[49]

Intelligent design and scientism

The need to rethink ID's critiques of theistic evolution is perhaps most evident in the tensions that exist between this critique and the ID movement's broader thought. First, the insistence on the importance of scientific evidence is in tension with the ID proponent's own reliance on non-scientific rationality. Second, the insistence on scientific evidence is also in tension with the movement's goal of criticizing scientism and defending religious rationality.

The first tension springs from the fact that the ID theorists recognize the existence of many other reasons for believing in God besides biological design

47 Johnson 1993b.

48 Dembski 1999a, 110.

49 Dembski and Witt 2008; Dembski 2010; influenced by Dawkins (1991).

arguments. However, if such broad reasons are available to the ID proponents, they should also be available to theistic evolutionists. ID proponents themselves do not believe that their own arguments prove the existence of God or the Christian doctrine on creation. God as 'being, consciousness and bliss' is far more than just an intelligent designer, and the doctrine of creation is also about the radical metaphysical dependence on all that exists on God as the 'ground of being' or 'being itself', not just about God as a the orderer of nature. Since ID proponents nevertheless believe (on theological and philosophical grounds) that the designer is God, and believe in the doctrine of creation, this means that they must acknowledge the validity of non-scientific reasons for belief despite their insistence on the necessity of scientific evidence.

The ID movement should even acknowledge the rationality of purely intuitive and philosophical belief in a designer of the cosmos. As I argued in Chapter 7, the ID movement sees the design argument as a defence of an ancient design intuition. However, if humans have found out the truth intuitively or even through philosophical design arguments before the advent of modern science, then this implies that true beliefs in the existence of the designer can arise without science. Since it would be incredible for these beliefs to be correct if they had been formed randomly, ID must also recognize these non-scientific methods and cognitive mechanisms to be reliable. It could of course be that this natural perception of design requires a further elaboration and defence to remain credible in our contemporary situation. However, it requires further arguments from the ID theorists to show that this defence has to be scientific rather than philosophical. Because of the great theological depth of the doctrine of creation, it seems more credible to think that philosophical and theological defences of this idea are more important than scientific ones.

As seen in Chapter 3, the ID theorists also recognize the possibility of cosmic design arguments, and it is difficult to see why just a naturalistic theory of biological origins would make these impossible in principle. On the ID theorists' understanding it is possible to see that the removal of the biological design argument would weaken the case for design, since it removes one level of design arguments. It also makes it difficult to argue that gaps in the abilities of known natural processes increase the plausibility of the biological design inference. However, it could be argued that more cosmic fine-tuning is required for Darwinian evolution than no Darwinian evolution, and thus the fine-tuning argument arguably becomes stronger as the gaps-based arguments diminish in power. Thus it seems that the wholesale rejection of evidence for design requires more than just a naturalistic theory of biological origins can provide.

Sometimes this is recognized in the ID literature. For example, Wiker and Witt argue that the cosmic evidence of design is 'Darwin-proof', meaning that a theory of biological evolution cannot refute it.[50] Even Johnson, who believes that the logic behind Darwinian evolutionary theory also leads to the rejection

50 Wiker and Witt 2006, 238.

of cosmic design arguments, sees broad reasons for opposing naturalism: 'reality is simply too rational and beautiful ever to be forced into the narrow categories that materialism can comprehend'.[51] The rationality and beauty of reality in its harmonious natural laws, the possibility of science, the fine-tuning of the universe, the complexity of biological organisms and even the glimpses of something greater in the arts and religious experience all speak of the reality of the 'intelligent designer' for proponents of ID.[52]

Unfortunately this kind of broad view of the issues tends to disappear when proponents of ID dialogue with theistic evolutionists. Applied consistently, this all should demonstrate to proponents of ID that there can be a great difference between theistic evolutionism and atheistic evolutionism. Theists do not necessarily have to present scientific reasons for belief; rather, theological and philosophical reasons are also important and valuable. There are many theistic evolutionists who have developed robust natural theologies and theologies of nature, which the ID movement has not interacted with in detail.

The second tension is between the ID movement's emphasis of the importance of scientific evidence and its goal of defending religious rationality and critiquing scientism. Cunningham has argued that ID's project presupposes scientism just as the new atheism does.[53] However, I find that insofar as ID comes close to scientism in its critique of theistic evolutionism, this is actually in tension with the movement's broader ideas. The ultimate theological purpose of the ID movement is to refute materialistic scientism, not to affirm it. Thus Dembski identifies scientific evidence for ID as the 'bridge between science and theology',[54] presupposing that Christian theology is a rational enterprise. Johnson has termed the ID movement a 'wedge' which can destroy the pretensions of scientific materialism and open up room for a broader conception of rationality which includes religion and theology.[55]

Johnson's opposition to scientism is sometimes so clear that Pennock actually identifies critiques his views as an example of the postmodernistic critique of science.[56] Johnson argues that if room is made for a designer within science, then the possibility of rationality outside of science also becomes credible. But this seems odd. If there is rationality outside of science, then why the insistence that belief in creation absolutely must have scientific support? Why not criticize scientism also on philosophical grounds? The ID movement plainly accepts the ideas that (1) the case for design is broader than biology, and (2) it can be rational to believe something even based on non-scientific reasons. Applied consistently, these principles would seem to lend themselves also to the justification of a theistic view of evolution.

51 Johnson 2000, 152.
52 See Moreland, ed. (1994), as well as Dembski and Licona, eds (2010) for such discussion.
53 Cunningham 2010, 278.
54 Dembski 1999a.
55 Johnson 2000.
56 Pennock 2010.

Rejecting the temptation of scientism

The ID theorists themselves insist that ID is not a form of scientism. Thus Richards explains the emphasis on scientific reasons as partly a strategic choice: science has immense cultural authority and far greater public credibility than religion or philosophy.[57] Dembski explains that the emphasis is because science is the 'only universally valid form of knowledge in our culture'.[58] And so, to be universally appealing, ID proponents attempt to oppose the atheistic use of science by scientific arguments, rather than philosophical and theological arguments. In challenging the scientific theory of Darwinian evolution, they want to say that their alternative is also scientific so as to present it as a rational and objective, rather than a pseudoscientific view. Their insistence on the necessity of science in influencing popular culture does not mean that they themselves accept science as the only habitat of rationality.

It seems clear to me that proponents of ID do accept the existence of rationality outside of science. However, in ID's critique of theistic evolutionism, this emphasis on the necessity of scientific reasons does not appear merely a strategic choice but takes on larger significance. For example, in the critiques against Lamoureux and Conway Morris, proponents of ID argue that the views of theistic evolutionists differ only superficially from naturalistic evolutionism, because the science is the same. It is as if other differences are meaningless. The philosophical and theological reasons theistic evolutionists present in defence of their position are dismissed as unconvincing and unimportant, and are rarely even interacted with. At this point, the ID proponent's arguments give the impression that the movement itself values scientific reasons far above religious and philosophical ones just as our broader culture does. Here the fears of critics like Cunningham seem to be confirmed.

There is a danger in this insistence on primarily scientific reasons in defence of religious belief. From a Christian perspective, the supposition that religious and philosophical reasons for belief have little value is surely a large problem in our culture to be confronted, rather than a reality that needs to be accepted for strategic reasons. Because of the implicit devaluing of philosophical and religious reasons in the critique of theistic evolutionism, the ID movement does seem to be flirting with scientism in this critique. But making science the primary arbiter of religious truths is theologically problematic, because (1) most Christian doctrines cannot be demonstrated within the narrow confines of what scientism counts as rational, (2) religious rationality is in actual practice based on much broader grounds and (3) the doctrines of God and creation are about much more than just design, as the ID movement itself acknowledges. Thus accepting scientism as the criterion of rationality would make typical Christian religious beliefs irrational. Because at least most ID proponents want

57 Richards (ed.) 2010, 260–270.

58 Dembski 1998c, 26–27.

to defend traditional religious beliefs, they should emphasize the existence of good philosophical and religious reasons for belief in design and creation, rather than insisting that theistic evolutionists and other religious believers must provide scientific evidence before their views can be substantially different from those of atheistic evolutionists.

Dembski's argument that ID is required to counter the atheists' use of evolutionary science as an argument against religious belief is problematic for related reasons. Both the ID proponents and theistic evolutionists recognize that the 'Darwinism' used as a weapon for atheism is not just a scientific theory but also a metaphysical worldview. But if this is true, then the weapon also has a philosophical component, and is not composed just of science. It follows that philosophical arguments can and must be used to dismantle the weapon. Again, powerful philosophical arguments against materialistic scientism indeed exist, so it is difficult to see why the ID theorists seem in many comments to see ID as the only durable answer to this use of Darwinism.

Theistic evolutionism does not need to be fideism, though it can also be fideism. The tradition of natural theology formulates a much broader idea of divine general revelation and evidence than ID. For example, whereas Johnson relates passages like Romans 1:20 primarily to the biological design argument, the text itself is actually quite ambiguous about the precise way God's power and wisdom are manifested. Biological and cosmic design arguments are not mentioned. Paul's text is closely following the apocryphal *Book of Wisdom* 13: 1–9, which has very general things to say:

> But all men are vain, in whom there is not the knowledge of God: and who by these good things that are seen, could not understand him that is, neither by attending to the works have acknowledged who was the workman: But have imagined either the fire, or the wind, or the swift air, or the circle of the stars, or the great water, or the Sun and Moon, to be the gods that rule the world. With whose beauty, if they, being delighted, took them to be gods: let them know how much the Lord of them is more beautiful than they: for the first author of beauty made all those things.

Many theistic evolutionists also retain this broad sense that nature points to God, expressed either in the terms of a natural theology, or in a theology of nature. Dialogue with the tradition of natural theology could help proponents of ID broaden their vision of natural revelation to include phenomena like beauty and existence itself.[59] Also, this dialogue could help proponents of ID to more clearly recognize that theistic evolutionists also typically see divine design in the order of the universe, but only claim that this is a philosophical and theological, rather than a scientific view.

59 Roberts 2003.

The temptation of scientism need not be fatal to the ID movement, because the movement's design argument does not presume scientism in any of its premises. So, the ID movement could abandon its critique of theistic evolutionism in general and turn away from the temptation of scientism without abandoning any part of the design arguments that are at the core of the movement's thought. The movement could also continue to insist that scientific evidence in support of belief in creation is valuable, and simultaneously acknowledge that belief in creation does not depend on the failure of Darwinism or the existence of scientific arguments in its favour. Giving up the critiques of theistic evolutionism analysed in this chapter also will not mean that the ID theorists will have to give up all of their critique of individual arguments for theistic evolutionism, or that the movement could not fall back on traditional biblical critiques of evolutionary theory, such as the insistence on the importance of a historical Adam and a historical Fall (which many theistic evolutionists, though not all, reject).[60]

Rather, rejecting the temptation of scientism would be in line with the ID movement's own broader argumentation, as well as its broader goals. Accepting theistic evolutionism as a rational position, and recognizing it as an ally against atheistic interpretations of evolution would also be in line with ID's 'big tent' strategy and its emphasis on the importance of an open evaluation of scientific evidence. Adopting the broader argument against scientism would lead to a more theologically and philosophically robust ID movement and would help answer the suspicion of many critics that religious and moral concerns about evolution influence the ID theorists' evaluation of the empirical evidence too much. Furthermore, ID's recognition of the rationality of other positions in this way could lead to a less polemical overall atmosphere of discussion.

Summary

It seems to me that while the theological rejection of theistic evolutionism is important for many proponents of ID, the arguments against theistic evolutionism are rarely developed very far in the ID literature. Proponents of ID are much more concerned with criticizing naturalistic understandings of evolution, and are puzzled why all theists have not joined in.

Ultimately much of ID's critique of theistic evolutionism is problematic and is in tension with the movement's broader ideas. While the ID movement admits the possibility that God could have created life through some sort of evolutionary process, it also understands Darwinian evolution as a worldview that is by definition atheistic. Here it seems to me that they do not adequately respond to arguments for separating between Darwinian evolutionary biology as a scientific discipline and Darwinism as a worldview. ID's critique of theistic evolutionism even comes close to scientism, because it assumes that theistic

60 For discussion, see Caneday, Barrett and Gundry, eds (2013).

evolutionism should differ from the Darwinian worldview on the level of science before it can differ in any meaningful way. Nevertheless, there are also grounds within ID itself for believing that belief in design and belief in evolution can be rationally combined.

Proponents of ID would do well to more clearly emphasize the value of philosophical and theological arguments in the discussion about theistic evolution. Furthermore, as implied by their argument from divine freedom, God could have used the process of Darwinian evolution in creating life, and it is up to empirical science to find out what happened. The admission of the possibility of the empirical and theological possibility of theistic evolutionism would help create a theologically more secure basis for ID and help quell the suspicion that ID is strongly driven by theologically motivated scepticism of evolution.

Afterword

Towards better discussion of Intelligent Design

In my analysis of the cognitive terrain of the discussion on ID, I have gone through a large amount of material to identify the core of the ID movement's argumentation and how ID relates to and differs from naturalism and theistic evolutionism. I have discovered that when one scratches the surface of the debate over science, fundamental philosophical and theological disagreements are revealed. This study has touched on issues like the relationship of rational everyday beliefs and scientific inquiry, the definition of science, the qualities of good explanations, the problems of good and evil, the fundamental nature of reality, what are theologically credible understandings of divine action and so on. Such issues are significant motivations not only for proponents of ID but also for many of ID's critics. I do not mean to argue that such philosophical and theological reasons are not valuable, quite the opposite. I have argued that these philosophical and theological differences should be openly acknowledged and discussed.

My primary aim with this study has been to build understanding across different positions, but in the course of the study, I have also discovered tensions and problems in many arguments. Many of these problems are not beyond remedy, however. Accordingly, I want to close the study by summarizing some ideas that I believe will benefit proponents and critics of ID. I will mention only some general ideas; the previous chapters also contain much discussion about how to best formulate, defend and criticize design arguments.

Ideas for proponents of ID

The design argument should be integrated into a broader worldview

Intelligent Design has sought to present a minimalistic argument for design while avoiding getting deeply into the complex philosophical and theological work of integrating this argument to a broader worldview. I am not opposed to books and articles focusing just on forms of the design argument. In academic discussion, it is often valuable to focus on developing just one argument and to analyse its evidential force as closely as possible. But at some point we do also need to ask how the design argument relates to other ideas in order to evaluate the overall plausibility of design. Thinkers of the ID movement have their own ideas about this, and some have written about the matter. But largely readers of ID literature are still left to connect the philosophical and theological dots themselves.

It seems to me that properly defending even the design argument would require attending to debate over worldviews. Proponents of ID themselves acknowledge that philosophical and theological differences have a large impact on how credible design argument seem to be, and my analysis of the design argument's logic support this understanding. However, while many proponents of ID do present ID as part of such a broader worldview, the reader usually gains only glimpses of it, since ID proponents develop the design argument in isolation from theology and philosophy in an effort to be scientifically neutral. Nevertheless, in my judgment combining ID into a more robust theology of nature would help strengthen the argument.

Resources from the discussion over natural theology and the discussion over the relationship of theology and the natural sciences could also help make ID's design arguments more robust. Dialogue with these traditions would lead to acknowledging that design arguments are just one among several theistic arguments and reasons for belief. This in turn might help proponents of ID realize that theistic evolutionists also do not need to be fideists, but they can believe that the Creator does reveal himself in some indirect way in nature.

Be careful not to undervalue philosophical and theological reasons

Proponents of ID have argued that the design argument should be regarded as a scientific argument. One of ID's core arguments for this inclusive definition of science is simply that science should be a search for truth, and so any good argument beginning from empirical premises should be considered scientific.

Whether ID could be a science depends on our definition of science. The definition of science is a complex philosophical matter, and it has proven difficult to find strict demarcation criteria for excluding ID's claim. I myself would gladly use a broad definition of science, which would also qualify philosophy, theology and the humanities as sciences. But if such a broad definition is not adopted, then whether ID is science or not is really beside the point. Certainly there are many good empirical arguments which are nevertheless not part of the natural sciences but are rather more properly the domain of disciplines like psychology or history. Even if ID is simply a philosophical or theological argument, its premises and evidence should still be examined and found convincing. Accordingly, I suggest that proponents of ID should incorporate the critique of epistemic scientism into their programme, just as they have criticized moral and ontological scientism.

The critique of scientism also has implications for ID's critique against theistic evolutionism. Proponents of ID find it worrisome that theistic evolutionists do not necessarily differ from atheistic evolutionists on the level of scientific theory. Sometimes these critiques make it seem as if only scientific differences would matter. Here ID's rhetorical strategy grants scientism too much ground, however, and this plays against the movement's broad cultural goals. When considered more broadly, ID's argumentation assumes that theological and philosophical differences and reasons are also important, and I have suggested that proponents of ID should consistently apply this also to their dialogue with theistic evolutionists. Once scientism is rejected, the separation theistic evolutionists make between evolution as a scientific theory and atheistic evolutionism as a worldview will hopefully become more credible also to proponents of ID.

If proponents of ID can accept the in principle possibility of theistic evolutionism, and the idea that the rationality of religious belief does not depend on the success of the biological design argument, then it will be easier for ID to avoid the charge that it is just a God of the gaps argument. This would also be more in line with ID's original vision of a 'big tent' uniting, rather than dividing opponents of naturalism. Overall I would like to see proponents of ID interact more with how theistic evolution is developed on the scholarly level, as well as with literature on natural theology.

Ideas for critics of ID

There is no 'silver bullet' to stop ID: criticisms should be more modest

I see nothing wrong in principle in using theological and philosophical arguments against ID. The following are commonly used examples of such arguments: 'ID is not science, so it is not worthy of consideration', 'ID is a God of the gaps-argument', 'appeals to design cannot be explanatory unless the designer is identified', 'a good designer would never create such an imperfect world' and so on.

However, I suggest the strength of these kinds of principles is often overstated and they need to be reformulated. In each case it is possible to formulate a different theological and philosophical position that would allow for something like ID's design arguments to be quite rational. For example, it is indeed possible to argue that the natural sciences should be methodologically naturalistic. But unless we assume that only things that can be studied by the natural sciences exist (which would be scientism), then it is possible for some argument to be rational, even if it is outside the natural sciences. This means that merely classifying ID as a non-scientific argument is not enough to refute it. Rather, we must criticize ID's logic and understanding of the evidence. It is not that no good critiques of ID do not exist. Throughout this study, I have attempted to show what lines of argument I believe are best for critics. But there are also many bad critiques of ID, based on criteria that prejudge the issue too heavily against ID, and that are too vulnerable to objections.

Theologically, it may be argued that ID does not capture the whole breadth of the doctrine of creation, but on the other hand it is not meant to. Claims that ID is heretical overstate the case against ID, and are too unaccepting of the diversity within the Christian tradition. It seems possible to conceive a world in which questions like the origin of life are indeed the proper limit of natural explanations. The idea that science could have limits is not strange to theistic evolutionists: for example, the explanation of cosmic fine-tuning and the rationality of the cosmos are often believed to be properly beyond the capacity of the natural sciences to explain. It is theologically possible that God could have created the world in a way that does not respect the traditional division of tasks between theology and the natural sciences. Claims about the limits of the natural sciences should be based on our experience of what kinds of question science is good at solving.

In the theology and science community, it is broadly accepted that God's creative acts are free and we need empirical research to find out what sort of world God did create. Applying this thinking to the question of ID means that theistic evolutionists should primarily also use the empirical evidence against ID, rather than depending too heavily on theological arguments. Of course, theological arguments can continue to be used to show why theological explanations are more at home in the level of metaphysics, rather than the natural sciences. Theological arguments can also continue to be used to show the compatibility of evolution and creation, and to point out tensions in ID's theological argumentation. Accepting that consonance between theology and the natural sciences is in principle possible, and even accepting that evidence can be relevant for many kinds of religious faith, one can still attempt to argue that ID seeks for this consonance in a problematic way.

Theistic evolutionists can defend the compatibility of design and evolution

The mainstream of the scientific community agrees that evolution has happened, though there continues to be much significant disagreement of the particulars. For laypersons, the testimony of experts is indeed usually a good reason to believe in scientific theories. But in the case of evolution, this is made more difficult by the fact that evolution is often presented as an idea that conflicts with theological and intuitive belief in the createdness and designedness of life. We can be reticent to accept the testimony of experts when that testimony goes against things that seem obvious to our experience and to our own community. In such cases, we can be inclined to think that the experts are not really experts at all.

Being clearer about the difference between scientific theories and their philosophical interpretations may help offset such suspicions. While many, particularly in the new atheist movement, argue that science and evolutionary biology naturally tend to support atheism, theistic evolutionists have presented good arguments for believing that the science can be separated from such metaphysical conclusions. Rather, it can be argued that the overall wider teleology of nature still makes good sense in the theistic perspective. Realizing that this kind of broad belief in creation is possible also as an evolutionist may help make scientists' testimony about science more easily acceptable.

Making the case against ID in a more humble manner, as I mentioned previously, would also increase the credibility of testimony about evolution to laypersons. Critics of ID are suspicious that proponents of ID are distorting the science because of their theological and philosophical motivations. Making the theological and philosophical case against ID in such strong terms can similarly cause those who are on the fence to mistrust the evolutionists, and to lend credibility to ID's argument that belief in evolution is not primarily motivated by science. Sometimes critiques of ID are much too simplistic, relying on ideas like the lack of difference between micro- and macroevolution, or on too simplistic ideas about what science is. This can in the end also create a lack of trust in readers who get more familiar with the academic discussion that is actually going on about these topics.

I have certainly also met quite a few polemical writings while reading theology and philosophy of religion. However, I have also met many people who can have profound respect for the arguments and people on the other side of some hotly debated issue, like the existence of God or the fundamental natural of reality. Neither theists nor atheists have to assume that the other side is completely irrational in their argumentation; rather, a level of mutual respect is possible even despite our disagreements. I believe the discussion over ID would also benefit from more emphasis on attempting to find areas of agreement and acknowledging the good points made by the other side.

I began this study be referring to the widespread intuition that the order of nature somehow testifies of the existence, power and wisdom of a Creator. The useful arrangements, rational ordering and beauty of nature can be understood as a 'problem of natural good' for naturalistic atheism. If there is no Creator, then why is there so much good in the world? The ID movement provides its own defence of the design argument, but this broad idea of the problem of good has historically far deeper roots, and can also be embraced by theistic evolutionists. Here there is room for further theological work to incorporate the idea of design in nature and 'the problem of natural good' into a proper theology of nature, taking into account the theological and philosophical problems identified in this study. This type of a theology of nature would argue that the order of nature has properties that help make talk of a Creator intelligible, just as the question 'Why is there something rather than nothing?' is often conceived to do.

Bibliography

Adamson, Donald 1995 *Blaise Pascal: Mathematician, Physicist and Thinker About God*. New York, NY: St Martin.

Alberts, Bruce 1998 'The Cell as a Collection Overview of Protein Machines: Preparing the Next Generation of Molecular Biologists'. *Cell*.Vol. 92. 291–294.

Alexander, Denis 2008 *Creation or Evolution: Do We Have to Choose?* Toronto, ON: Monarch Books.

——— 2009 'Evolution, Intelligent and Designed'. *Intelligent Faith: A Celebration of 150 Years of Darwinian Evolution*. Eds John Quenby and John MacDonald Smith. Winchester, UK: O Books. 7–22.

Alston, William 1989 *Divine Nature and Human Language: Essays in Philosophical Theology*. Ithaca, NY: Cornell University Press.

——— 1991 *Perceiving God: The Epistemology of Religious Experience*. Ithaca, NY: Cornell University Press.

——— 1994 'Divine Action: Shadow or Substance?' *The God Who Acts: Philosophical and Theological Explorations*. Ed. Thomas F. Tracy. University Park, PA: Pennsylvania University Press. 41–62.

——— 2005 'Two Cheers for Mystery'. *God and the Ethics of Belief: New Essays in the Philosophy of Religion*. Eds Andrew Dole Andrew and Andrew Chignell. Cambridge, UK: Cambridge University Press.

Ariew, Andre 2002 'Platonic and Aristotelian Roots of Teleological Arguments'. *Functions: New Essays in the Philosophy of Psychology and Biology*. Eds Andre Ariew, Robert Cummins and Mark Perlman. New York, NY: Oxford University Press. 7–32.

Axe, Douglas 2004 'Estimating the Prevalence of Protein Sequences Adopting Functional Enzyme Folds'. *Journal of Molecular Biology*. Vol. 341. No. 5. 1295–1315.

——— 2010a 'The Case Against a Darwinian Origin of Protein Folds'. *BIO-Complexity*. Vol. 1. No. 1.

——— 2010b 'The Limits of Complex Adaptation: An Analysis Based on a Simple Model of Structured Bacterial Populations'. *BIO-Complexity*. Vol. 1. No. 4.

——— 2011 'Correcting Four Misconceptions about my 2004 Article in JMB'. Biologic Institute Website. Available at <http://www.biologicinstitute.org>. Accessed on 20 May 2014.

——— 2012 'Darwin's Little Engine That Couldn't'. *Science and Human Origins*. Eds Ann Gauger, Douglas Axe and Casey Luskin. Seattle, WA: Discovery Institute Press. 31–43.

Ayala, Francisco 2006 *Darwin and Intelligent Design*. Minneapolis, MN: Fortress Press.

——— 2007 *Darwin's Gift to Science and Religion*. Washington, DC: Joseph Henry Press.

——— 2008 'Darwin's Gift to Science and Religion: Commentaries and Responses'. *Theology and Science.* Vol. 6. No. 2. 179–196.

Banner, Michael C. 1990 *The Justification of Science and the Rationality of Religious Belief.* Oxford, UK : Oxford University Press.

Barbour, Ian 1997 *Religion and Science: Historical and Contemporary Issues*. San Francisco, CA: HarperOne.

Barham, James 2012 'William Dembski Interview'. *The Best Schools Blog.* Available at <http://www.thebestschools.org/blog/2012/01/14/william-dembski-interview/>. Accessed on 20 May 2014.

Barr, James 1994 *Biblical Faith and Natural Theology.* The Gifford Lectures for 1991: Delivered in the University of Edinburgh. New York, NY: Oxford University Press.

Barrett, Justin 2004 *Why Would Anyone Believe in God?* Lanham, ML: Altamira Press.

Barrow, John D 2002 *The Constants of Nature: The Numbers that Encode the Secrets of the Universe.* New York, NY: Random House.

Barrow, John D. and Tipler, Frank 1986 *The Anthropic Cosmological Principle.* Oxford, UK: Oxford University Press.

Barrow, John D., Conway Morris, Simon, Freeland, Stephen and Harper, Charles (Eds) 2008 *Fitness of the Cosmos for Life: Biochemistry and Fine-Tuning.* Cambridge, UK: Cambridge University Press.

Beckwith, Francis J. 2003 *Law, Darwinism and Public Education: The Establishment Clause and the Challenge of Intelligent Design.* New York, NY: Rowman & Littlefield.

Behe, Michael 1997a 'Michael Behe's Response to Boston Review Critics'. *Discovery Institute.* Available at <http://www.discovery.org/csc/>. Accessed on 20 May 2014.

——— 1997b 'The Sterility of Darwinism'. *Boston Review.* February/March.

——— 1998 'Tulips and Dandelions & A Response to Rebecca Fliestra'. *Books & Culture: A Christianity Today Review.* September/October.

——— 1999a 'Review. God After Darwin: A Theology of Evolution'. *Metaviews.* December 4.

——— 1999b 'Comments on Denis Lamoureux's Essays'. *Darwinism Defeated? The Johnson-Lamoureux Debate on Biological Origins.* Eds Phillip Johnson and Denis Lamoureux. Vancouver, BC: Regent College Publishing. 103–108.

——— 2000a 'Intelligent Design is Not Creationism: Response to "Not (Just) in Kansas Anymore"' by Eugenie C. Scott, Science (May 2000)'. *Science Online.* July 7.

——— 2000b 'Philosophical Objections to Intelligent Design: Response to Critics'. *Discovery Institute.* July 31. Available at <http://www.discovery.org/ csc/>. Accessed on May 20, 2014.

——— 2000g 'Correspondence with Science Journals: Response to Critics Concerning Peer Review'. *Discovery Institute.* August 2. Available at <http://www.discovery.org/csc/>. Accessed on 20 May 2014.

——— 2001a 'Reply to My Critics: A Response to Reviews of Darwin's Black Box: The Biochemical Challenge to Evolution'. *Biology & Philosophy.* Vol. 16. No. 5. 685–709.

——— 2001b 'Molecular Machines: Experimental Support for the Design Inference'. *Intelligent Design Creationism and Its Critics: Philosophical, Theological and Scientific Perspectives.* Ed. Robert Pennock. Cambridge, MA: The MIT Press. 241–256.

——— 2003 'Design in the Details: The Origin of Biomolecular Machines'. *Darwinism, Design & Public Education.* Eds J.A. Campbell and S.C. Meyer. Lansing, MI: Michigan State University Press. 287–302.

——— 2004a 'Irreducible Complexity: Obstacle to Darwinian Evolution'. *Debating Design: From Darwin to DNA.* Eds W.A. Dembski and M. Ruse. Cambridge: Cambridge University Press. 352–370.

——— 2004b 'Simulating Evolution by Gene Duplication of Protein Features that Require Multiple Amino Acid Residues'. *Protein Science*.Vol. 13. 2651–2664.

——— 2006a *Darwin's Black Box. 10th Anniversary edition*. New York, NY: The Free Press.

——— 2006b 'From Muttering to Mayhem: How Phillip Johnson Got Me Moving'. *Darwin's Nemesis: Phillip Johnson and the Intelligent Design Movement*. Ed. William A. Dembski. Downer's Grove, IL: InterVarsity Press.

——— 2006c 'Whether Intelligent Design is Science: A Response to the Opinion of the Court in Kitzmiller v Dover Area School District'. *Discovery Institute*. February 3. Available at <http://www.discovery.org/csc/>. Accessed on 24 January 2014.

——— 2007a *The Edge of Evolution: The Search for the Limits of Darwinism*. New York, NY: The Free Press.

——— 2007b 'Responses to Reviews of the Edge of Evolution'. *Michael Behe's Blog*. 24 June–16 July. Available at <http://behe.uncommondescent.com/>. Accessed on 20 May 2014.

——— 2007c 'Kenneth R. Miller and the Problem of Evil'. *Michael Behe's Blog*. 24 October–26 October. Available at <http://behe.uncommondescent.com/>. Accessed on 20 May 2014.

——— 2009 'Waiting Longer for Two Mutations'. *Genetics*.Vol. 181. 819–820.

——— 2010 'Experimental Evolution, Loss-of-Function Mutations, and "The First Rule of Adaptive Evolution"'. *The Quarterly Review of Biology*.Vol. 85. No. 4. 419–45.

Bergmann, Michael 2009 'Skeptical Theism and the Problem of Evil'. *The Oxford Handbook of Philosophical Theology*. Eds Thomas P. Flint and Michael C. Rea. Oxford: Oxford University Press. 374–399.

Berlinski, David 2009 *The Devil's Delusion: Atheism and its Scientific Pretensions*. London: Basic Books.

Berlinski, David and Klinghoffer, David 2010 *The Deniable Darwin and Other Essays*. Seattle, WA: Discovery Institute Press.

Bird, Alexander 2005 'Abductive Knowledge and Holmesian Inference'. *Oxford Studies in Epistemology*. Eds Tamar Szabo Gendler and John Hawthorne. Oxford: Oxford University Press. 1–31.

——— 2007 'Inference to the Only Explanation'. *Philosophy and Phenomenological Research*. Vol. 74. 424–432.

——— 2010 'Eliminative Abduction – Examples from Medicine'. *Studies in History and Philosophy of Science*.Vol. 41. 345–352.

Bishop, Robert 2013 'God and Methodological Naturalism in the Scientific Revolution and Beyond'. *Perspectives on Science and Christian Faith*.Vol. 65. No. 1. 10–23.

Boethius, Anicius Manlius Severinus 1973 [524] *The Consolation of Philosophy*. Cambridge, MA: Harvard University Press.

Bonhoeffer, Dietrich 1997 *Letters and Papers from Prison. New Greatly Enlarged Edition*. New York, NY: Touchstone.

Boudry, Maarten, Blancke, Stefaan and Braeckman, Johan 2012 'Grist to the Mill of Anti-Evolutionism: The Failed Strategy of Ruling the Supernatural Out of Science by Philosophical Fiat'. *Science & Education*.Vol. 21. 1151–1165.

Bowler, Peter J. 2009 *Evolution: The History of an Idea. 25th Anniversary Edition*. Berkeley, CA: University of California Press.

Boyd, Gregory A. 2001 *Satan and the Problem of Evil: Constructing a Trinitarian Warfare Theodicy*. Downers Grove, IL: IVP Academic.

Bridges, J.T. 2012 *An Analysis of the Neo-Darwinism/Intelligent Design Debate Based on an Eclectic Philosophy of Science Grounded in Thomistic Realism*. Doctoral Dissertation for the Southern Evangelical Seminary.

Brockman, John (Ed.) 2006 *Intelligent Thought: Science Versus the Intelligent Design Movement.* New York, NY: Vintage Books.

Brooke, John Hedley 1991 *Science and Religion: Some Historical Perspectives*. Cambridge: Cambridge University Press.

——— 2002 'Natural Theology'. *Science and Religion: a Historical Introduction.* Ed. Gary Ferngren. Baltimore, MA: The John Hopkins University Press.

——— 2010 'Learning from the Past'. *God, Humanity and the Cosmos. Second Edition, Revised and Expanded as a Companion to the Science – Religion Debate.* Ed. Christopher Southgate. London: T & T Clark International. 63–81.

Brown, James Robert and Fehige, Yiftach 2011 'Thought Experiments'. *The Stanford Encyclopedia of Philosophy* (Fall 2011 Edition). Ed. Edward N. Zalta. Available at <http://plato.stanford.edu/archives/fall2011/entries/thought-experiment/>.

Brunner, Emil and Barth, Karl 2002[1934] *Natural Theology: Comprising "Nature and Grace" by Professor Emil Brunner and the Reply "Nein" by Dr. Karl Barth.* Eugene, OR: Wipf & Stock Publishers.

Bube, Richard H. 1971 'Man Come of Age: Bonhoeffer's Response To The God-Of-The-Gaps'. *Journal of the Evangelical Theological Society.* Vol. 14. No. 3. 203–220.

Campbell, John Angus and Meyer, Stephen C. (Eds) 2004 *Darwinism, Design & Public Education.* Lansing, MI: Michigan State University Press.

Campbell, Neil A. and Reece, Jane B. (Eds) 2007 *Biology. 8th edition.* Upper Saddle River, NJ: Pearson.

Caneday, Ardel B., Barrett, Matthew and Gundry, Stanley N. (Eds) 2013 *Four Views on the Historical Adam.* Counterpoints: Bible and Theology. Grand Rapids, MI: Zondervan.

Carroll, John W. 2010 'Laws of Nature'. *The Stanford Encyclopedia of Philosophy* (Spring 2012 Edition). Ed. Edward N. Zalta Available at <http://plato.stanford.edu/archives/spr2012/entries/laws-of-nature/>.

Carroll, Sean B. 2006 *Endless Forms Most Beautiful: The New Science of Evo-Devo.* New York, NY: W.W. Norton Company.

Carroll, Sean M. 2003 'Why Almost All Cosmologists Are Atheists'. Faith and Philosophy. Vol. 20. No. 5. 622–635.

Carroll, Sean M., Ortlund, Eric A. and Thornton, Joseph W. 2011 'Mechanisms for the Evolution of a Derived Function in the Ancestral Glucocorticoid Receptor'. *PLoS Genetics.* 2011 June; 7(6): e1002117.

Chalmers, A.F. 1982 *What Is This Thing Called Science? Adn Assessment of the Nature and Status of Science and Its Methods.* 2nd edition. St Lucia: University of Queensland Press.

Chignell, Andrew 2009 '"As Kant has Shown . . .": Analytic Theology and the Critical Philosophy'. *Analytic Theology: New Essays in the Philosophy of Religion.* Eds Oliver D. Crisp and Michael C. Rea. Oxford: Oxford University Press. 117–135.

Clark, Kelly James 2014 *Religion and the Sciences of Origins: Historical and Contemporary Discussions.* New York, NY: Palgrave Macmillan.

Clayton, Philip and Simpson, Zachary (Eds) 2006 *The Oxford Handbook of Religion and Science.* Oxford: Oxford University Press.

Cleaver, Gerald (forthcoming) 'Multiverse: God's Indeterminicy in Action'. Saturn Conference Proceedings 2014. Ed. Robert J. Russell.

Cleland, Carol E. 2011 'Prediction and Explanation in Historical Natural Science'. *British Journal of the Philosophy of Science.* Vol. 62. No. 3. 551–582.

Cobb, John B (Ed.) 2008 *Back to Darwin: A Richer Account of Evolution.* Grand Rapids, MI: William B. Eerdmans Publishing Co.

Collins, Francis S. 2007 *The Language of God: A Scientist Presents Evidence for Belief.* New York, NY: The Free Press.

Collins, Robin 2003 'Six Solid Cases of Fine-Tuning'. *God and Design: The Teleological Argument and Modern Science.* Ed. Neil. A. Manson. London: Routledge. 178–199.

——— 2005a 'Hume, Fine-Tuning and the "Who Designed God?" Objection'. *In Defence of Natural Theology: A Post-Humean Assessment.* Eds James F. Sennett and Douglas Groothuis. Downers Grove, IL: InterVarsity Press. 175–199.

——— 2005b 'The Many-Worlds Hypothesis as an Explanation of Cosmic Fine-Tuning: An Alternative to Design?' *Faith and Philosophy.* Vol. 22. No. 5. 654–666.

——— 2006 'A Critical Evaluation of the Intelligent Design Program: An Analysis and a Proposal'. *Home Page of Robin Collins.* Available at <http://home.messiah.edu/~rcollins/Intelligent%20Design/INTELL3.htm>. Accessed on 15 May 2013.

——— 2009 'Divine Action and Evolution'. *The Oxford Handbook of Philosophical Theology.* Eds Thomas P. Flint and Michael C. Rea. Oxford: Oxford University Press. 241–261.

——— 2012 'The Teleological Argument'. *The Blackwell Companion to Natural Theology.* Eds William Lane Craig and J.P. Moreland. Malden, MA: Wiley-Blackwell.

Comfort, Nathaniel C. (Ed.) 2007 *The Panda's Black Box: Opening up the Intelligent Design Controversy.* Baltimore, ML: The Johns Hopkins University Press.

Conway Morris, Simon 2005 *Life's Solution: Inevitable Humans in a Lonely Universe.* Cambridge: Cambridge University Press.

——— 2009 'The Predictability of Evolution: Glimpses into a Post-Darwinian World'. *Naturwissenschaften.* Vol. 96. 1313–1337.

Corabi, Joseph 2009 'Intelligent Design and Theodicy'. *Religious Studies.* Vol. 45. No. 1. 21–35.

Coulson, Charles A. 1958 *Science and the Idea of God.* Cambridge, UK: Cambridge University Press.

Coyne, Jerry 2005 'The Case Against Intelligent Design'. Edge.org. Wed. Nov. 13. Available at <http://www.edge.org/conversation/the-case-against-intelligent-design>. Accessed on 24 January 2014.

——— 2007 'The Great Mutator'. *The New Republic.* June 18.

——— 2009 *Why Evolution is True.* London: Penguin Books.

——— 2015 *Faith Versus Fact: Why Science and Religion Are Incompatible.* New York, NY: Viking Penguin.

Craig, William Lane 2003 'Design and the Anthropic Fine-Tuning of the Universe'. *God and Design. The Teleological Argument and Modern Science.* Ed. Neil. A. Manson. London: Routledge. 155–177.

——— 2007 'Naturalism and Intelligent Design'. *Intelligent Design: William A. Dembski & Michael Ruse in Dialogue.* Ed. Robert Stewart. Minneapolis, MN: Fortress Press.

——— 2008 'God is Not Dead Yet: How Current Philosophers Argue for His Existence'. *Christianity Today.* July 2008.

Craig, William and Copan, Paul 2004 *Creation out of Nothing: A Biblical, Philosophical and Scientific Exploration.* Grand Rapids, MI: Baker Academic.

Craig, William and Moreland, J.P. (Eds) 2010 *The Blackwell Companion to Natural Theology.* Oxford: Blackwell Publishing.

Cunningham, Conor 2010 *Darwin's Pious Idea: Why the Ultra-Darwinists and Creationists Both Get it Wrong.* London: Wm. B. Eerdmans Publishing Company.

Darwin, Charles 2009 [1859] *On the Origin of Species.* Oxford: Oxford University Press.

——— 2012 [1860] 'Letter to Asa Gray, dated 22 May, 1860'. Available at <http://www.darwinproject.ac.uk/entry-2814>. Accessed on 20 May 2014.

Davidson, Eric H. 2006 *The Regulatory Genome: Gene Regulatory Networks In Development and Evolution*. Burlington, MA: Elsevier.

——— 2011 'Evolutionary Bioscience as Regulatory Systems Biology'. *Developmental Biology*. Vol. 357. No. 1. 35–40.

Davies, Paul 1992 *The Mind of God: Science and the Search for Ultimate Meaning*. London: Simon & Schuster.

——— 2006 *The Goldilocks Enigma: Why is the Universe Just Right for Life?* London: Penguin Books.

Davis, Percival and Kenyon, Dean H. 1993 *Of Pandas and People: The Central Question of Biological Origins*. 2nd Edition. Richardson, TX: Foundation for Thought and Ethics.

Dawes, Gregory A. 2007 'What is Wrong with Intelligent Design?' *International Journal for Philosophy of Religion*. Vol. 61. No. 2. 69–81.

——— 2009 *Theism and Explanation*. New York, NY: Routledge.

Dawkins, Richard 1991 *The Blind Watchmaker: How the Evidence of Evolution Reveals a Universe without Design*. London: Penguin.

——— 2006a *The God Delusion*. London: Bantam Press.

——— 2009 *The Greatest Show on Earth: The Evidence for Evolution*. New York, NY: The Free Press.

De Cruz, Helen and De Smedt, Johan 2015 *A Natural History of Natural Theology: The Cognitive Science of Theology and Philosophy of Religion*. Cambridge, MA: The MIT Press.

De Duve, Christian 1984 *A Guided Tour of the Living Cell*. New York, NY: Scientific American.

Dembski, William A. 1994 'On the Very Possibility of Intelligent Design'. *The Creation Hypothesis: Scientific Evidence for an Intelligent Designer*. Ed. J.P. Moreland. Downers Grove, IL: InterVarsity Press.

Dembski, W. and Licona, M. (Eds) 2010 *Evidence for God: 50 Arguments for Faith from the Bible, History, Philosophy and Science*. Grand Rapids, MI: Baker Books.

Dembski, W. and Meyer, Stephen C. 1998 'Fruitful Interchange or Polite Chitchat? The Dialogue Between Science and Theology'. *Zygon*. Vol. 33. No. 3. 415–430.

Dembski, W. and Wells, J. 2007 *The Design of Life: Discovering Signs of Intelligence in Biological Systems*. Richardson, TX: Foundation for Thought and Ethics.

——— 2008 *How to be an Intellectual Fulfilled Atheist (Or Not)*. Wilmington, DL: Intercollegiate Studies Institute.

Dembski, W. Downes, J. and Frederick, W. (Eds) 2008 *The Patristic Understanding of Creation: An Anthology of Writings from the Church Fathers on Creation and Design*. Riesel, TX: Erasmus Press.

Dembski, William A. and Marks, Robert J. II. 2009 'Conservation of Information in Search: Measuring the Cost of Success'. *IEEE Transactions on Systems, Man and Cybernetics A, Systems & Humans*. Vol. 5. No. 5. 1051–1061.

Dembski, William and Ruse, Michael (Eds) 2004 *Debating Design: From Darwin to DNA*. Cambridge: Cambridge University Press.

——— 1998a *The Design Inference: Eliminating Chance Through Small Probabilities*. Cambridge Studies in Probability, Induction and Decision Theory. Cambridge: Cambridge University Press.

——— 1998b 'The Intelligent Design Movement'. *Cosmic Pursuit Magazine*, Spring 1998.

——— 1998c 'Introduction: Mere Creation'. *Mere Creation: Science, Faith and Intelligent Design*. Ed. William A. Dembski. Downers Grove, IL: InterVarsity Press.

——— 1998d 'Intelligent Science and Design'. *First Things*. No. 86. 21–27.

——— 1999a *Intelligent Design: The Bridge Between Science and Theology*. Downers Grove, IL: InterVarsity Press.

——— 1999b 'The Last Magic. Review of the Applicability of Mathematics as a Philosophical Problem by Mark Steiner'. *Books & Culture*. Vol. 5. No. 4.

——— 2000a 'Intelligent Design Is Not Optimal Design'. *The Leadership University Website*. Available at <http://www.leaderu.com>. Accessed on 24 January 2014.

——— 2000b 'Intelligent Design Coming Clean'. *DesignInference.com*. Available at <http://www.designinference.com>. Accessed on 7 August 2014.

——— 2002a *No Free Lunch: Why Specified Complexity Cannot Be Purchased Without Intelligence*. Lanham: Rowman & Littlefield Publishers.

——— 2002b 'Detecting Design in the Natural Sciences'. Article commissioned for POISK. Design Inference Website. Available at <http://www.designinference.com>. Accessed on 29 December 2013.

——— 2003a 'Making the Task of Theodicy Impossible? Intelligent Design and the Problem of Evil'. *The Design Inference*. Available at <http://www.designinference.com>. Accessed on 29 December 2013.

——— 2003b 'The Chance of the Gaps'. *God and Design: The Teleological Argument and Modern Science*. Ed. Neil A. Manson. London: Routledge. 251–274.

——— 2004a *The Design Revolution: Answering the Toughest Questions About Intelligent Design*. Downer's Grove, IL: Intervarsity Press.

——— 2004b 'Irreducible Complexity Revisited'. *The Design Inference*. Available at <http://www.designinference.com>. Accessed on 29 December 2013.

——— 2004c 'Conway Morris Solution'. *The Design Inference*. Available at <http://www.designinference.com>.

——— 2005a 'Allen Orr in the New Yorker: A Response'. *The Design Inference*. Available at <http://www.designinference.com>. Accessed on 29 December 2013.

——— 2005b 'Specification: The Pattern That Signifies Intelligence'. *The Design Inference*. Available at <http://www.designinference.com>. Accessed on 29 December 2013.

——— 2009 *The End of Christianity: Finding a Good God in an Evil World*. Nashville, TN: B & H Academic.

——— 2011 'BioLogos and Theistic Evolution: Selling the Product'. *Patheos Website*. Available at <http://www.patheos.com>. Accessed on 29 December 2013.

——— 2013 'Evil, Creation and Intelligent Design'. *God and Evil: The Case for God in a World Filled with Pain*. Eds Chad Meister and James K. Dew Jr. Downer's Grove, IL: IVP Books. 259–269.

——— 2014 *Being as Communion: A Metaphysics of Information*. Farnham: Ashgate.

Dembski, William A. (Ed.) 1998 *Mere Creation: Science, Faith and Intelligent Design*. Downers Grove, IL: InterVarsity Press.

——— 2004 *Uncommon Dissent: Intellectuals Who Find Darwinism Unconvincing*. Wilmington, DL: ISI Books. 153–176.

——— 2006 *Darwin's Nemesis: Phillip Johnson and the Intelligent Design Movement*. Downers Grove, IL: InterVarsity Press.

Dennett, Daniel 1995 *Darwin's Dangerous Idea*. New York, NY: Simon & Schuster.

Dennett, Daniel and Plantinga, Alvin 2011 *Science and Religion: Are They Compatible?* Oxford: Oxford University Press.

——— 2006a *Breaking the Spell: Religion as a Natural Phenomenon*. New York, NY: Viking.

——— 2006b 'The Hoax of Intelligent Design and How It Was Perpetrated'. *Intelligent Thought: Science Versus the Intelligent Design Movement*. Ed. John Brockman. New York, NY: Vintage Books. 33–49.

Denton, Michael 1986 *Evolution: A Theory in Crisis*. Bethesda, ML: Adler & Adler 1986.

——— 1998 *Nature's Destiny: How the Laws of Biology Reveal Purpose in the Universe*. New York, NY: The Free Press.

——— 2004 'An Anti-Darwinian Intellectual Journey: Biological Order as an Inherent Property of Matter'. *Uncommon Dissent: Intellectuals Who Find Darwinism Unconvincing*. Ed. W.A. Dembski. Wilmington, DL: ISI Books. 153–176.

——— 2013 'The Types: A Persistent Structuralist Challenge to Darwinian Pan-Selectionism'. *Bio-Complexity*. 2013: 3. 1–18. doi:10.5048/BIO-C.2013.3.

DePoe, John 2014 'The Epistemic Framework for Skeptical Theism'. *Skeptical Theism: New Essays*. Eds Trent Dougherty and Justin P. McBrayer. Oxford: Oxford University Press. 32–44.

De Ridder, Jeroen2014a 'Science and Scientism in Popular Science Writing'. *Social Epistemology Review and Reply Collective*.Vol. 3. No. 12. 23–39.

——— 2014b 'Design Discourse and the Cognitive Science of Design'. *Philosophia Reformata*.Vol. 79. No. 1. 37–53.

Desmond, Adrian and Moore, James 1991 *Darwin: The Life of a Tormented Evolutionist*. New York, NY: W.W. Norton.

DeVries, Paul 1986 'Naturalism in the Natural Sciences'. *Christian Scholar's Review*.Vol. 15. 388–396.

DeWeese, Garry 2013 'Natural Evil: A Free Process Defence'. *God and Evil: The Case for God in a World Filled with Pain*. Eds Chad Meister and James K. Dew Jr. Downer's Grove, IL: IVP Books.

Dewolf, David K., West, John G., Casey, Luskin and Witt, Jonathan (Eds) 2006 *Traipsing into Evolution: Intelligent Design and the Kitzmiller V Dover Decision*. Seattle, WA: Discovery Institute Press.

Discovery Institute 2003 '"The Wedge Document": How Darwinist Paranoia Fueled an Urban Legend'. *Discovery Institute*. Available at <http://www.discovery.org/csc/>. Accessed on 29 December 2013.

——— 2005 'The Truth about Discovery Institute and "Theocracy"'. *Discovery Institute*. Available at <http://www.discovery.org/csc>. Accessed on 29 December 2013.

——— 2015 'What is Intelligent Design?' *Discovery Institute*. Available at <http://www.intelligentdesign.org/whatisid.php>. Accessed on 12 June 2015.

Dobzhansky, Theodosius 1973 'Nothing in Biology Makes Sense Except in the Light of Evolution'. *American Biology Teacher*.Vol. 35. No. 3, 125–129.

Doolittle, W. Ford 2013 'Is Junk DNA Bunk? A Critique of ENCODE'. *Proceedings of the National Academy of Sciences*.Vol. 110. No. 14. 5294–5300.

Doran, Chris 2009 'From Atheism to Theodicy to Intelligent Design: Responding to the Work of Francisco J. Ayala'. *Theology and Science*.Vol. 7. No. 4. 337–344.

——— 2010 'Intelligent Design: It's Just Too Good to Be True'. *Theology and Science*.Vol. 8. No. 2. 223–237.

Dougherty, Trent 2014a *The Problem of Animal Pain*. London: Palgrave McMillan.

——— 2014b 'Evil and the Problem of Anomaly'. *Oxford Studies in Philosophy of Religion*. Vol. 5. Ed. Jonathan Kvanvig. Oxford: Oxford University Press. DOI:10.1093/acprof:oso/9780198704768.001.0001

——— Forthcoming. 'Evidence in Theology'. *The Oxford Handbook of the Epistemology of Theology*. Eds William J. Abraham and Frederick D. Aquinio. Oxford: Oxford University Press.

Dougherty, Trent and McBrayer, Justin P. (Eds) 2014 *Skeptical Theism: New Essays*. Oxford: Oxford University Press.

Dougherty, Trent and Pruss, Alexander 2014 'Evil and the Problem of Anomaly'. *Oxford Studies in Philosophy of Religion*. Ed. Jonathan L. Kvanvig. Vol. 5. 49–87.

Draper, Paul 2002 'Irreducible Complexity and Darwinian Gradualism: A Reply to Michael Behe'. *Faith and Philosophy*. Vol. 19. No. 1. 3–21.

Draper, Paul and Dougherty, Trent 2014 'Explanation and the Problem of Evil'. *The Blackwell Companion to the Problem of Evil*. Eds McBrayer, Justin P. and Howard-Snyder, Daniel. Oxford: Blackwell. 71–87.

Drees, Willem B. 2006 'Religious Naturalism and Science'. *The Oxford Handbook of Religion and Science*. Ed. Philip Clayton. Oxford: Oxford University Press. 108–123.

Drummond, Henry 2008 [1883] *The Lowell Lectures on the Ascent of Man*. Radford, VA: Wilder Publications.

Durrett, Rick and Schmidt, Deena 2008 'Waiting for Two Mutations: With Applications to Regulatory Sequence Evolution and the Limits of Darwinian Evolution'. *Genetics*. Vol. 180. 1501–1509.

Earman, John 2000 *Hume's Abject Failure: The Argument Against Miracles*. Oxford: Oxford University Press.

Edis, Taner 2006 'Grand Themes, Narrow Constitutiency'. *Why Intelligent Design Fails: A Scientific Critique of the New Creationism*. Eds Matt Young and Taner Edis. New Brunswick, NJ: Rutgers University Press. 9–19.

Elsberry, Wesley 2007 'Logic and Math Turn to Smoke and Mirrors'. *Scientists Confront Intelligent Design and Creationism*. Eds Andrew J. Petto and Laurie R. Godfrey. New York, NY: W.W. Norton & Co. 250–271.

Elsberry, Wesley and Shallit, Jeffrey 2003 'Information theory, Evolutionary Computation, and Dembski's "Complex Specified Information"'. *Antievolution.org*. Available at <http://www.antievolution.org>. Accessed on 29 December 2013.

ENCODE Project Consortium 2012 'An Integrated Encyclopedia of DNA Elements in the Human Genome'. *Nature*. Vol. 489. 57–74.

Evans, Stephen C. 2010 *Natural Signs and Knowledge of God: A New Look at Theistic Arguments*. Oxford: Oxford University Press.

——— 2014 'Moral Arguments for the Existence of God', *The Stanford Encyclopedia of Philosophy* (Summer 2014 Edition). Ed. Edward N. Zalta. Available at <http://plato.stanford.edu/archives/sum2014/entries/moral-arguments-god/>. Accessed on 21 October 2015.

Falk, Darrel 2009 'On Reducing Irreducible Complexity, part II'. *Beliefnet: Science and the Sacred*. Available at <http://blog.beliefnet.com/scienceandthesacred/>. Accessed on 24 October 2013.

Ferngren, Gary B (Ed.) 2002 *Science and Religion: A Historical Introduction*. Baltimore, MA: The John Hopkins University Press. 2002.

Feser, Edward 2008 *The Last Superstition: A Refutation of the New Atheism*. South Bend, IN: St Augustine's Press.

——— 2010 'Teleology: A Shopper's Guide'. *Philosophia Christi*. Vol. 12. No. 1. 142–159.

Flew, Antony and Varghese, Roy Abraham 2007 *There Is a God: How the World's Most Notorious Atheist Changed His Mind*. London: HarperOne.

Flint, Thomas P. and Rea, Michael C. 2009 *The Oxford Handbook of Philosophical Theology*. Oxford: Oxford University Press.

Fodor, Jerry and Piattelli-Palmarini, Massimo 2011 *What Darwin Got Wrong*. London: Profile Books.

Forrest, Barbara 2001 'The Wedge at Work: How Intelligent Design Creationism is Wedging its Way into the Cultural and Academic Mainstream'. *Intelligent Design Creationism and Its Critics: Philosophical, Theological and Scientific Perspectives*. Ed. Robert T. Pennock. Cambridge, MA: The MIT Press. 5–53.

Forrest, Barbara and Gross, Paul 2004 *Creationism's Trojan Horse: The Wedge of Intelligent Design*. Oxford: Oxford University Press.

Freeman, Scott and Herron, John C. 2007 *Evolutionary Analysis*. Fourth Edition. Upper Saddle River, NJ: Pearson Prentice Hall.

Ganssle, Gregory E. 2012 '"God of the Gaps" Arguments'. *The Blackwell Companion to Science and Christianity*. Eds J.B. Stump and Alan G. Padgett. Oxford: Blackwell. 130–139.

Garcia, Robert K. and King, Nathan L. (Eds) 2009 *Is Goodness without God Good Enough? A Debate on Faith, Secularism and Ethics*. Lanham, ML: Rowman & Littlefield.

Gauger, Ann 2012 'On Enzymes and Teleology'. *Evolution News and Views*. Available at <http://www.evolutionnews.org>. Accessed on 17 June 2013.

Gauger, Ann and Axe, Douglas 2011 'The Evolutionary Accessibility of New Enzyme Functions: A Case Study from the Biotin Pathway'. *Bio-Complexity*. No. 1. 1–17.

——— 2013 'Natural Selection's Reach'. *The Biologic Institute*. Available at <http://www.biologicinstitute.org>. Accessed on 28 August 2013.

Gauger, Ann, Axe, Douglas and Luskin, Casey 2012 *Science & Human Origins*. Seattle, WA: Discovery Institute Press.

Gender, Tamar Szabó and Hawthorne, John (Eds) 2002 *Conceivability and Possibility*. Oxford: Clarendon Press.

Giberson, Karl W. 2009 'Evolution and the Problem of Evil'. *Beliefnet: Science and the Sacred*. Available at <http://blog.beliefnet.com>. Accessed on 24 October 2013.

Giberson, Karl W. and Artigas, Mariano 2009 *Oracles of Science: Celebrity Scientists versus God and Religion*. Oxford: Oxford University. 32–33.

Giberson, Karl W. and Collins, Francis S. 2011 *The Language of Science and Faith: Straight Answers to Genuine Questions*. Downer's Grove, IL: InterVarsity Press.

——— 2013 'Evil, Creation and Evolution'. *God and Evil: The Case for God in a World Filled with Pain*. Eds Chad Meister and James K. Dew Jr. Downer's Grove, IL: IVP Books.

Giberson, Karl W. and Yerxa, Donald A. 2002 *Species of Origins: America's Search for a Creation Story*. Lanham, Md: Rowman & Littlefield.

Gishlick, Alan 2006 'Evolutionary Paths to Irreducible Systems: The Avian Flight Apparatus'. *Why Intelligent Design Fails: A Scientific Critique of the New Creationism*. Eds Matt Young and Taner Edis. New Brunswick, NJ: Rutgers University Press. 58–71.

Glass, David H. 2012a 'Darwin, Design and Dawkins' Dilemma'. *Sophia*. Vol. 51. No. 1. 31–57.

——— 2012b 'Can Evidence for Design be Explained Away?' *Probability in the Philosophy of Religion*. Eds V. Harrison and J. Chandler. Oxford: Oxford University. 77–102.

Gliboff, Sander 2000 'Paley's Design Argument as an Inference to the Best Explanation, or Dawkins Dilemma'. *Studies in the History and Philosophy of Biological and Biomedical Sciences*. Vol. 31. No. 4. 579–597.

Godfrey-Smith, Peter 2007 'Information in Biology'. *The Cambridge Companion to the Philosophy of Biology*. Eds David L. Hull and Michael Ruse. Cambridge: Cambridge University Press. 103–119.

Godfrey-Smith, Peter and Sterelny, Kim 2008 'Biological Information'. *The Stanford Encyclopedia of Philosophy* (Fall 2008 Edition). Ed. Edward N. Zalta. Available at <http://plato.stanford.edu/archives/fall2008/entries/information-biological/>. Accessed on October 21, 2015.

Goetz, Stewart and Taliaferro, Charles 2008 *Naturalism. Interventions*. Grand Rapids, MI: William B. Eerdmans Publishing.

Gonzales, Guillermo and Richards, Jay W. 2004 *The Privileged Planet: How Our Place in the Cosmos Is Designed for Discovery*. Washington, DC: Regnery Publishing.

Gould, Stephen Jay and Lewontin, Richard 1979 'The Spandrels of San Marco and the Panglossian Paradigm: A Critique of the Adaptationist Programme'. *Proceedings of the Royal Society B.* Vol. 205. No. 1161. 581–598.

Gould, Stephen Jay 1980 *The Panda's Thumb.* New York, NY: Norton.

——— 1989 *Wonderful Life: The Burgess Shale and the Nature of History.* New York, NY: W.W. Norton.

——— 1992 'Impeaching a Self-Appointed Judge'. *Scientific American.* Vol. 261. No. 1. 79–84.

——— 2002 *Rocks of Ages: Science and Religion in the Fullness of Life.* New York, NY: Ballantine Books.

Greene, Brian 2005 *The Fabric of the Cosmos: Space, Time and the Texture of Reality.* New York, NY: Vintage Books.

Gregersen, Niels. 2009. 'Special Divine Action and the Quilt of Laws: Why the Distinction Between Special and General Divine Action Cannot be Maintained.' *Scientific Perspectives on Divine Action: Twenty Years of Challenges and Progress.* Ed. Robert J. Russell, Nancey Murphy & William R. Stoeger. Berkeley, CA: CTNS. 179–199.

Griesemer, James 2008 'Origins of Life Studies'. *The Oxford Handbook of Philosophy of Biology.* Ed. Michael Ruse. Oxford: Oxford University Press. 263–290.

Guthrie, Stewart Elliott 2006 'Intelligent Design as Illusion'. *Free Inquiry.* Vol. 26. No. 3. 40–44.

Haack, Susan 2003 *Defending Science – Within Reason: Between Scientism and Cynicism.* Amherst, NY: Prometheus Books.

Häggvist, Karl 1996 *Thought Experiments in Philosophy.* Stockholm Studies in Philosophy 18. Stockholm : Almqvist & Wiksell International.

——— 2013 'Six Signs of Scientism'. *Skeptical Inquirer.* Vol. 37. No. 6. 40–46.

Hall, Alexander W. 2013 'Natural Theology in the Middle Ages'. *The Oxford Handbook of Natural Theology.* Eds Russell Re Manning, John Hedley Brooke and Fraser Watts. Oxford: Oxford University Press. 57–74.

Halvorson, Hans 2014 'Why Methodological Naturalism?' Preprint article. Phil Sci Archive. Available at <http://philsci-archive.pitt.edu/11003/1/metnat3.pdf>. Accessed on 3 September 2014.

Hannam, James 2011 *The Genesis of Science: How the Christian Middle Ages Launched the Scientific Revolution.* Washington, DC: Regnery Publishing.

Hardwick, Charley D. 1996 *Events of Grace: Naturalism, Existentialism, and Theology.* Cambridge: Cambridge University Press.

Harman, Gilbert 2004 'Practical Aspects of Theoretical Reasoning'. *The Oxford Handbook of Rationality.* Eds Afred E. Mele and Piers Rawling. Oxford: Oxford University Press.

Harold, Franklin 2001 *The Way of the Cell: Molecules, Organisms and the Order of Life.* Oxford: Oxford University Press.

Harrison, Peter 2015 *The Territories of Science and Religion.* Chicago, IL: University of Chicago Press.

Hart, David Bentley 2003 *The Beauty of the Infinite: The Aesthetics of Christian Truth.* Grand Rapids, MI: Wm. B. Eerdmans Publishing Co.

——— 2005 *The Doors of the Sea: Where Was God in the Tsunami?* Grand Rapids, MI: Wm. B. Eerdmans Publishing Co.

——— 2010 *Atheist Delusions: The Christian Revolution and Its Fashionable Enemies.* New Haven, CT: Yale University Press.

——— 2013 *Being, Consciousness and Bliss.* New Haven, CT: Yale University Press.

Harvey, Allan 2000 'What Does God of the Gaps Mean?' *Allen Harvey's Homepage.* Available at <http://steamdoc.s5.com/writings/gaps.html>. Accessed on 11 December 2013.

Haught, John 2003 *Deeper than Darwin: The Prospect for Religion in an Age of Evolution.* Boulder, CL: Westview Press.

——— 2004 'Darwin, Design and Divine Providence'. *Debating Design: From Darwin to DNA.* Eds William A. Dembski and Michael Ruse. Cambridge: Cambridge University Press. 229–244.

——— 2008 'Is Fine-Tuning Remarkable?' *Fitness of the Cosmos for Life: Biochemistry and Fine-Tuning.* Eds John Barrow, Simon Conway Morris, Stephen Freeland and Charles Harper. Cambridge: Cambridge University Press. 31–48.

——— 2009 'Theology and Evolution: How Much Can Biology Explain?' *The Believing Primate: Scientific, Philosophical and Theological Reflections on the Origin of Religion.* Eds Michael J. Murray and Jeffrey Schloss. Oxford: Oxford University Press. 246–264.

Hawking, Stephen and Mlodinow, Leonard 2010 *The Grand Design.* New York, NY: Bantam Books.

Hick, John 1978 *Evil and the God of Love.* Revised Ed. San Francisco, CA: Harper & Row.

Himma, Kenneth 2005 'The Application-Conditions for Design Inferences: Why the Design Arguments Need the Help of Other Arguments for God's Existence'. *International Journal for Philosophy of Religion.* Vol. 57. No. 1. 1–33.

Holder, Rodney 2012 *The Heavens Declare: Natural Theology and the Legacy of Karl Barth.* West Conshohocken, PA: Templeton Press.

Holmes, Stephen R. 2007 'The Attributes of God'. *Oxford Handbook of Systematic Theology.* Eds John Webster, Kathryn Tanner and Iain Torrance. Oxford: Oxford University Press. 54–71.

Hooyakas, Reijer 1977 *Religion and the Rise of Modern Science.* Edinburgh: Scottish Academy Press.

Hossenfelder, Sabine 2013 'Minimal Length Scale Scenarios for Quantum Gravity'. *Living Reviews Relativity.* Vol. 16. No. 2.

Hough, Adrian 2006 'Not a Gap in Sight: Fifty Years of Charles Coulson's Science and Christian Belief'. *Theology.* Vol. 109. No. 847. 21–27.

Howard-Snyder, Daniel (Ed.) 1996 *The Evidential Argument from Evil.* Bloomington, IN: Indiana University Press.

Howson, Colin and Urbach, Peter 2006 *Scientific Reasoning. The Bayesian Approach.* 3rd ed. Chicago: Open Court.

Hull, David L. 1991 'The God of the Galapagos'. *Nature.* Vol. 352. August. 485–486.

Hume, David 1999 [1779] *Dialogues and Natural History of Religion.* Oxford World's Classics. New York, NY: Oxford University Press.

Hunter, Cornelius G. 2001 *Darwin's God: Evolution and the Problem of Evil.* Ada, MI: Brazos Press.

——— 2010 'The Problem of Evil Atheism'. *Darwin's God Blog.* April 18. Available at <http://darwins-god.blogspot.fi/2010/04/problem-of-evil-atheism.html>. Accessed on 24 October 2010.

Hurd, Gary S. 2004 'The Explanatory Filter, Archaeology and Forensics'. *Why Intelligent Design Fails: A Scientific Critique of the New Creationism.* Eds Matt Young and Taner Edis. Picataway, NJ: Rutgers University Press.

Hurlbutt, Robert H. III 1985 *Hume, Newton and the Design Argument. Revised edition.* London: University of Nebraska Press.

Illustra Media 2003 *Unlocking the Mystery of Life.* Documentary Programme. La Mirada, CA: Illustra Media.

——— 2005 *The Privileged Planet.* Documentary Programme. La Mirada, CA: Illustra Media.

Iranzo, Valeriano 2007 'Abduction and Inference to the Best Explanation'. *Theoria*. Vol. 60. 339–346.

Järnefelt, Elisa 2013 *Created by Some Being Theoretical and Empirical Exploration of Adults' Automatic and Reflective Beliefs about the Origin of Natural Phenomena*. Doctoral Dissertation. University of Helsinki, Faculty of Arts, Department of World Cultures.

Johnson, Philip 1993a *Darwin on Trial*. 2nd ed. Downers Grove, Illinois: InterVarsity Press.

——— 1993b 'Creator or Blind Watchmaker?' *First Things*. January Issue.

——— 1995 *Reason in the Balance*. Downers Grove, Illinois: InterVarsity Press.

——— 1997 'The Unraveling of Scientific Materialism'. *First Things*. Vol. 77. (November 1997). 22–25.

——— 1999 'The Wedge: Breaking the Modernist Monopoly on Science'. *Touchstone Magazine*. July/August 1999.

——— 2000 *The Wedge of Truth: Splitting the Foundations of Naturalism*. Downer's Grove, IL: InterVarsity Press.

——— 2007 'Intelligent Design in Biology: The Current Situation and Future Prospects'. *Think. The Royal Institute of Philosophy.* February 19.

Johnson, Phillip and Lamoureux, Denis (Eds) 1999 Darwinism Defeated? The Johnson-Lamoureux Debate on Biological Origins. Vancouver, BC: Regent College Publishing.

Johnson, Phillip and Reynolds, John Mark 2010 *Against all Gods: What's Right (and Wrong) About the New Atheists*. Downer's Grove, IL: IVP Books.

Johnson, Susan C. 2003 'Detecting Agents'. *Philosophical Transactions of the Royal Society*. Vol. 358. No. 1431. 549–559.

Jones, John E. 2005 *Tammy Kitzmiller, et al. v. Dover Area School District, et al. Memorandum Opinion. Case 4:04-cv-02688-JEJ. Document 342.* The United States Disctrict Court for the Middle State of Pennsylvania.

Joyce, James 2003 'Bayes's Theorem'. *The Stanford Encyclopedia of Philosophy* (Winter 2003 Edition). Ed. Edward N. Zalta. Available at <http://plato.stanford.edu/archives/win2003/entries/bayes-theorem/>.

Juthe, A. 2005 'Argument by Analogy'. *Argumentation*. Vol. 19. 1–27.

Kant, Immanuel 1957 [1781] *Critique of Pure Reason*. Translation by N.K. Smith. London: Macmillan.

Keener, Craig 2011 *Miracles: The Credibility of the New Testament Accounts*. Vol. 1. Grand Rapids, MI: Baker Academic.

Kelemen, Deborah 2004 'Are Children "Intuitive Theists"? Reasoning About Purpose and Design in Nature'. *Psychological Science*. Vol. 15. No. 5. 295–301.

Kitcher, Phillip 1981 'Explanatory Unification'. *Philosophy of Science*. Vol. 48. 507–531.

——— 2007 *Living With Darwin: Evolution, Design and the Future of Faith*. New York: Oxford University Press.

Klinghoffer, David. (Ed.) 2010 *Signature of Controversy: Responses to Critics of Signature in the Cell*. Seattle, WA: Discovery Institute Press.

Knuuttila, Simo 1993 *Modalities in Medieval Philosophy*. London: Routledge.

Knuuttila, Simo and Sihvola, Juha (Eds) 2014 *Philosophical Psychology from Plato to Kant*. Studies in the History of Philosophy of Mind. Vol. 12. New York, NY: Springer.

Koistinen, Timo 2000 *Philosophy of Religion or Religious Philosophy? A Critical Study of Contemporary Anglo-American Approaches*. Scriften der Luther-Agricola-Gesellschaft 49. Helsinki: Luther-Agricola-seura.

Kojonen, Erkki Vesa Rope 2013 'Tensions in Intelligent Design's Critique of Theistic Evolutionism'. *Zygon*. Vol. 48. 251–273.

——— 2015 'Luottamus toisten todistukseen perustana Jumala- ja evoluutiouskolle'. *Teologinen Aikakauskirja — The Finnish Journal of Theology*. No. 1. 23–37.

——— Forthcoming. 'The God of the Gaps, Natural Theology and Intelligent Design.' *The Journal of Analytic Theology.*

Koons, Robert C. 2003 'Science and Theism: Concord, Not Conflict'. *The Rationality of Theism*. Eds Paul Copan and Paul K. Moser. London: Routledge.

Koperski, Jeffrey 2003 'Intelligent Design and the End of Science'. *American Catholic Philosophical Quarterly*. Vol. 77. No. 4. 567–588.

——— 2005 'Should We Care about Fine-Tuning?' *British Journal for the Philosophy of Science*. Vol. 56. No. 2. 303–319.

——— 2008 'Two Bad Ways to Attack Intelligent Design and Two Good Ones'. *Zygon*. Vol. 43. No. 2. 433–449.

——— 2015 *The Physics of Theism: God, Physics and the Philosophy of Science*. Oxford: Wiley-Blackwell.

Korthof, Gert 1998 'Nature's Destiny'. *Was Darwin Wrong Website*. Available at <http://wasdarwinwrong.com/kortho29.htm>. Accessed on 17 June 2013.

——— 2005 'Common Descent: It's All or Nothing'. *Why Intelligent Design Fails: A Scientific Critique of the New Creationism*. Eds Matt Young and Taner Edis. New Brunswick, NJ: Rutgers University Press.

Kretzmann, Norman 1991 'A General Problem of Creation: Why Would God Create Anything at All?' *Being and Goodness: The Concept of the Good in Metaphysics and Philosophical Theology*. Ed. Scott MacDonald. Ithaca, NY: Cornell UP, 1991. 208–228.

——— 1999 *The Metaphysics of Creation: Aquinas' Natural Theology in Summa Contra Gentiles*. Oxford: Oxford University Press.

Kroeker, Esther 2014 'Where the Conflict Really Lies: Plantinga's Reidian Discourse'. *Philosophia Reformata*. Vol. 79. No. 1. 21–36.

Labody, Guus 2015 'A Defense of Partisan Science: An Assessment of Stenmark's Non-Partisan Science'. *Theology & Science*. Vol. 13. No. 1. 79–88.

Lackey, Jennifer and Sosa, Ernest (Eds) 2006 *The Epistemology of Testimony*. Oxford: Clarendon Press, 2006.

Ladyman, James 2011 'The Scientistic Stance: The Empirical and Materialist Stances Reconciled'. *Synthese*. Vol. 178. No. 1. 87–98.

Lakatos, Imre 1977 *The Methodology of Scientific Research Programmes: Philosophical Papers. Volume 1*. Cambridge: Cambridge University Press.

Laland, Kevin, Uller, Tobias, Feldman, Marc, Sterelny, Kim, Müller, Gerd B, Moczek, Armin, Jablonka, Eva, Odling-Smee, John, Wray, Gregory A., Hoekstra, Hopi E., Futuyama, Douglas J., Lenski, Richard E., Mackay, Trudy F.C., Schluter, Dolph and Strassman, Joen E. 2014 'Does Evolutionary Biology Need a Rethink? Researchers Are Divided Over What Processes Should Be Considered Fundamental'. *Nature*. Vol. 514. 9 October. 161–164.

Lamoureux, Denis 2008 *Evolutionary Creation: A Christian Approach to Evolution*. London: Lutterworth Press.

——— 2013 'Response from the Evolutionary View'. *Four Views on the Historical Adam*. Eds Matthew Barrett, Ardel B. Caneday and Stanley N. Gundry. Grand Rapids, MI: Zondervan. 176–183.

Larmer, Robert 2002 'Is There Anything Wrong with 'God-of-the-Gaps' Reasoning?' *International Journal for Philosophy of Religion*. Vol. 52. No. 3. 129–142.

——— 2003 'Is Methodological Naturalism Question-Begging?' *Philosophia Christi*. Vol. 5. No. 1.

——— 2014 *The Legitimacy of Miracle*. Lanham, ML: Lexington Books.

Leech, David and Visala, Aku 2011 'The Cognitive Science of Religion: Implications for Theism?' *Zygon*. Vol. 46. No. 1. 47–64.

Leisola, Matti 2013 *Evoluutiouskon ihmemaassa*. Lahti: Datakirjat.

Lennox, John C. 2007 *God's Undertaker: Has Science Buried God?* Oxford: Lion.

Leslie, John 1989 *Universes*. London: Routledge.

Lewis, C.S. 2001 *Mere Christianity*. New York, NY: HarperSanFrancisco.

Lewontin, Richard 1997 'Billions and Billions of Demons. Review of Carl Sagan: The Demon-Haunted World'. *The New York Times Book Reviews*. 9 January 1997.

Lindberg, David C. 2003 'Galileo, the Church, and the Cosmos'. *When Science and Christianity Meet*. Eds David C. Lindberg & Ronald Numbers. Chicago, IL: The University of Chicago Press. 33–60.

Lipton, Peter 2004 *Inference to the Best Explanation*. London: Routledge.

Livingston, James C. 2007 *Religious Thought in the Victorian Age*. London: Continuum International Publishing.

Loesberg, Jonathan 2007 'Kant, Hume, Darwin, and Design: Why Intelligent Design Wasn't Science Before Darwin and Still Isn't'. *The Philosophical Forum*. Vol. 38. No. 2. 95–123.

Luoma, Tapio 2002 *Incarnation and Physics: Natural Science in the Theology of Thomas F. Torrance*. Oxford: Oxford University Press.

Luskin, Casey 2008 'ID Does Not Address Religious Claims About the Supernatural'. Opposing views.com. Available at <http://www.opposingviews.com>. Accessed on 10 May 2013.

——— 2014 'Phys.org: Specialized Retinal Cells Are a "Design Feature," Showing that the Argument for Suboptimal Design of the Eye "Is Folly"'. *Evolution News and Views*. 8 August. Available at <http://www.evolutionnews.org>. Accessed on 25 June 2015.

Mackie, J.L. 1982 *The Miracle of Theism: Arguments for and against the Existence of God*. Oxford: Clarendon.

Manson, Neil A. (Ed.) 2003 *God and Design. The Teleological Argument and Modern Science*. London: Routledge.

——— 2009 'The Fine-Tuning Argument'. *Philosophy Compass*. Vol. 4. No. 1. 271–286.

Margulis, Lynn 1999 *Symbiotic Planet: A New Look at Evolution*. New York, NY: Basic Books.

Marshall, Charles R. 2013 'When Prior Belief Trumps Scholarship'. *Science*. Vol. 341. No. 6152. 1344.

Masel, Joanna 2014 'What Can Evolutionary Biologists Learn from Creationists?' *Scientia Salon*, 2014. Available at <http://scientiasalon.wordpress.com>. Accessed on 29 June 2015.

Matzke, Nick 2006 'Evolution in (Brownian) Space: A Model for the Origin of the Bacterial Flagellum'. *Talkdesign.org*. Available at <www.talkdesign.org>. Accessed on 29 June 2015.

——— 2013 'Meyer's Hopeless Monster, Part II'. *Panda's Thumb Blog*. Available at <http://pandasthumb.org>. Accessed on 29 December 2013.

Mayr, Ernst 2002 *What Evolution Is: From Theory to Fact*. London: Phoenix.

McCauley, Robert N. 2012 *Why Religion Is Natural and Science Is Not*. Oxford: Oxford University Press.

McCord Adams, Marilyn 2014 'What's Wrong with the Ontotheological Error?' *Journal of Analytic Theology*. Vol. 2. 10.12978/jat.2014–1.120013000318a.

McCullough, Ross 2013 'God and the Gaps'. *First Things*. April 2013.

McDaniel, Jay and Bowman, Donna (Eds) 2006 *Handbook of Process Theology*. Danvers, MA: Chalice Press.

McFadden, Johnjoe 2000 *Quantum Evolution: How Physics' Weirdest Theory Explains Life's Biggest Mystery*. New York, NY: Norton.

McGrath, Alister 2001 *A Scientific Theology, Vol. 1: Nature*. Edinburgh: T & T Clark.

——— 2002 *A Scientific Theology, Vol. 2: Reality*. Edinburgh: T & T Clark.

——— 2003 *A Scientific Theology, Vol. 3: Theory*. Edinburgh: T & T Clark.

——— 2008 *The Open Secret: A New Vision for Natural Theology*. Oxford: Blackwell Publishing.

——— 2009 *A Fine-Tuned Universe: The Quest for God in Science and Theology*. Louisville, KN: Westminster John Knox Press.

——— 2010 *Science & Religion: A New Introduction*. 2nd Edition. Oxford: Wiley-Blackwell.

——— 2011 *Darwinism and the Divine: Evolutionary Thought and Natural Theology*. Oxford: Wiley-Blackwell.

McGrew, Lydia 2004 'Testability, Likelihoods and Design'. *Philo*. Vol. 7. No. 1. 5–21.

McGrew, Timothy 2009 'The Argument from Miracles: A Cumulative Case for the Resurrection of Jesus of Nazareth'. *The Blackwell Companion to Natural Theology*. Eds J.P. Moreland and William Lane Craign. Oxford: Blackwell. 593–662.

——— 2013 'Miracles'. *Stanford Encyclopedia of Philosophy* (Spring 2013 Edition). Ed. Edward N. Zalta. Available at <http://plato.stanford.edu/archives/spr2013/entries/miracles/>.

McGrew, Timothy, McGrew, Lydia and Vestrup, Eric 2003 'Probabilities and the Fine-Tuning Argument: A Sceptical View'. *God and Design. The Teleological Argument and Modern Science*. Ed. Neil A. Manson. London: Routledge.

Melander, Peter 1997 *Analyzing Functions: An Essay on a Fundamental Notion in Biology*. Umeå Studies in the Humanities 138. Umeå: Umeå Universitet Tryckeri.

Menuge, Angus 2004a 'Who's Afraid of ID? A Survey of the Intelligent Design Movement'. *Debating Design*. Eds William A. Dembski and Michael Ruse. Cambridge: Cambridge University Press. 32–51.

——— 2004b *Agents under Fire: Materialism and the Rationality of Science*. Lanham: Rowman & Littlefield Publishers.

Meyer, Stephen C. 1999a 'The Scientific Status of Intelligent Design: The Methodological Equivalence of Naturalistic and Non-Naturalistic Origins Theories'. *Science and Evidence for Design in the Universe. Proceedings of the Wethersfield Institute. Vol. 9*. Eds W.A. Dembski and Stephen C. Meyer. San Francisco, CA: Ignatius Press. 151–212.

——— 1999b 'Evidence for Design in Physics and Biology: From the Origin of the Universe to the Origin of Life'. *Science and Evidence for Design in the Universe. Proceedings of the Wethersfield Institute. Vol. 9*. Eds W.A. Dembski & Stephen C. Meyer. San Francisco, CA: Ignatius Press. 53–112.

——— 1999c 'The Return of the God Hypothesis'. *Journal of Interdisciplinary Studies*. Vol. 11. 1–38.

——— 2004a 'Intelligent Design: The Origin of Biological Information and the Higher Taxonomic Categories'. *Proceedings of the Biological Society of Washington*. Vol. 117. No. 2. 213–239.

——— 2004b 'DNA and the Origin of Life: Information, Specification and Explanation'. *Darwinism, Design and Public Education*. Eds J.A Campbell and S.C. Meyer. Lansing, MI: Michigan University Press. 233–285.

——— 2006 'A Scientific History – and Philosophical Defence – of the Theory of Intelligent Design'. *Religion Staat Gesellschaft*. Berlin: Duncker & Humbolt, 7. Jahrgang. Heft 2. 203–247.

——— 2009 *Signature in the Cell: DNA and the Evidence for Intelligent Design*. San Francisco, CA: HarperOne.

——— 2010 'The Difference It Doesn't Make'. *God and Evolution: Protestants, Catholics and Jews Explore Darwin's Challenge to Faith*. Ed. J.W. Richards. Seattle, WA: Discovery Institute Press. 147–164.

——— 2013 *Darwin's Doubt: The Explosive Origin of Animal Life and the Case for Intelligent Design*. San Francisco, CA: HarperCollins.

Meyer, Stephen, Minnich, Scott, Moneymaker, Jonathan, Nelson, Paul and Seelke, Ralph 2007 *Explore Evolution: The Arguments for and Against Neo-Darwinism*. Melbourne: Hill House Publishers.

Miller, Keith 2010 'The Cambrian "Explosion", Transitional Forms and the Tree of Life'. *Biologos Institute*. Available at <http://biologos.org/blog/the-cambrian-explosion-transitional-forms-and-the-tree-of-life>. Accessed on 17 June 2013.

Miller, Kenneth 2002 *Finding Darwin's God: A Scientist's Search for Common Ground Between God and Evolution*. New York, NY: Harper Perennial.

——— 2007a 'Falling Over the Edge: Review of the Edge of Evolution'. *Nature*. Vol. 447. No. 28. 1055–1056.

——— 2007b 'Faulty Design: Review of the Edge of Evolution'. *Commonweal*. 12 October. 31–33.

Monton, Bradley 2006 'God, Fine-Tuning and the Problem of Old Evidence'. *British Journal of the Philosophy of Science*. Vol. 57. No. 2. 405–424.

——— 2009a *Seeking God in Science: An Atheist Defends Intelligent Design*. Toronto, ON: Broadview Press.

——— 2009b 'Pennock on Monton in U.S. News & World Report'. *Bradley Monton's Blog*. Available at <http://bradleymonton.wordpress.com>. Accessed on 7 August 2014.

——— 2013 'An Atheistic Defence of Christian Science'. *European Journal for Philosophy of Religion*. Vol. 5. No. 3. 43–54.

Moore, Randy and Decker, Mark D. 2008 *More than Darwin: An Encyclopedia of the People and Places of the Evolution-Creationism Controversy*. Westport, CT: Greenwood Press.

Moreland, J.P. (Ed.) 1994 *The Creation Hypothesis: Scientific Evidence for an Intelligent Designer*. Downers Grove, IL: IVP Books.

Moritz, Joshua M. (forthcoming) 'Contingency, Convergence, Constraints, and the Challenge from Theodicy in Creation's Evolution'. SATURN October 2014 conference proceedings. Ed. Robert J. Russell.

Morris, Thomas V. 1993 'Perfection and Creation'. *Reasoned Faith: Essays in Philosophical Theology in Honor of Norman Kretzmann*. Ed. Eleonore Stump. Ithaca, NY: Cornell University Press. 234–247.

Mullen, John Tholfsen 2004 *Design Arguments Within a Reidian Epistemology*. Nore Dame, Indiana: University of Notre Dame.

Murphy, George 2008 'Cross, Evolution and Theodicy: Telling it Like It Is'. *The Evolution of Evil*. Eds Gaymon Bennett, Martinez J. Hewlett, Ted Peters and Robert J. Russell. Göttingen: Vandhoeck & Ruprecht. 349–366.

Murphy, Nancey 1993 *Theology in an Age of Scientific Reasoning*. Cornell Studies in the Philosophy of Religion. Ithaca, NY: Cornell University Press.

Murray, Michael J. 2003 'Natural Providence (or Design Trouble)?' *Faith and Philosophy*. Vol. 20. No. 3. 307–327.

——— 2006 'Natural Providence: Reply to Dembski'. *Faith and Philosophy*. Vol. 23. No. 3. 337–341.

——— 2011 *Nature Red in Tooth and Claw: Theism and the Problem of Animal Suffering*. Oxford: Oxford University Press.

Murray, Paul D. 2010 'Truth and Reason in Science and Theology'. *God, the Humanity and Cosmos*. Ed. Christopher Southgate. 2nd ed. London: T & T Clark International. 92–115.

Murray, Paul D. and Wilkinson, David 2010 'The Significance of the Theology of Creation within Christian Tradition: Systematic Considerations'. *God, Humanity and the Cosmos*. 2nd Edition. Ed. Christopher Southgate. London:T & T Clark. 39–62.

Musgrave, Ian 2006 'The Evolution of the Bacterial Flagellum'. *Why Intelligent Design Fails: A Scientific Critique of the New Creationism*. Eds Matt Young and Taner Edis. New Brunswick, NJ: Rutgers University Press. 72–84.

Myers, P.Z. 2011 'How Not to Examine the Evolution of Proteins'. *Panda's Thumb Blog*. Available at <http://www.pandasthumb.org>. Accessed on 29 December 2013.

Nagasawa, Yujin 2010 *The Existence of God: A Philosophical Introduction*. New York, NY: Routledge.

Narveson, Jan 2003 'God by Design?' *God and Design: The Teleological Argument and Modern Science*. Ed. Neil A. Manson. London: Routledge. 88–103.

Nelson, Paul 1996 'The Role of Theology in Current Evolutionary Reasoning'. *Biology and Philosophy*. Vol. 11. 493–517.

Nelson, Paul and Gauger, Ann 2011 'Stranger than Fiction: The Riddle of Metamorphosis'. *Metamorphosis: The Case for Intelligent Design in a Nutshell Chrysalis*. Ed. David Klinghoffer. Seattle, WA: Discovery Institute Press. 28–42.

——— 2002 'Life in the Big Tent: Traditional Creationism and the Intelligent Design Community'. *Christian Research Journal*. Vol. 24. No. 4.

Newman, Robert C. 2001 'Creation, Creationism'. *Encyclopedia of Fundamentalism*. Ed. Brenda E. Brasher. New York, NY: Routledge.

Nielsen, Kai 2004 *Naturalism and Religion*. New York, NY: Prometheus Books.

Nieminen, Petteri, Mustonen, Anne-Mari and Ryökäs, Esko 2014 'Theological Implications of Young Earth Creationism and Intelligent Design: Emerging Tendencies of Scientism and Agnosticism'. *Theology and Science*. Vol. 12. No. 3. 260–284.

Niiniluoto, Ilkka 2002 *Critical Scientific Realism*. Oxford: Oxford University Press.

Noble, Denis 2008 *The Music of Life: Biology Beyond the Genome*. Oxford: Oxford University Press.

——— 2013 'Physiology Is Rocking the Foundations of Evolutionary Biology'. *Experimental Physiology*. 10.1113/expphysiol.2012.071134.

Numbers, Ronald 2003 'Science without God: Natural Laws and Christian Beliefs'. *When Science and Christianity Meet*. Eds Ronald Numbers and David C. Linberg. Chicago, IL: University of Chicago Press. 265–286.

——— 2006 *The Creationists: From Scientific Creationism to Intelligent Design*. Cambridge, MA: Harvard University Press.

O' Connor, J.J. and Robertson, E.F. 1996 'The Mathematical Discovery of the Planets'. *The History of Mathematics Archive, University of St. Andrews*. Available at: <http://www.history.mcs.st.and.ac.uk/PrintHT/Neptune_and_Pluto.html>. Accessed on 17 October 2013.

O' Connor, Robert 2003 'The Design Inference: Old Wine in New Wineskins'. *God and Design. The Teleological Argument and Modern Science*. Ed. Neil. A. Manson. London: Routledge. 66–87.

Oord, Thomas Jay 2010 'A Theologian Evaluates Intelligent Design'. *Thomas Jay Oord's Blog*. Available at <http://thomasjayoord.com/index.php/blog/archives/a_theologian_evaluates_intelligent_design_pt._1_of_3/>. Accessed on 22 January 2014.

Oppy, Graham 2002 'Paley's Argument for Design'. *Philo*. No. 5. 161–173.

——— 2006 *Arguing About Gods*. Cambridge, UK: Cambridge University Press.

Orr, Allen 1996 'Darwin v. Intelligent Design (Again)'. *Boston Review*. December/January Issue.

——— 1997 'H. Allen Orr Responds'. *Boston Review*. February/March Issue.

——— 2007 'A Mission to Convert. Review of "the God Delusion"'. *The New York Review of Books*. 11 January.

Overton, William 2009 [1981] 'United States District Court Opinion, McLean v. Arkansas Board of Education'. *But Is It Science? The Philosophical Question in the Creation/Evolution Controversy. Updated Edition*. Eds Robert Pennock and Michael Ruse. Amherst, NY: Prometheus Books. 379–311.

Padgett, Alan G. 2004 'Theologia Naturalis: Philosophy of Religion or Doctrine of Creation?' *Faith and Philosophy*. Vol. 21. No. 4. 493–502.

Paley, William 2006 [1802] *Natural Theology*. Oxford World's Classics. New York, NY: Oxford University Press.

Palmerino, Carla Rita 2011 'Galileo's Use of Medieval Thought Experiments'. *Thought Experiments in Methodological and Historical Contexts*. Eds Katerina Ierodiakonou and Sophie Roux. Leiden: Brill. 101–126.

Papineau, David 2009 'Naturalism'. *Stanford Encyclopedia of Philosophy* (Spring 2009 Edition). Ed. Edward N. Zalta. Available at <http://plato.stanford.edu/archives/spr2009/entries/naturalism/>.

Peacocke, Arthur 1993 *Theology for a Scientific Age: Being and Becoming, Divine and Human*. Enlarged edition. Minneapolis, MN: Fortress Press.

Peels, Rik 2015a 'A Conceptual Map of Scientism'. *Scientism: Problems and Prospects*. Eds Jeroen de Ridder, Rik Peels and René van Woudenberg. New York, NY: Oxford University Press.

——— 2015b 'Scientism and the Argument from Self-Referential Incoherence. Unpublished manuscript'.

——— 2015c 'Scientism and the Basing Problem'. *Science Unlimited? The Challenges of Scientism*. Eds Maarten Boudry and Massimo Pigliucci. Chicago, IL: Chicago University Press.

Peirce, C.S. 1955 *Philosophical Writings of Peirce*. Ed. Justus Buchler. New York: Dover.

Pelikan, Jaroslav 1971 *The Emergence of the Catholic Tradition (100–600). The Christian Tradition: A History of the Development of Doctrine. Vol. 1*. Chicago, IL: University of Chicago Press.

Penelhum, Terrence 2005 'Hume's Criticisms of Natural Theology'. *In Defence of Natural Theology: A Post-Humean Assessment*. Eds James F. Sennett and Douglas Groothuis. Downers Grove, IL: InterVarsity Press. 21–41.

Pennisi, Elizabeth 2010 'The Little Wasp That Could'. *Science*. Vol. 327. No. 5963. 260–262.

Pennock, Robert (Ed.) 2001 *Intelligent Design Creationism and Its Critics: Philosophical, Theological and Scientific Perspectives*. Cambridge, MA: The MIT Press.

Pennock, Robert and Ruse, Michael (Eds) 2009 *But Is It Science? The Philosophical Question in the Creation/Evolution Controversy. Updated Edition*. Amherst, NY: Prometheus Books.

Pennock, Robert 1999 *The Tower of Babel: The Evidence Against the New Creationism*. Cambridge, MA: MIT Press.

——— 2001 'The Wizards of ID: Reply to Dembski'. *Intelligent Design Creationism and Its Critics: Philosophical, Theological and Scientific Perspectives*. Ed. Robert Pennock. Cambridge, MA: The MIT Press. 645–667.

——— 2007 'The God of the Gaps: The Argument from Ignorance and the Limits of Methodological Naturalism'. *Scientists Confront Creationism: Intelligent Design and Beyond*. Eds Andrew J. Petto and Laurie R. Godfrey. New York, NY: W.W. Norton & Co. 309–338.

——— 2010 'The Postmodern Sin of Intelligent Design Creationism'. *Science & Education*. Vol. 19. No. 6–8. 757–778.

——— 2011 'Can't Philosophers Tell the Difference between Science and Religion? Demarcation Revisited'. *Synthese*. Vol. 178. No. 2. 177–206.

Penrose, Roger 2002 [1989] *The Emperor's New Mind: Concerning Computers, Minds and the Laws of Physics*. Oxford: Oxford University Press.

Perakh, Mark 2004 *Unintelligent Design*. New York: Prometheus Books.

Perakh, Mark and Young, Matt 2006 'Is Intelligent Design Science?' *Why Intelligent Design Fails: A Scientific Critique of the New Creationism*. Eds Matt Young and Taner Edis. New Brunswick, NJ: Rutgers University Press. 185–196.

Peters, Ted and Hallanger, Nathan (Eds) 2006 *God's Action in Nature's World: Essays in Honour of Robert John Russell*. London: Ashgate.

Peters, Ted and Hewlett, Martinez 2003 *Evolution from Creation to New Creation: Conflict, Conversation and Convergence*. Nashville, TN: Abingdon Press.

Peterson, Michael 1982 *Evil and the Christian God*. Grand Rapids, MI: Baker.

Petto, Andrew and Godfrey, Laurie R. (Eds) 2007 *Scientists Confront Creationism: Intelligent Design and Beyond*. New York, NY: W.W. Norton & Co.

Philipse, Herman 2012 *God in the Age of Science: A Critique of Religious Reason*. Oxford: Oxford University Press.

Phillips, D.Z. 1976 *Religion without Explanation*. Oxford: Blackwell.

——— 1994 *Wittgenstein and Religion*. Pallgrave: St Martin's Press.

Pigliucci, Massimo and Boudry, Maarten 2011 'Why Machine-Information Metaphors are Bad for Science and Science Education'. *Science & Education*. Vol. 20. No. 5. 453–471.

Pigliucci, Massimo and Müller, Gerd B. (Eds) 2010 *Evolution: The Extended Synthesis*. Cambridge, MA: The MIT Press.

Plantinga, Alvin 1977 *God, Freedom, and Evil*. Grand Rapids, MI: Eerdmans.

——— 1990 [1967] *God and Other Minds: A Study of the Rational Justification of Belief in God*. Ithaca, NY: Cornell University Press.

——— 1991 'When Faith and Reason Clash: Evolution and the Bible'. *Christian Scholar's Review*. Vol. 21. No. 1. 8–32.

——— 1997 'Methodological Naturalism?' *Perspectives on Science and Christian Faith*. Vol. 49. (September 1997). 143–154.

——— 2000 *Warranted Christian Belief*. New York, NY: Oxford University Press.

——— 2007 'The Dawkins Confusion: Naturalism ad Absurdum'. *Books & Culture. A Service of Christianity Today*. Vol. 13. No. 2.

——— 2011 *Where the Conflict Really Lies: Science, Religion and Naturalism*. New York, NY: Oxford University Press.

Pigliucci, Massimo 2013 'New Atheism and the Scientistic Turn in the Atheism Movement'. *Midwest Studies in Philosophy*. Vol. 37. No. 1. 142–153.

——— 2014 'New Atheism and the Scientistic Turn in the Atheism Movement'. *Midwest Studies in Philosophy*. Vol. 37. No. 1. 142–153.

Popper, Karl 1959 'On the Use and Misuse of Imaginary Experiments, Especially in Quantum Theory'. *The Logic of Scientific Discovery*. London: Hutchinson, 442–456.

——— 1964 *Conjectures and Refutations: The Growth of Scientific Knowledge*. London: Routledge.

Pust, Joel 2012 'Intuition'. *The Stanford Encyclopedia of Philosophy* (Winter 2012 Edition). Ed. Edward N. Zalta. Available at <http://plato.stanford.edu/archives/win2012/entries/intuition/>.

Quine, Willard Van Orman 1953 'Two Dogmas of Empiricism'. *From a Logical Point of View: Nine Logico-Philosophical Essays*. 2nd ed. Cambridge, MA: Harvard University Press. 20–46.

Quinn, Philip 2009 'Creationism, Methodology, and Politics'. *But Is It Science?: The Philosophical Question in the Creation/Evolution Controversy*. Eds Robert Pennock and Michael Ruse. Amherst, NY: Prometheus Books. 367–385.

Ratzsch, Del 2001 *Nature, Design and Science: The Status of Design in Natural Science*. Albany, NY: State University of New York Press.

——— 2002 'Design Theory and Its Critics: Monologues Passing in the Night. Review Article of: Robert T. Pennock (ed.), Intelligent Design Creationism and its Critics'. *Ars Disputandi. The Online Journal for Philosophy of Religion*. Vol. 2. Available at <http://www.arsdisputandi.org/>.

——— 2003 'Perceiving Design'. *God and Design. The Teleological Argument and Modern Science*. Ed. Neil. A. Manson. London: Routledge. 124–144.

——— 2004 'Stenmark, Plantinga and Scientific Neutrality'. *Faith and Philosophy*. Vol. 21. No. 3. 353–365.

——— 2005 'How Not to Critique Intelligent Design Theory: A Review of Niall Shanks: God, the Devil and Darwin'. *Ars Disputandi. The Online Journal for Philosophy of Religion*. Available at <http://www.arsdisputandi.org>.

——— 2006 'Science and Design'. An Interview by Hugo Holbling. *The Galilean Library*. Available at <http://www.galilean-library.org>. Accessed on 11 December 2013.

——— 2009 'Humanness in Their Hearts?' *The Believing Primate: Scientific, Philosophical and Religious Reflections on the Origin of Religion*. Eds Jeffrey Schloss and Michael Murray. Oxford: Oxford University. 215–245.

Ratzsch, Del and Koperski, Jeffrey 2015 'Teleological Arguments for God's Existence'. *Stanford Encyclopedia of Philosophy* (Spring 2015 Edition). Ed. Edward N. Zalta. Available at <http://plato.stanford.edu/archives/spr2015/entries/teleological-arguments/>.

Rea, Michael C. 2005 *World without Design: The Ontological Consequences of Naturalism*. Oxford: Oxford University Press.

Rees, Martin 2000 *Just Six Numbers: The Deep Forces that Shape the Universe*. London: Basic Books.

——— 2003 'Other Universes: A Scientific Perspective'. *God and Design: The Teleological Argument and Modern Science*. Ed. Neil A. Manson. London: Routledge. 211–220.

Richards, Jay W. (Ed.) 2010 *God and Evolution: Protestants, Catholics and Jews Explore Darwin's Challenge to Faith*. Seattle, WA: Discovery Institute Press.

——— 2007 'Can ID Explain the Origin of Evil?' *Salvo Magazine*. No. 4.

Ridley, Mark 2004 *Evolution*. Third Edition. Oxford: Blackwell.

Ritchie, Jack 2008 *Understanding Naturalism*. Stocksfield: Acumen.

Roberts, Michael 2003 'Intelligent Design: Some Geological, Historical and Theological Questions'. *Debating Design: From Darwin to DNA*. Eds Michael Ruse and William A. Dembski. Cambridge: Cambridge University Press. 275–293.

Rosenberg, Alex 2011 *The Atheist's Guide to Reality: Enjoying Life without Illusions*. New York, NY: W.W. Norton & Co.

Ross, Marcus R. 2005 'Who Believes What? Clearing Up Confusion About Intelligent Design and Young-Earth Creationism'. *Journal of Geoscience Education*. Vol. 53. No. 3. 319–323.

Rossi, Philip 2014 'Kant's Philosophy of Religion'. *Stanford Encyclopedia of Philosophy* (Fall 2014 Edition). Ed. Edward N. Zalta. Available at <http://plato.stanford.edu/archives/fall2014/entries/kant-religion/>.

Roth, Ariel A. 2001 'Ariel A. Roth, Biology'. *In Six Days: Why 50 Scientists Choose to Believe in Creation*. Ed. John F. Ashton. Green Forest, AR: Master Books. 86–101.

Rowland, Christopher 2013 'Natural Theology and the Christian Bible'. *The Oxford Handbook of Natural Theology*. Eds Russell Re Manning, John Hedley Brooke and Fraser Watts. Oxford: Oxford University Press. 23–37.

Runehov, Anne L.C. 2010 'Natural Theology or Theology of Nature and the Natural?' *The Human Project in Science and Religion. Copenhagen University Discussions in Science and Religion.* Eds Anne L.C. Runehov, Niels Henrik Gregersen and Jacob Wolf. Copenhagen: Publications from the Faculty of Theology No. 20.

Rusbult, Craig 2004 'God of the Gaps – What Does It Mean?' *American Scientific Affiliation.* Available at <http://www.asa3.org/ASA/education/origins/gaps2-cr.htm>. Accessed on 11 December 2013.

Ruse, Michael 2001 *Can a Darwinian be a Christian? The Relationship Between Science and Religion.* Cambridge: Cambridge University Press.

——— 2003 *Darwin and Design: Does Evolution Have a Purpose?* Cambridge, MA: Harvard University Press.

——— 2004 'The Argument from Design: A Brief History'. *Debating Design: From Darwin to DNA.* Ed. William A. Dembski and Michael Ruse. Cambridge: Cambridge University Press. 13–31.

——— 2007 'The Argument from Design'. *The Panda's Black Box: Opening up the Intelligent Design Controversy.* Ed. Nathaniel C. Comfort. Baltimore, ML: The Johns Hopkins University Press. 18–39.

——— 2009 'Witness Testimony Sheet: McLean v. Arkansas'. But Is It Science? The Philosophical Question in the Creation/Evolution Controversy. Updated Edition. Eds Robert Pennock and Michael Ruse. Amhurt, NY: Prometheus Books. 253–278.

——— 2011 'Darwinism and the Problem of Evil'. *The Huffington Post.* 11 March.

——— 2012 'Darwinism and Atheism: A Marriage Made in Heaven?' *The Blackwell Companion to Science and Christianity.* Eds James Stump and Alan Padgett. Malden, MA: Blackwell, 2012. 246–257.

Russell, Robert J. 2005 'Intelligent Design is Not Science and Does Not Qualify to be Taught in Public School Science Classes'. *Theology and Science.* Vol. 3. No. 2. 131–132.

——— 2006 'Quantum Physics and Divine Action'. *The Oxford Handbook of Religion and Science.* Eds Phillip Clayton and Zachary Simpson. Oxford: Oxford University Press. 579–595.

——— 2008 *Cosmology from Alpha to Omega: The Creative Mutual Interaction of Theology and Science.* Minneapolis, MN: Fortress Press.

——— 2013 'Recent Theological Interpretations of Evolution'. *Theology and Science.* Vol. 11. No. 3. 169–184.

Salmon, Wesley C. 1990 *Four Decades of Scientific Explanation.* Minneapolis, MN: University of Minnesota Press.

Sansom, Roger 2008 'Evolvability'. *The Oxford Handbook of Philosophy of Biology.* Ed. Michael Ruse. Oxford: Oxford University Press. 138–160.

Sarkar, Sahotra 2007 *Doubting Darwin? Creationist Designs on Evolution.* Oxford: Wiley-Blackwell.

——— 2011 'The Science Question in Intelligent Design'. *Synthese.* Vol. 178. No. 2. 291–305.

Saunders, Nicholas 2003 *Divine Action and Modern Science.* Cambridge: Cambridge University Press.

Savuoja, Ari 2007 *Mikä on ihme ja mitä ihmeistä voidaan tietää? Keskustelu ihmeistä uusimmassa englanninkielisessä uskonnonfilosofiassa.* Dissertation in the Philosophy of Religion. Helsinki: University of Helsinki.

Schöenborn, Christoph 2007 *Chance or Purpose? Creation, Evolution and a Rational Faith.* Ft. Collins, CO: Ignatius Press.

Schupbach, Jonah 2005 'Paley's Inductive Inference to Design. A Response to Graham Oppy'. *Philosophia Christi.* Vol. 7. No. 2. 491–502.

Scott, Eugenie C. 1999 'The Creation/Evolution Continuum'. *NCSE Reports*.Vol. 19. No. 4. 16–17, 23–25.

——— 2004 *Evolution vs. Creationism: An Introduction*. Westport, CT: Greenwood Press.

Sedley, David 2007 *Creationism and Its Critics in Antiquity*. Sather Classical Lectures 66. Berkeley, CA: University of California Press.

Sennett, James F. 2005 'Hume's Stopper and the Natural Theology Project'. *In Defence of Natural Theology: A Post-Humean Assessment*. Eds James F. Sennett and Douglas Groothuis. Downers Grove, IL: InterVarsity Press. 82–104.

Sepkoski, David 2008 'Macroevolution'. *The Oxford Handbook of Philosophy of Biology*. Ed. Michael Ruse. Oxford: Oxford University Press. 211–237.

Shanks, Niall 2004 *God, the Devil and Darwin: A Critique of Intelligent Design Theory*. Oxford: Oxford University Press.

Shapiro, James A. 2011 *Evolution: A View from the 21st Century*. Upper Saddle River, NJ: FT Press.

Shaw, William H. and Ashley, L.R. 1983 'Analogy and Inference'. *Dialogue*.Vol. 22. 415–432.

Shoshtak, Seth 2005 'SETI and Intelligent Design'. *Space.com*. December 1. Available at <http://www.space.com/1826-seti-intelligent-design.html>. Accessed on 29 December 2013.

Simon, Dan 2013 *Evolutionary Optimization Algorithms*. Oxford: Wiley-Blackwell.

Snoke, David 2001 'In Favor of God-of-the-Gaps-Reasoning'. *Perspectives on Science and the Christian Faith*.Vol. 53. No. 9. 152–158.

Sober, Elliott 2004 'The Design Argument'. *Debating Design: From Darwin to DNA*. Eds Michael Ruse and William A. Dembski. Cambridge: Cambridge University Press. 98–129.

——— 2007 'Intelligent Design and the Supernatural: The "God of the Extraterrestrials" Reply'. *Faith and Philosophy*.Vol. 24. No. 1. 72–82.

——— 2008 *Evidence and Evolution: The Logic Behind the Science*. Cambridge: Cambridge University Press.

——— 2011 'Why Methodological Naturalism?' *Biological Evolution — Facts and Theories, A Critical Appraisal 150 Years after The Origin of Species*. Eds G. Aulette, M. LeClerc and R. Martinez. Rome: Gregorian Biblical Press. 359–378.

——— 2014 'Evolutionary Theory, Causal Completeness, and Theism: The Case of "Guided' Mutation"'. *Evolutionary Biology – Conceptual, Ethical, and Religious Issues*. Eds D. Walsh and P. Thompson. Cambridge: Cambridge University Press. 31–44.

Sober, Elliott; Fitelson, Branden and Stephens, Christopher 1999 'How Not to Detect Design – A Review of William Dembski's *The Design Inference*'. *Philosophy of Science*, 1999, 66: 472–488.

Sorensen, Roy A. 1992 *Thought Experiments*. Oxford: Oxford University Press.

Sorri, Jaakkom 2013 'Aukkojen Jumala?' *Areiopagi.fi — The Meeting of Science, Theology and Philosophy*. Available at <http://www.areiopagi.fi/aukkojen-jumala/>. Accessed on 20 November 2013.

Southgate, Christopher2011 'Re-reading Genesis, John, and Job: A Christian Response to Darwinism'. *Zygon*.Vol. 46. No. 2. 370–395.

Southgate, Christopher (ed.) 2010 *God, Humanity and the Cosmos: A Textbook in Science and Religion*. 3rd Edition. London: T & T Clark.

Spitzer, Robert J. 2010 *New Arguments for the Existence of God*. Grand Rapids, MI: Eerdmans.

Stafford, Tim 1997 'The Making of a Revolution'. *Christianity Today*. 41 (8 December).

Steiner, Michael 1999 *The Applicability of Mathematics as a Philosophical Problem*. Cambridge, MA: Harvard University Press.

Stenger, Victor J. 2006 'Is the Universe Fine-Tuned for Us?' *Why Intelligent Design Fails: A Scientific Critique of the New Creationism*. Eds Matt Young and Taner Edis. New Brunswick, NJ: Rutgers University Press. 172–184.

——— 2011 *The Fallacy of Fine-Tuning: Why the Universe Is Not Designed for Us*. Amherst, NY: Prometheus.

Stenmark, Mikael 1995 *Rationality in Science, Religion and Everyday Life: A Critical Evaluation of Four Models of Rationality*. Notre Dame, IN: University of Notre Dame Press.

——— 2001 *Scientism: Science, Ethics and Religion*. Burlington: Ashgate Publishing Co.

——— 2004 *How to Relate Science and Religion: A Multi-Dimensional Model*. Grand Rapids, MI: Wm. B. Eerdmans Publishing Co.

Stewart, Robert (Ed.) 2007 *Intelligent Design: William A. Dembski & Michael Ruse in Dialogue*. Minneapolis, MN: Fortress Press.

Stoeger, William R. 2010 'God, Physics and the Big Bang'. *The Cambridge Companion to Science and Religion*. Ed. Peter Harrison. Cambridge: Cambridge University Press.

Stump, Eleonore 2010 *Wandering in Darkness: Narrative and the Problem of Suffering*. Oxford: Oxford University Press.

Susskind, Leonard 2006a *The Cosmic Landscape: String Theory and the Illusion of Intelligent Design*. New York, NY: Back Bay Books.

——— 2006b 'The Good Fight'. *Intelligent Thought: Science Versus the Intelligent Design Movement*. Ed. John Brockman. New York, NY: Vintage Books. 24–32.

Swinburne, Richard 1993 *The Coherence of Theism*. Oxford: Clarendon.

——— 1998 *Providence and the Problem of Evil*. Oxford: Oxford University Press.

——— 2003 *The Resurrection of God Incarnate*. Oxford: Oxford University Press.

——— 2004a *The Existence of God*. Oxford: Oxford University Press.

——— 2004b 'Natural Theology, Its "Dwindling Probabilities" and "Lack of Rapport"'. *Faith and Philosophy*. Vol. 21. No. 4. 533–546.

——— 2004c 'The Argument From Nature Reassessed'. *Debating Design: From Darwin to DNA*. Eds William A. Dembski and Michael Ruse. Cambridge: Cambridge University Press. 298–310.

——— 2011a 'Why Hume and Kant Were Mistaken in Rejecting Natural Theology'. *Presentation at the Philosophy of Religion in the 21st Century Conference*. Cracow, Poland. 27 June.

——— 2011b 'God as the Simplest Explanation of the Universe'. *European Journal of Philosophy of Religion*. Vol. 2. No. 1. 1–24.

Taliaferro, Charles 1994 *Consciousness and the Mind of God*. Cambridge: Cambridge University Press.

——— 2012 'The Project of Natural Theology'. *The Blackwell Companion to Natural Theology*. Eds William Lane Craig and J.P. Moreland. Oxford: Blackwell. 1–23.

Thaxton, Charles, Bradley, Walter and Olson, Roger 1992 [1984] *The Mystery of Life's Origin: Reassessing Current Theories*. Dallas, TX: Lewis and Stanley.

Thornhill, R.H. and Ussery, D.W. 2000 'A Classification of Possible Routes of Darwinian Evolution'. *Journal of Theoretical Biology*. Vol. 203. No. 2. 111–116.

Todd, Scott C. 1999 'A View from Kansas on That Evolution Debate'. *Nature*. Vol. 401. 423.

Tooley, Michael 2013 'The Problem of Evil'. *Stanford Encyclopedia of Philosophy* (Summer 2013 Edition). Ed. Edward N. Zalta. Available at <http://plato.stanford.edu/archives/sum2013/entries/evil/>.

Trigg, Roger 1993 *Rationality in Science*. Oxford: Blackwell.

Tracy, Thomas F. 2006 'Theologies of Divine Action', *The Oxford Handbook of Religion and Science*. Eds Phillip Clayton and Zachary Simpson. Oxford: Oxford University Press. 596–611.

Trout, J.D. 2002 'Explanation and the Sense of Understanding'. *Philosophy of Science*. Vol. 69. No. 2. 212–233.

Turner, Denys 2004 *Faith, Reason and the Existence of God*. Cambridge: Cambridge University Press.

Vainio, Olli-Pekka 2010 *Beyond Fideism: Negotiable Religious Identities*. Burlington, VT: Ashgate.

Vainio, Olli-Pekka and Visala, Aku 2013 'Mitä ateismi on? Katsaus nykyaikaisen ateismin muotoihin'. *Teologinen Aikakauskirja*. Vol. 118. Nos 5–6. 401–415.

Van Inwagen, Peter 1991 'The Problem of Evil, the Problem of Air, and the Problem of Silence'. *Philosophical Perspectives 5: Philosophy of Religion*. Ed. J. Tomberlin. Atascadero, CA: Ridgeview Publishing.

——— 1998 'Modal Epistemology'. *Philosophical Studies*. Vol. 92. 67–84.

——— 2008 *The Problem of Evil*. Oxford: Oxford University Press.

Van Till, Howard 2000 'Partnership: Science & Christian Theology as Partners in Theorizing'. *Science and Christianity: Four Views*. Ed. Richard F. Carlson. Downers Grove, IL: InterVarsity Press.

——— 2001 'The Creation: Intelligently Designed or Optimally Equipped?' *Intelligent Design Creationism and Its Critics: Philosophical, Theological and Scientific Perspectives*. Ed. Robert Pennock. Cambridge, MA: The MIT Press. 487–512.

Van Woudenberg, René 2005 'Intuitive Knowledge Reconsidered'. *Basic Belief and Basic Knowledge: Papers in Epistemology*. Eds René van Woudenberg, S. Roeser and R. Rood. Heusetamm nr Frankfurt: Ontos Verlag. Sivut. 15–39.

Venema, Dennis 2011 'Evolution and the Origin of Biological Information'. *BioLogos Institute*. Available at <biologos.org>. Accessed on 17 June 2013.

——— 2012 'The Evolutionary Origins of Irreducible Complexity'. *Biologos Institute*. Available at <http://biologos.org>. Accessed on 28 August 2013.

Visala, Aku 2011 *Naturalism, Theism and the Cognitive Study of Religion: Religion Explained?* Burlington, VT: Ashgate.

Von Wachter, Daniel 2014 'Defending Design Arguments against Plantinga'. *Philosophia Reformata*. Vol. 79. No. 1. 54–65.

Wagner, Andrew 2007 *Robustness and Evolvability in Living Systems*. Princeton, NJ: Princeton University Press.

Wainwright, William J. 2009 'Theology and Mystery'. *Oxford Handbook of Philosophical Theology*. Eds Thomas P. Flint and Michael C. Rea. Oxford: Oxford University Press. 78–102.

Walsh, Denis 2008 'Teleology'. *The Oxford Handbook of Philosophy of Biology*. Ed. Michael Ruse. Oxford: Oxford University Press. 113–137.

Walton, Douglas 2009 *Arguments from Ignorance*. University Park, PA: Penn State University Press.

Ward, Keith 2002 'Believing in Miracles'. *Zygon*. Vol. 37. 741–750.

——— 2003 'Theistic Evolution'. *Debating Design: From Darwin to DNA*. Eds W.A. Dembski and M. Ruse. Cambridge: Cambridge University Press. 261–274.

——— 2007 *Divine Action: Examining God's Role in an Open and Emergent Universe*. London: Templeton Press.

——— 2008 *The Big Questions in Science and Religion*. West Conshohocken, PA: Templeton Foundation Press.

Wells, Jonathan 2002a *Icons of Evolution*. Washington, DC: Regnery Publishing.

——— 2002b 'Critics Rave over Icons of Evolution: A Response to Published Reviews'. *Discovery Institute*. Available at <http://www.discovery.org/csc/>.

——— 2010 'Darwin of the Gaps'. *God and Evolution: Protestants, Catholics and Jews Explore Darwin's Challenge to Faith*. Ed. Jay W. Richards. Seattle, WA: Discovery Institute Press. 117–128.

——— 2011 *The Myth of Junk DNA*. Seattle, WA: Discovery Institute Press.

West, John G. 2007 *Darwin Day in America: How Our Politics Have Been Dehumanized in the Name of Science*. Wilmington, DL: Intercollegiate Studies Institute.

West, John G. (Ed.) 2012 *The Magician's Twin: C.S. Lewis of Science, Scientism and Society*. Seattle, WA: Discovery Institute Press.

Whewell, William 1834 *Astronomy and General Physics Considered with Reference to Natural Theology*. London: William Pickering.

White, Roger 2003 'Fine-Tuning and Multiple Universes'. *God and Design: The Teleological Argument and Modern Science*. Ed. Neil A. Manson. London: Routledge. 229–250.

White, Thomas Joseph 2010 *The Analogy of Being: Invention of the Antichrist or Wisdom of God?* Grand Rapids, MI: Wm. B. Eerdmans Publishing Company.

Whitehead, Alfred North 1926 *Science and the Modern World*. New York, NY: Macmillan.

Wieland, Carl 2002 'AIG's Views on the Intelligent Design Movement'. *Answers in Genesis*. Available at <http://www.answersingenesis.org>. Accessed on 29 December 2013.

Wigner, Eugene P. 1960 'The Unreasonable Effectiveness of Mathematics in the Natural Sciences'. *Communications on Pure and Applied Mathematics*. Vol. 13. 1–14.

Wiker, Benjamin and Witt, Jonathan 2006 *A Meaningful World: How the Arts and Sciences Reveal the Genius of Nature*. Downers Grove, IL: IVP Academic.

Wiker, Benjamin 2002 *Moral Darwinism: How We Became Hedonists*. Downers Grove, IL: InterVarsity Press.

——— 2009 'The Problem of Evil'. *Crisis Magazine*. April 22. Available at <http://www.crisismagazine.com/2009/the-problem-of-evil>. Accessed on 24 October 2013.

Wildman, Wesley 2004 'The Divine Action Project, 1988–2003'. *Theology and Science*. Vol. 2. No. 1. 31–75.

Wilkes, Kathleen V. 1988 *Real People: Personal Identity without Thought Experiments*. Oxford: Oxford University Press.

Wilkins, John S. and Elsberry, Wesley R. 2001 'The Advantages of Theft Over Toil: The Design Inference and Arguing from Ignorance'. *Biology & Philosophy*. Vol. 16. No. 5. 711–724.

Williams, Thomas 2005 'The Doctrine of Univocity of True and Salutary'. *Modern Theology*. Vol. 21. No. 4. 575–585.

——— 2013 'Saint Anselm'. *The Stanford Encyclopedia of Philosophy* (Spring 2013 Edition). Ed. Edward N. Zalta. Available at <http://plato.stanford.edu/archives/spr2013/entries/anselm/>.

Winter, Ralph 2013 'Where Darwin Scores Higher than Intelligent Design'. *William Carey International Development Journal*. Vol. 4. No. 20. 31–35.

Witt, Jonathan 2005a 'The Origin of Intelligent Design: A Brief History of the Scientific Theory of Intelligent Design'. *Discovery Institute*. Available at <http://www.discovery.org/csc/>. Accessed on 29 December 2013.

——— 2005b 'Book Review: Creationism's Trojan Horse'. *Philosophia Christi*. Vol. 7. No. 2. 517–519.

——— 2007 'Hoyle Uses the Term "Intelligent Design" in a 1982 Work Making a Design Inference for the Origin of Life'. *Evolution News*. Discovery Institute. Available at <http://www.evolutionnews.org/>. Accessed on 29 December 2013.

——— 2009 'Panning God: Darwinism's Defective Argument against Bad Design'. 4truth.net. Available at: <http://www.4truth.net>. Accessed on 25 June 2015.

Wolterstorff, Nicholas 2009 'How Philosophical Theology Became Possible within the Analytic Tradition of Philosophy'. *Analytic Theology: New Essays in the Philosophy of Religion*. Eds Oliver D. Crisp and Michael C. Rea. Oxford: Oxford University Press. 155–168.

Wood, Todd C. 2011 'Protein Evolution in Bio-Complexity'. *Todd's Blog*. Available at <toddcwood.blogspot.fi>. Accessed on 17 June 2013.

Woodward, James 2003 *Making Things Happen: A Theory of Causal Explanation*. Oxford: Oxford University Press.

——— 2011 'Scientific Explanation'. *The Stanford Encyclopedia of Philosophy* (Winter 2011 Edition). Ed. Edward N. Zalta. Available at <http://plato.stanford.edu/archives/win2011/entries/scientific-explanation/>.

Woodward, Thomas 2003 *Doubts about Darwin: A History of Intelligent Design*. Grand Rapids, MI: Baker Books.

——— 2006 *Darwin Strikes Back: Defending the Science of Intelligent Design*. Grand Rapids, MI: Baker Books.

Wright, Larry 1976 *Teleological Explanations: An Etiological Analysis of Goals and Functions*. London: University of California Press.

Wykstra, Stephen J. 2001 'Religious Beliefs, Metaphysical Beliefs and the Historiography of Science'. *Osiris*. Vol. 16. 29–46.

Yaffe, Gideon 2003 'Thomas Reid'. *Stanford Encyclopedia of Philosophy*. Stanford University. Available at <http://plato.stanford.edu/entries/reid/>. Accessed on 24 January 2014.

Yerxa, Donald 2002 'Phillip Johnson and the Origins of the Intelligent Design Movement, 1977–1991'. *Perspectives on Science and the Christian Faith*. Vol. 54. No. 1. 47–52.

Ylikoski, Petri 2001 *Understanding Interests and Causal Explanations*. Helsinki: University of Helsinki.

Yockey, Hubert P. 2005 *Information Theory, Evolution and the Origin of Life*. Cambridge: Cambridge University Press.

Young, Matthew and Edis, Taner (Eds) 2006 *Why Intelligent Design Fails: A Scientific Critique of the New Creationism*. New Brunswick, NJ: Rutgers University Press.

Zagzebski, Linda Trinkaus 2012 *Epistemic Authority: A Theory of Trust, Authority, and Autonomy in Belief*. Oxford: Oxford University Press.

Index

Printed in Great Britain
by Amazon

61130328R00136